HAZARDS 3

SURE...OSX3

MIMU

VENIDAS 43RD

SNAPPER KRAZY

V·EXP

✝ Cholo Writing ✝
Latino Gang Graffiti in Los Angeles

✝

François Chastanet

Dokument

Press

✝

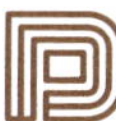

editor François Chastanet photographs
François Chastanet & Howard Gribble
texts Chaz Bojórquez, François Chastanet
& Howard Gribble proofreader Perrine
Saint Martin graphic design François
Chastanet foreword calligraphy Chaz
Bojórquez, wall inscription with flat brush,
Mexico City, 2007 color balance, pre-press
photo settings Per Englund. Text is set in
Scala, typeface drawn by Martin Majoor in
1991, titles in Wallau Halbfett, typeface drawn
by Rudolf Koch in 1930. Printed on Munken
Lynx 120g by Dimograf, Bielsko-Biala,
Poland. *Cholo Writing: Latino Gang Graffiti
in Los Angeles* second edition ISBN 978-91-
88369-85-7, copyright 2024 Dokument
Press, Årstavägen 26, 120 52 Årsta, Sweden,
e-mail hello@dokumentpress.com, website
www.dokumentpress.com

Los Angeles may have the longest history of street writing in the world. Some say that an earlier style of LA graffiti goes back to the 1930s when the Latino shoeshine boys marked their names on the walls with daubers to stake out their spot on the sidewalk.

Before the invention of the spray cans, most LA graffiti was painted with paint and a brush, and the young men who lived by the Los Angeles River would use sticks and paint with the tar seeping from the ground. Those tar tags still exist today and trace our graffiti history back to the 1940s.

East LA graffiti has its own unique format called *placas* or «plaques», symbols of territorial street boundaries. Placas are graffiti painted walls with the names of a gang and its members, mostly painted on the limits or edges of their communities. They are pledges of allegiance to their neighborhood. Placas encourage gang strength, create an aura of exclusivity, and are always painted in blackletters. The squarish, prestigious font used was called «Old English», a typeface meant to present a formal document to the public. All the names from a gang were written in lines that were flushed left and right, or names were stacked line over line and centered. Great care was taken to make them straight and clean. This layout or format is based on an ancient formula that demanded a headline, body copy, and a logo. These three major building blocks of corporate and public advertising can also describe the type layout from ancient Sumerian clay tablets to *The Constitution of the United States* and the modern layout of *The Los Angeles Times*. The headline states the gang or street name, the body copy is your roll call list of everyone's gang name, and the logo refers to the person who wrote it by adding his tag to the end of the placa [pages 19, 22, 25, 27, 35]. This tradition of type, names and language has rarely deviated drastically and has been handed down from generation to generation. This style of writing, we now call «Cholo Graffiti». Cholo is much more than just graffiti. It's a lifestyle. It exists only in the Southwest United States, but the best graffiti comes from East Los Angeles. This style of graffiti is written «by the neighborhood for the neighborhood». To quote Joseph Rodríguez (*East Side Stories: Gang Life in East LA*, PowerHouse Books, 1998), «la vida loca, or the crazy life,

is what they call the barrio gang experience». This is a major difference between Cholo and New York wild style graffiti. In Los Angeles the graffiti is based on culture and race. In Cholo writing only one person writes for the whole gang and you tag only within your own territory. In New York graffiti, the emphasis is on being more of an individual and not about ethnic identity, where «getting up» all-city or all-state with your tag is more important than the group.

«Racism and poverty created the gangs, we had to protect ourselves», said old time Zoot Suiter El Chava from HOYO MARAVILLA gang in the 1940s. In those times, Latino Zoot Suiters were defining their Americanism. Zooters were not accepted by the Anglo-Americans as true citizens, where language (Spanish) and skin color segregated you to the bottom of society. In the 1920s there were illegal mass deportations to Mexico of Mexican-American citizens who were trying to unionize their labor. In Downtown Los Angeles, my mother witnessed the public beatings of Latino Zooters by white US servicemen during World War II. The sailors would follow the Latinos into their neighborhoods to attack them. To protect themselves, the Latinos formed gangs based on which neighborhood they lived in. Gang names like 18 TH STREET, WHITE FENCE, ALPINE STREET, CLOVER STREET and AVENUES referred to actual locations and streets that still exist today. Latino Zooters were swinging to their own styles, their hair done in big Pompadours and their bodies draped in tailor-made suits with the pants starting under the armpits. They spoke *caló*, their own language, a cool jive of half-English half-Spanish rhythms. The term applied loosely to the spoken slang of gypsies and bullfighters in Mexico and Spain used at that time. Out of this 1940s Zoot Suiter experience came lowriders (a parallel car culture to the Anglo Hot Rod scene of the 1950s), gangster culture (Zoot Suiters from the 1940s, Pachucos in the 1950s, Cholos and Vatos of the 1960–70s, all these names are the same people, today we call them Home Boys). The Zooter experience also gave us tag names, and finally a unique style of East Los Angeles graffiti, called Cholo. The Mexican-American gangs were the first and Original Gangsters, hence the moniker OG. In the 1980s the Black gangsters adapted the dress code of the Home Boys, even copying the style of lowrider cars. The only difference would be their choice of «Western» serif typeface for their own graffiti. The renowned Black gangs, the Bloods and Crips, were

mere copies of Cholo culture. Even today
the Mexican gang members largely outnumber
the different Blacks gangs in LA county.

We must give credit to the gangs
for their steadfastness in keeping with
the graffiti traditions. Cholo type is stronger
today than ever before, and it has grown
into an international influence. In the graffiti
world, painting «battles» have taken place
between Japanese calligraphers and East LA
writers. This unique typeface has taken a very
long journey from a European prototype to
its use as a symbol of pride for an American
gangster culture. To have remained intact
is formidable, and its future usage is
in the hands of the next generation.

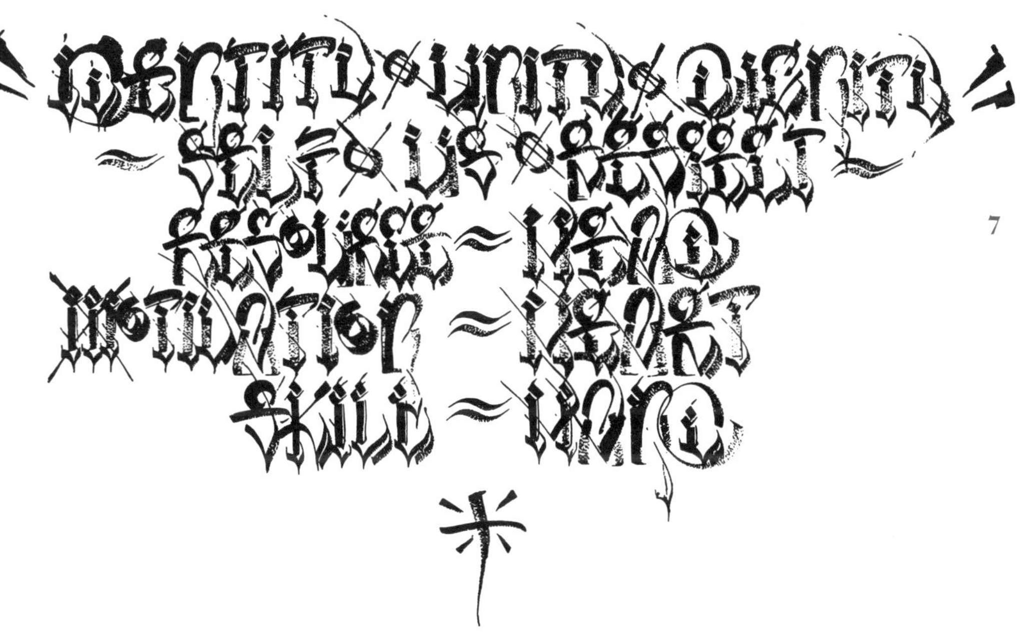

« IDENTITY × UNITY × DIGNITY »
— SELF × US × RESPECT —
RESOURCE — HEAD
MOTIVATION — HEART
SKILL — HAND
†

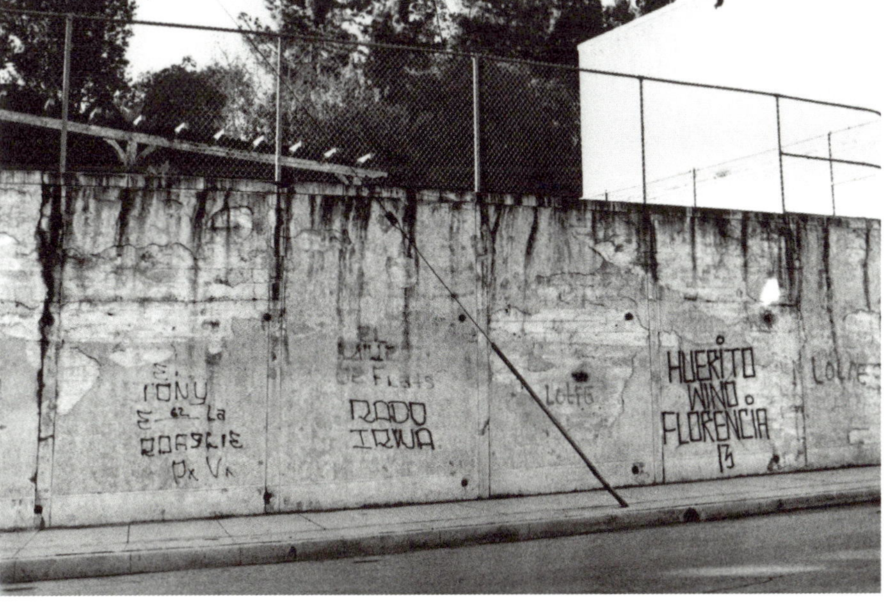

EL
TONY
E — 62 — La
(EAST 1962 LOS ANGELES)
ROSALIE
P × V ×
(POR VIDA)

EL
MIKE
DE FLATS

RADO
IRWA

HUERITO
WINO
FLORENCIA
13

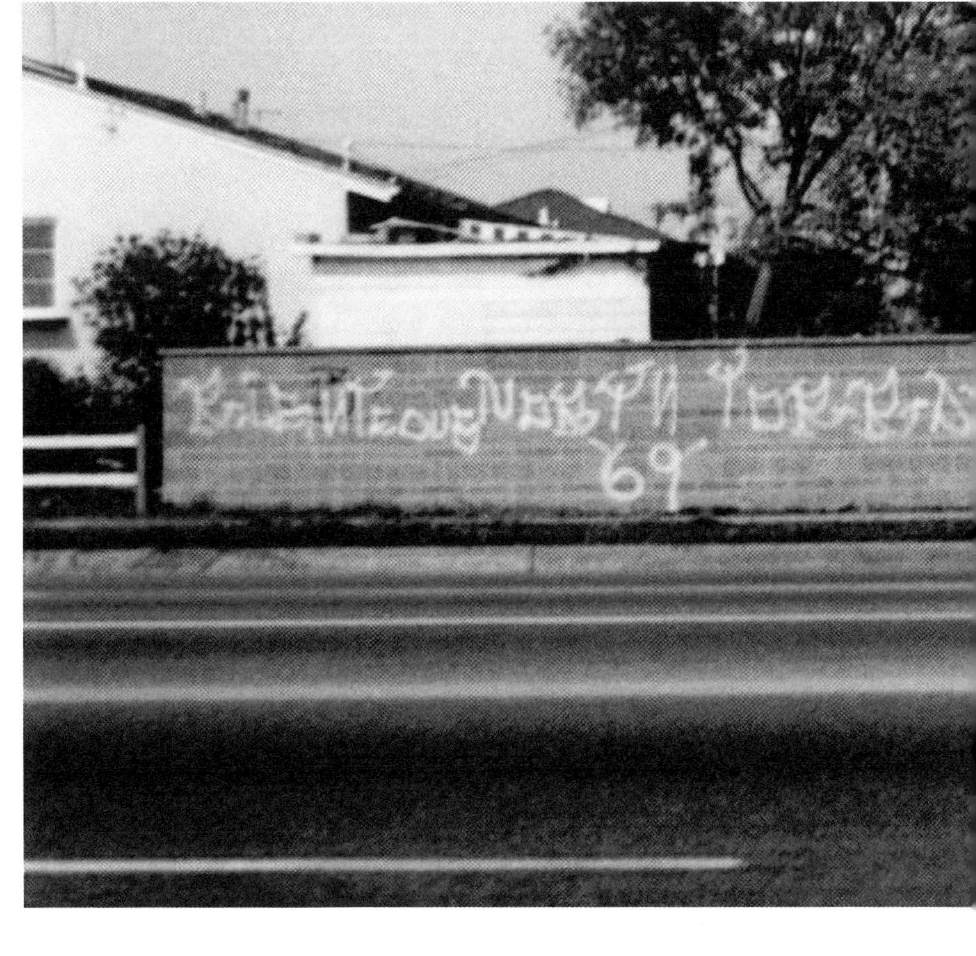

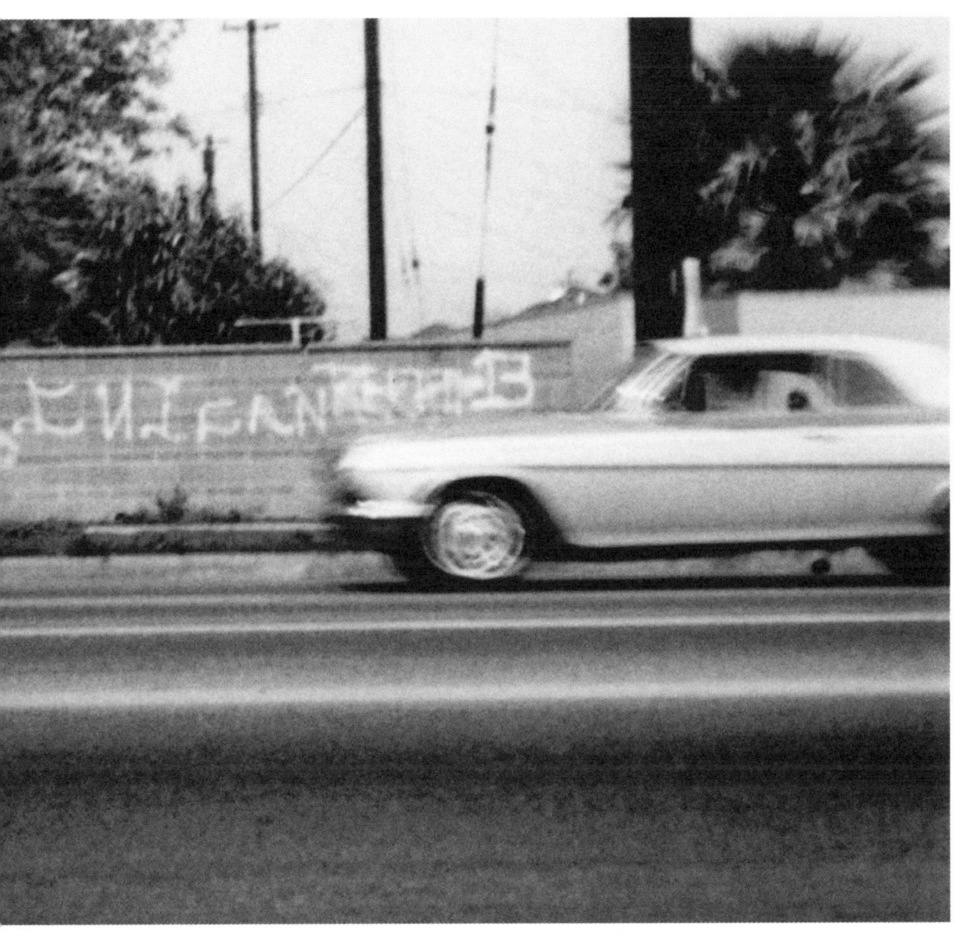

RIGHTEOUS NORTH TORRANCE CHICAN[OS] 13
'69'

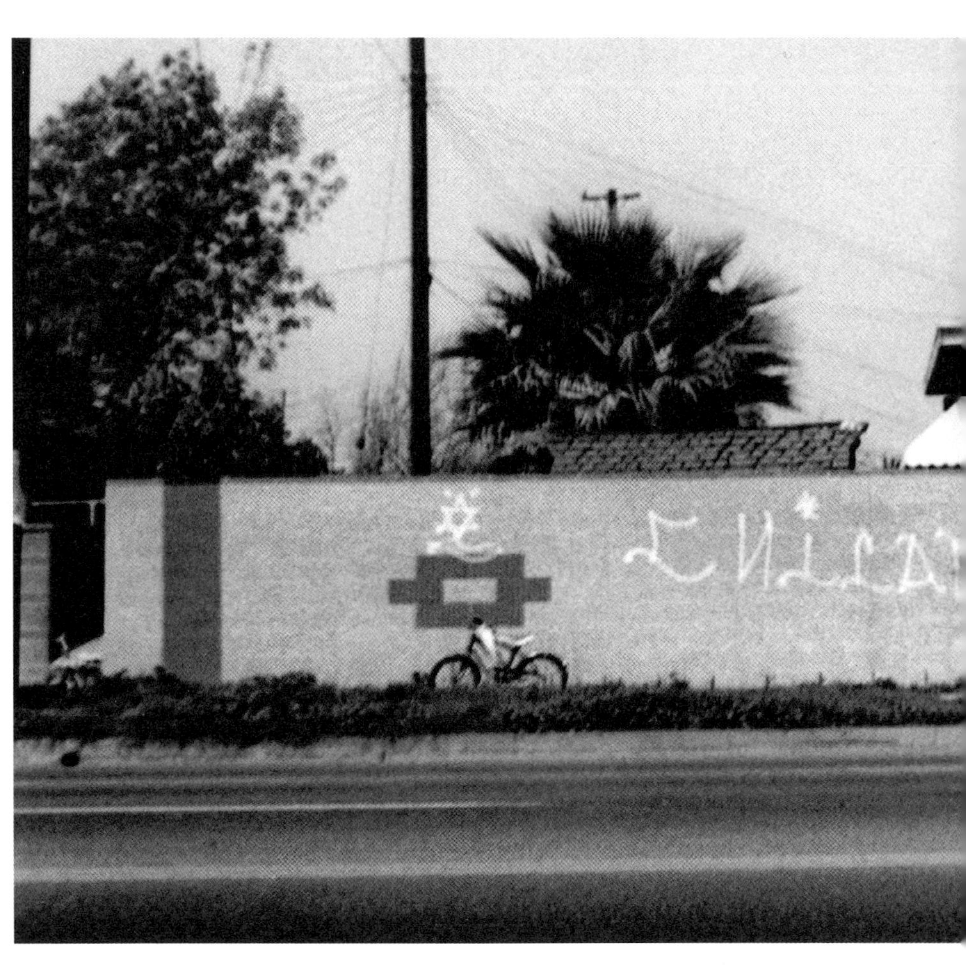
CHICA

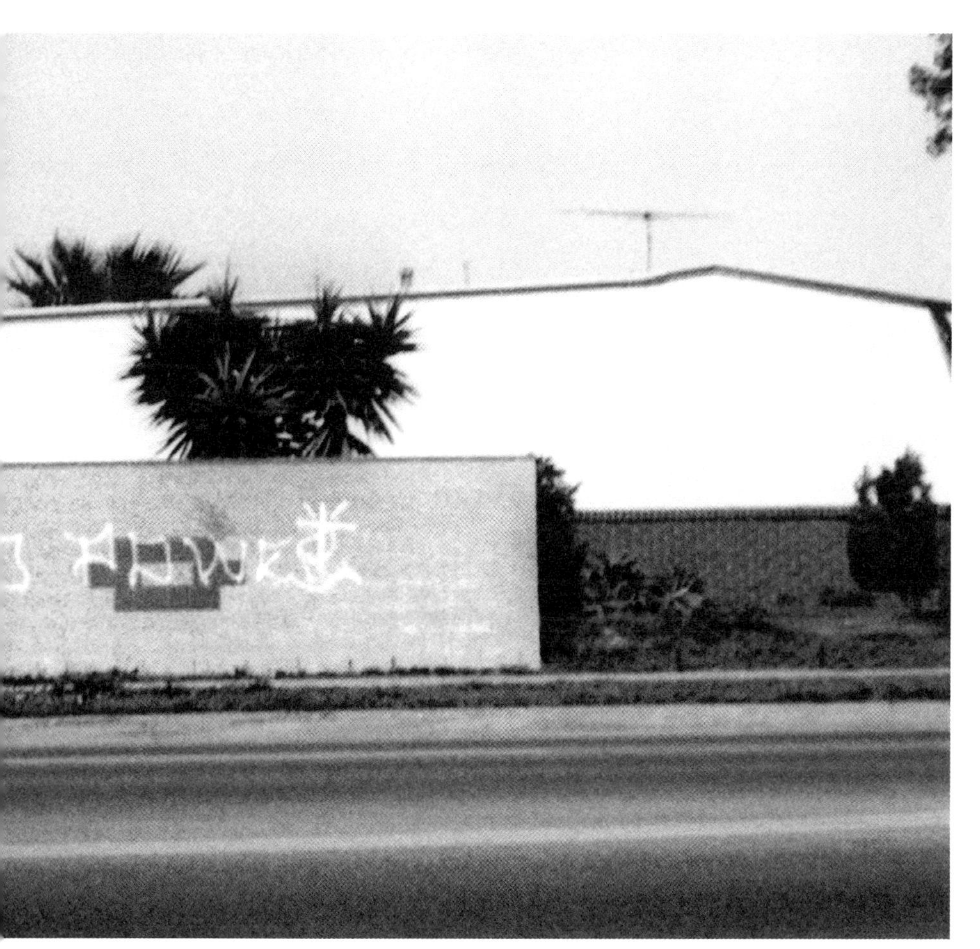

✶ CHICANO POWER † (PACHUCO CROSS)

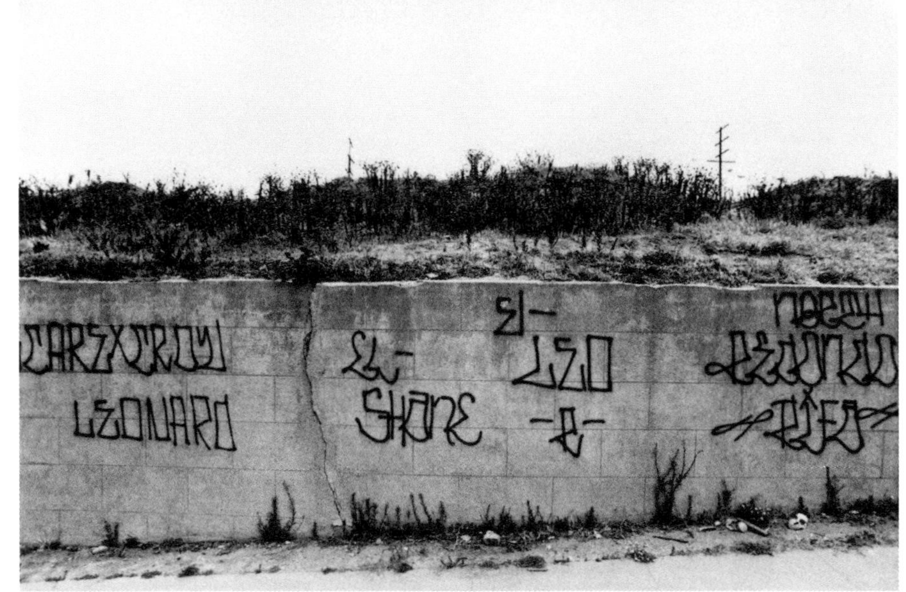

[S]CARE×CROW   EL—   EL—   NORTH
LEONARD   SHaNE   LEO   REDONDO
                           —R—   —RIFa—
                           (RIFA)

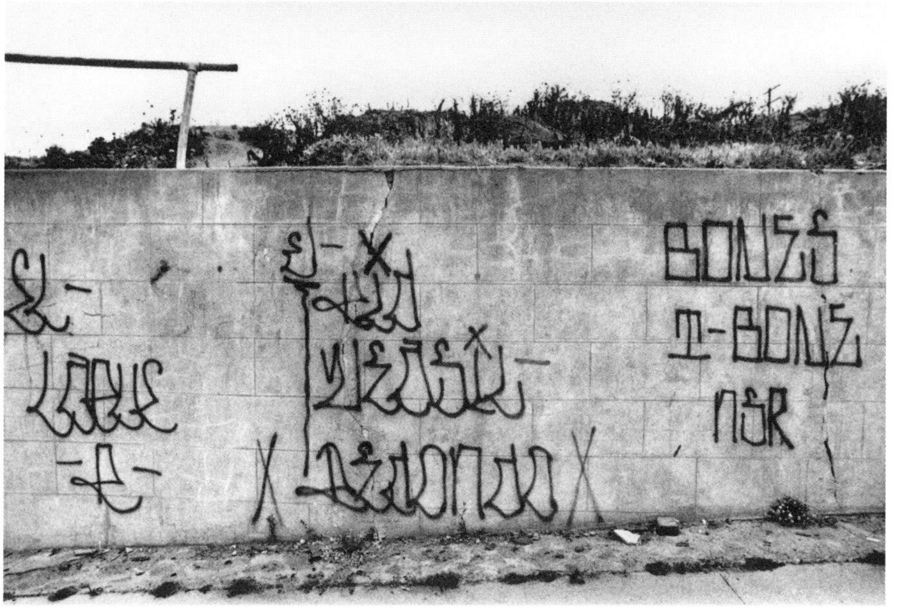

EL —
LARVE
— R —
(RIFA)

EL —
KID
WEASIL —
×REDONDO×

BONES
T-BONE
NSR

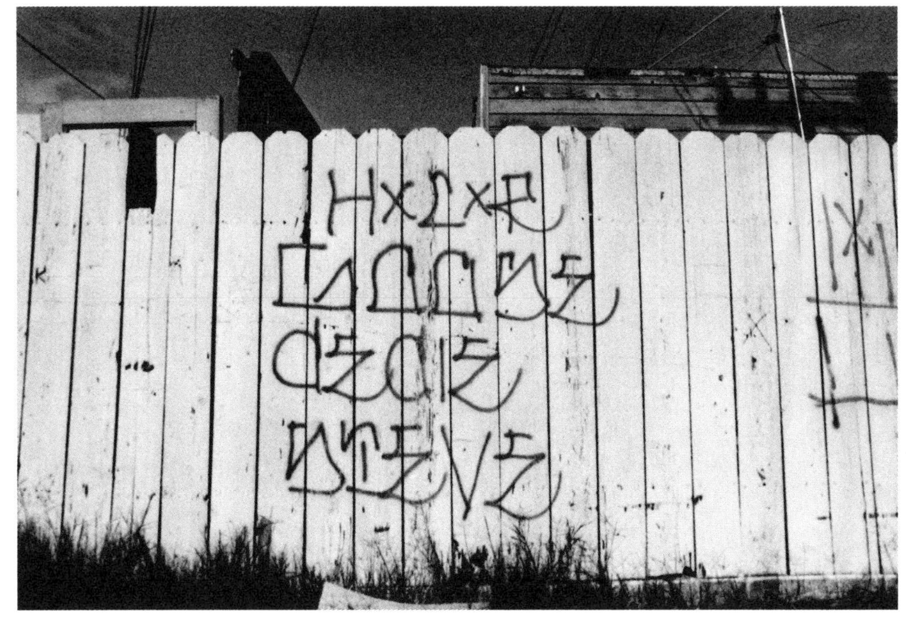

H×C×R
(HARBOR CITY RIFA)
GOOSE
dedie
STEVE

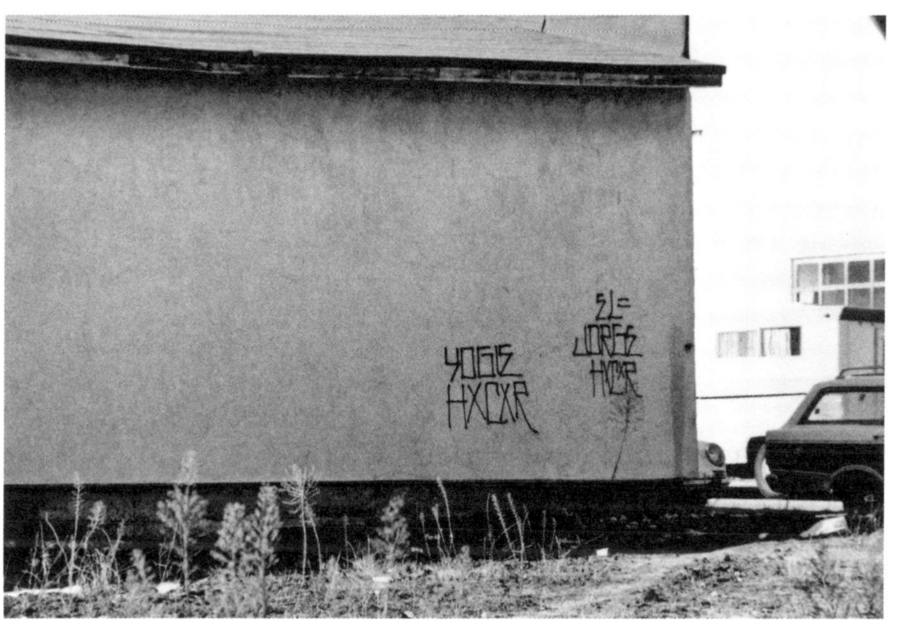

YOGIE   EL=
H×C×R   JORGE
(HARBOR   H×C×R
CITY RIFA)

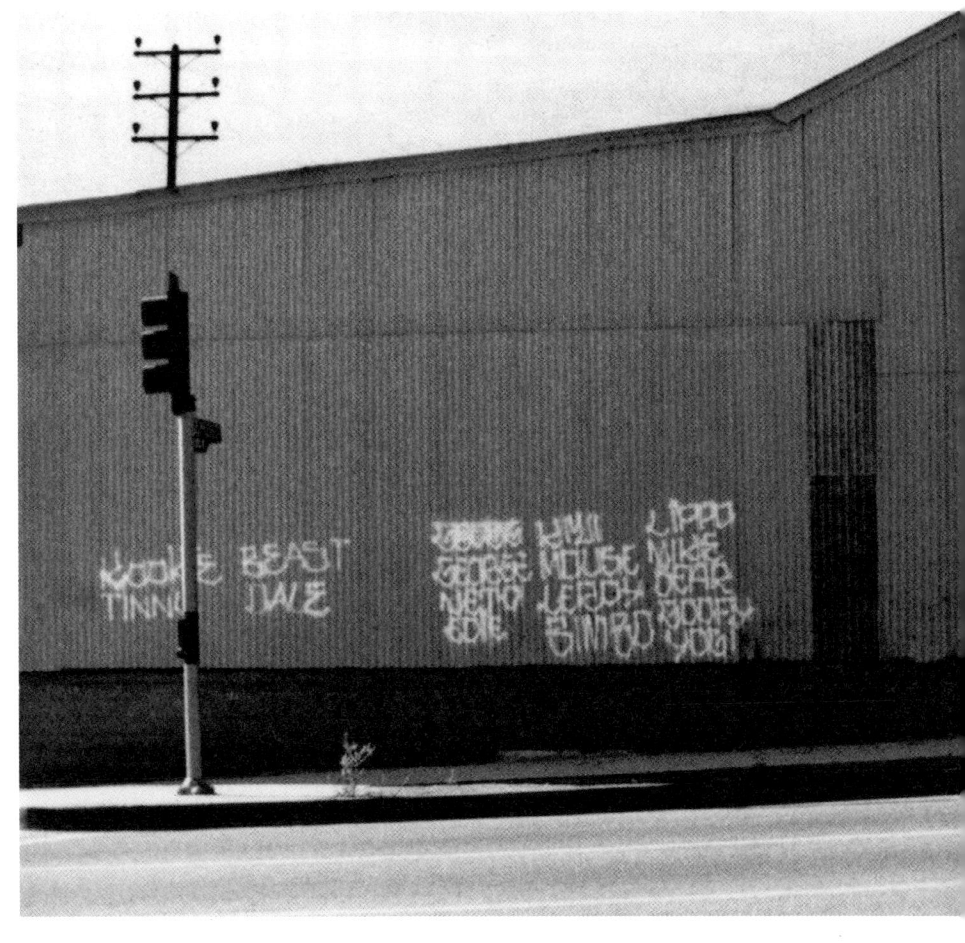

KOOKIE	BEAST	—	KIWI	LIPPO
TINNY	DALE	GEORGE	MOUSE	MIKE
		NETO	LEROY	BEAR
		EDIE	BIMBO	GOOFY
				YOGI

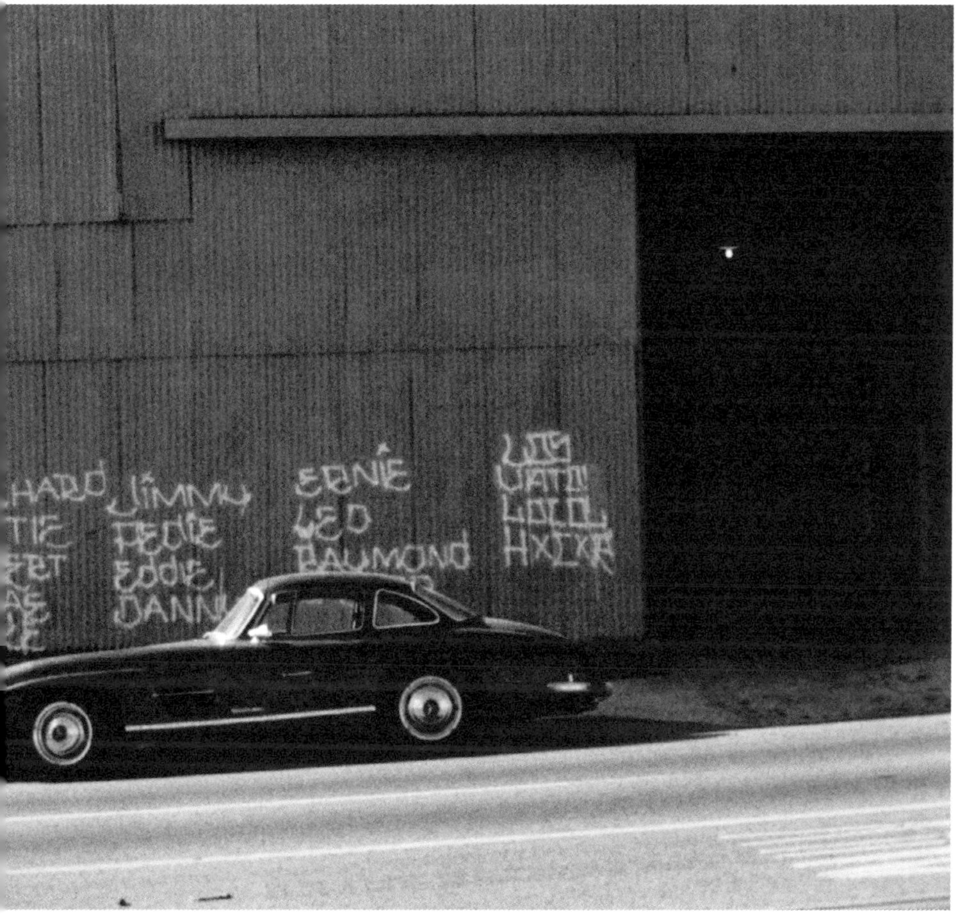

RICHARD   JIMMY   ERNIE   LOS
ARTIE   PEDIE   LEO   VATOS
ALBERT   EDDIE   RAYMOND   LOCOS
RENAE   DANNY   H×C×R
MIKE

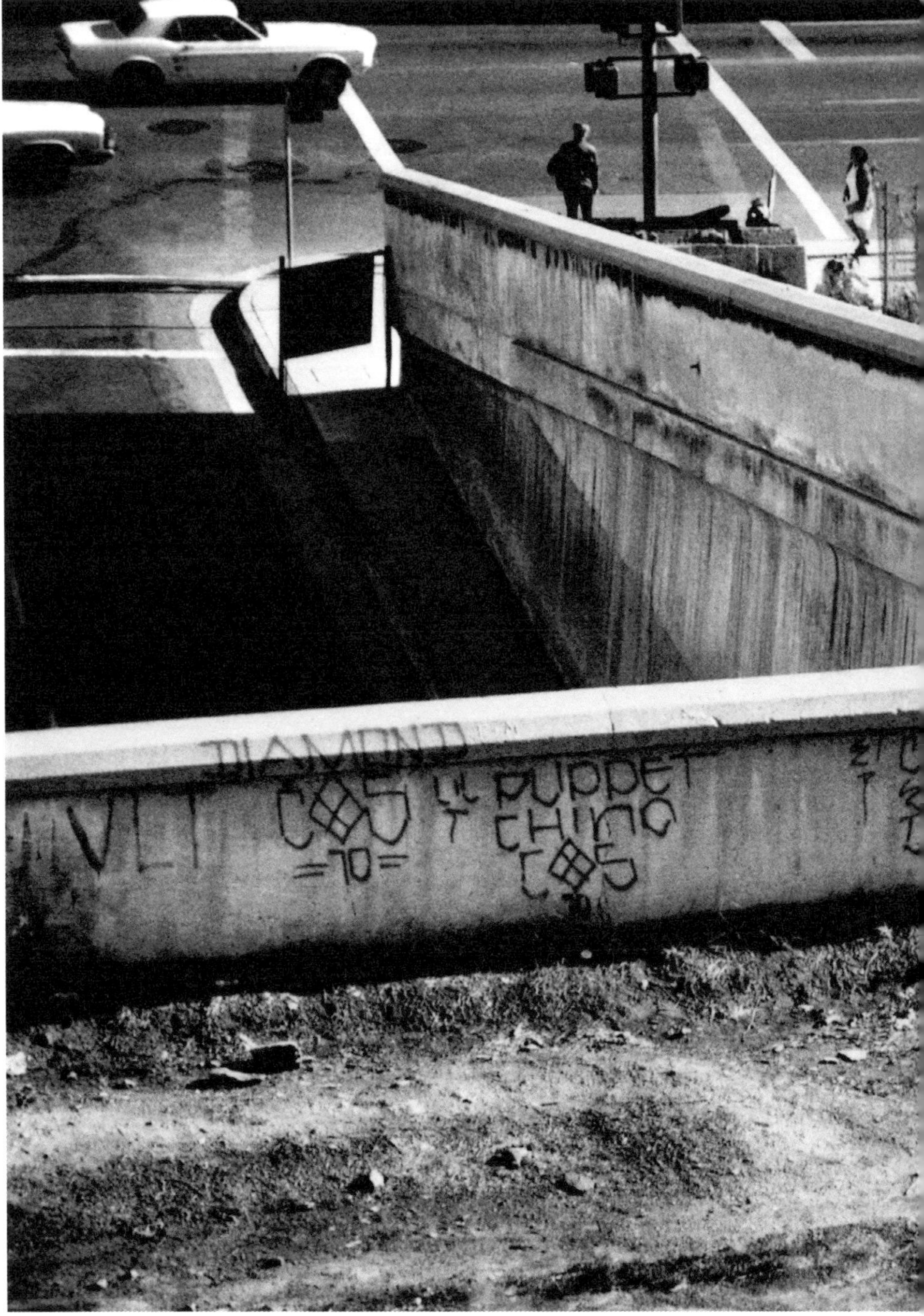

DIAMOND
VLT
PUPPET
THING

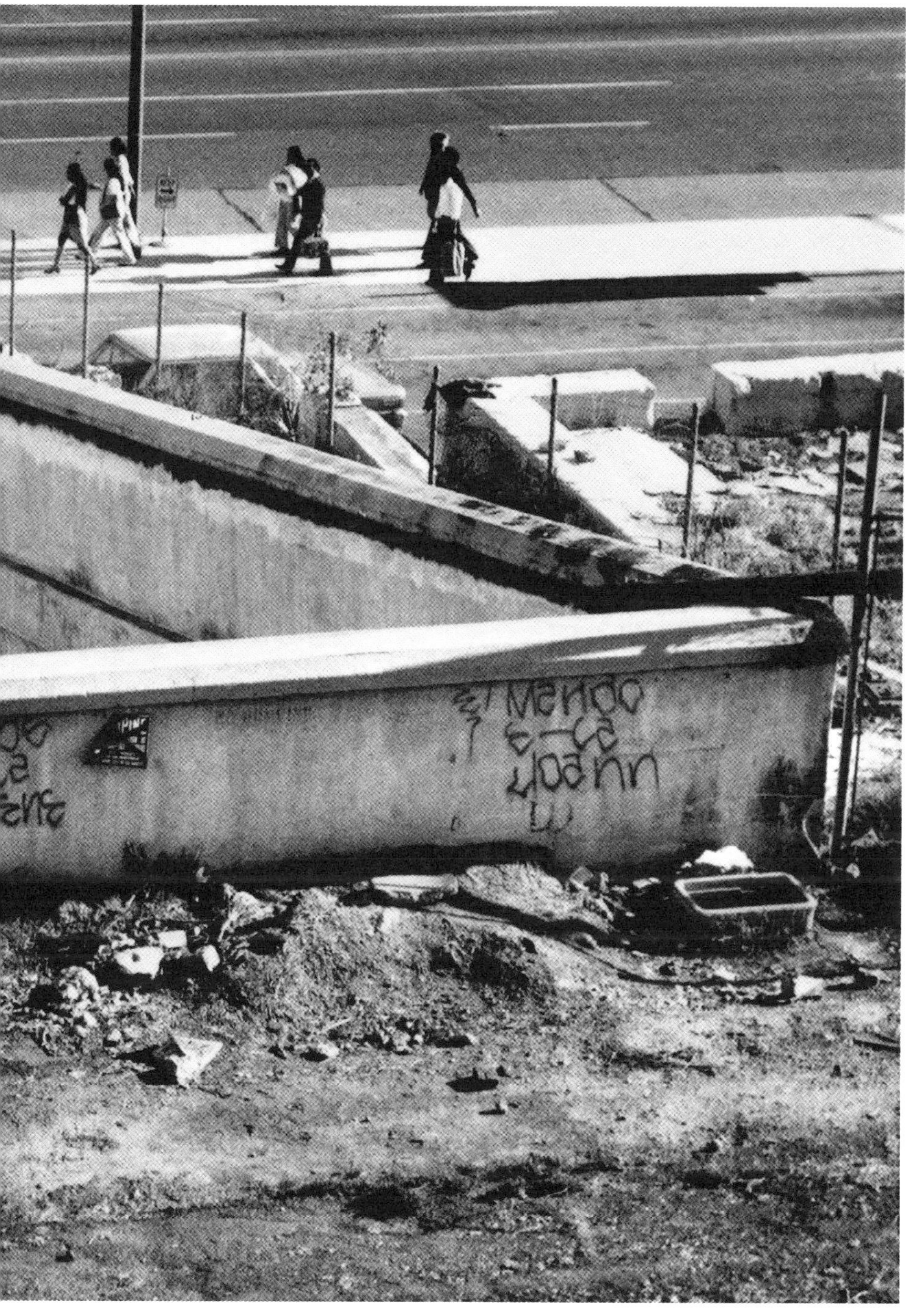

DIAMOND	LIL PUPPET	EL CARLOS	EL MANDO
C◊S	CHINO	E — LA	E — LA
(CON SAFOS)	C◊S	DARLENE	JOANN
=70=	70		

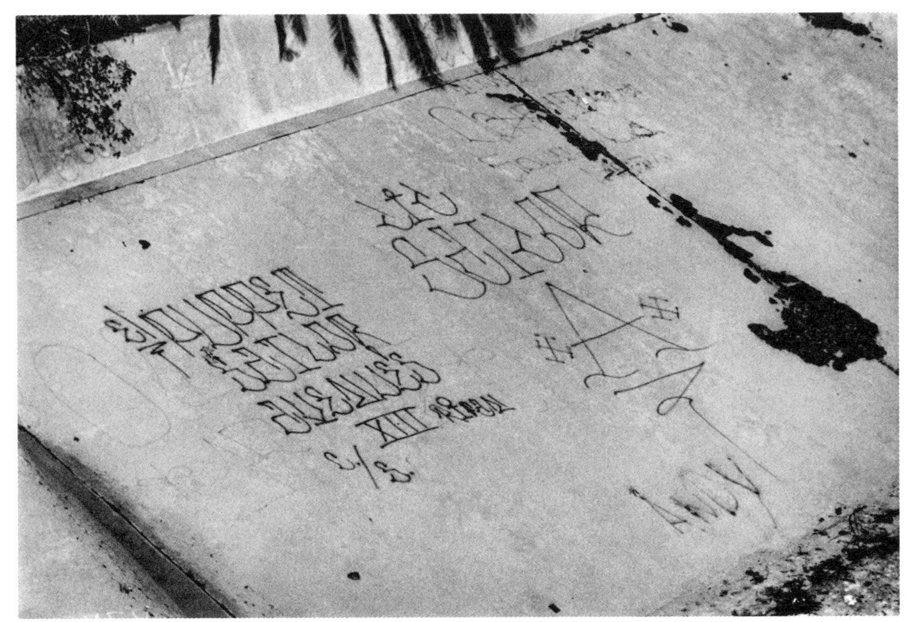

EL PUPPET   LIL
SAILOR   SAILOR
AVENUES   *A*
C./S. XIII RIFAN
(CON SAFOS)

NITE OWL   BILLY   13
AVENUE'S   E×S XIII   *BILL*
               (EAST SIDE 1967
               THIRTEEN)

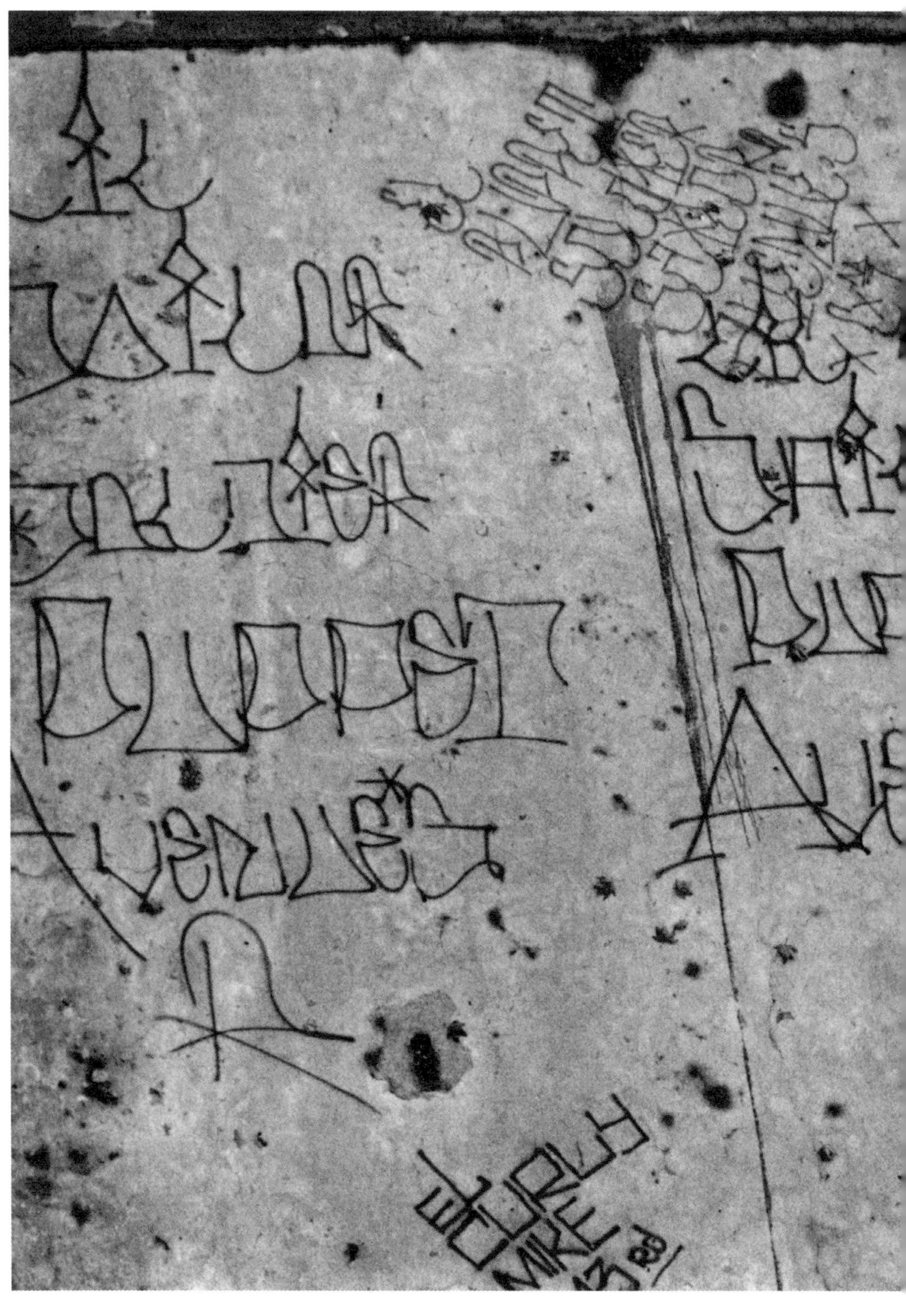

LIL   EL   EL PUPPET
SAILOR   CURLY   SOLDIER
SOLDIER   MIKE   SAILOR
PUPPET   43 RD   AVENUES
AVENUES   ×C×M×
R   XIII

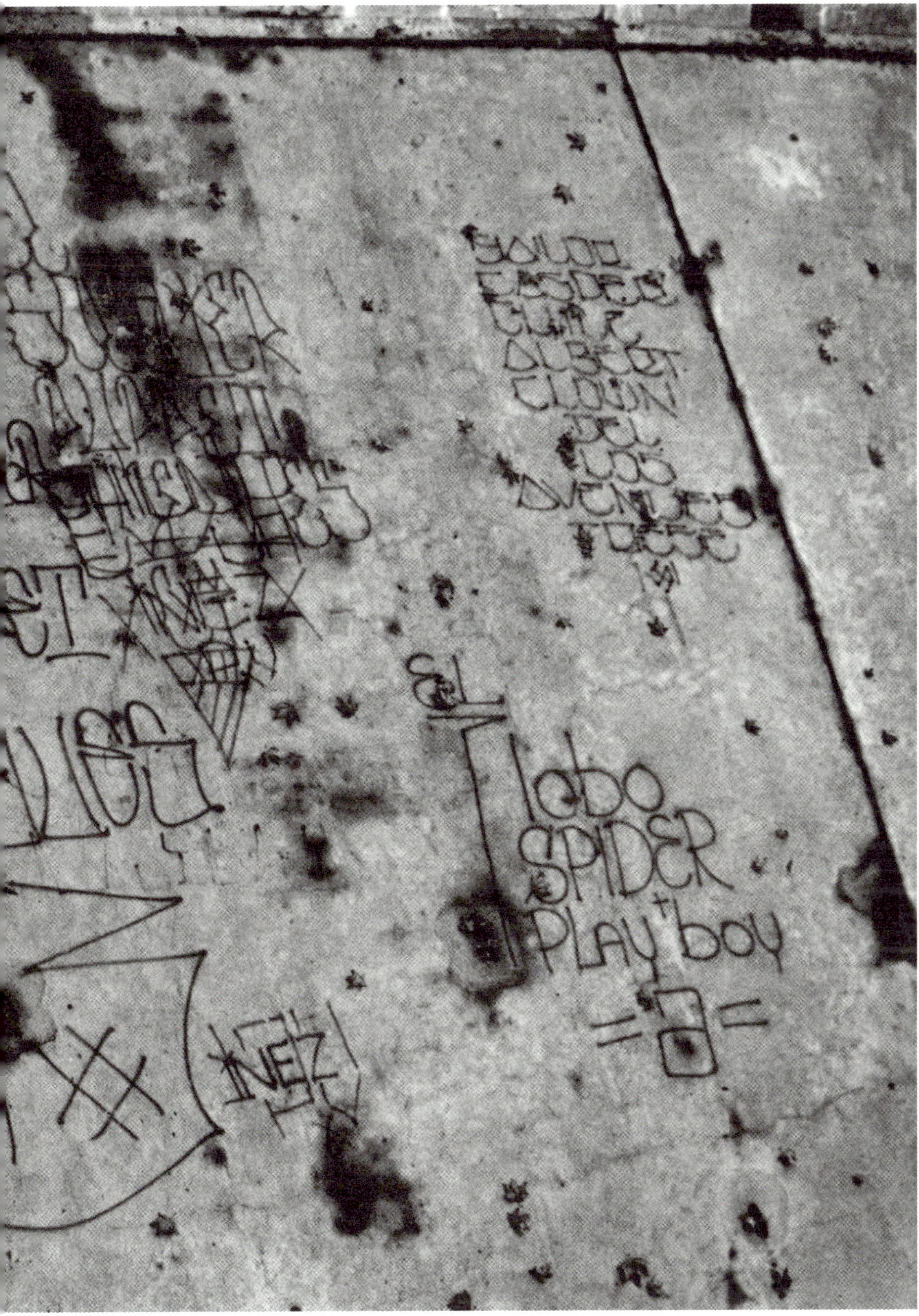

LIL | EL SOLDIER | EL | SAILOR | / DEL
SAILOR | PUPPET | LOBO | CASPER | LOS
PUPPET | AVENUES | SPIDER | CHILE | AVENUES
AVENUES | ×C×M× | PLAYBOY | ALBERT | TRESE
1#3 | XIII | = a = | CLOWN / | |∗|
INEZ / PV
(POR VIDA)

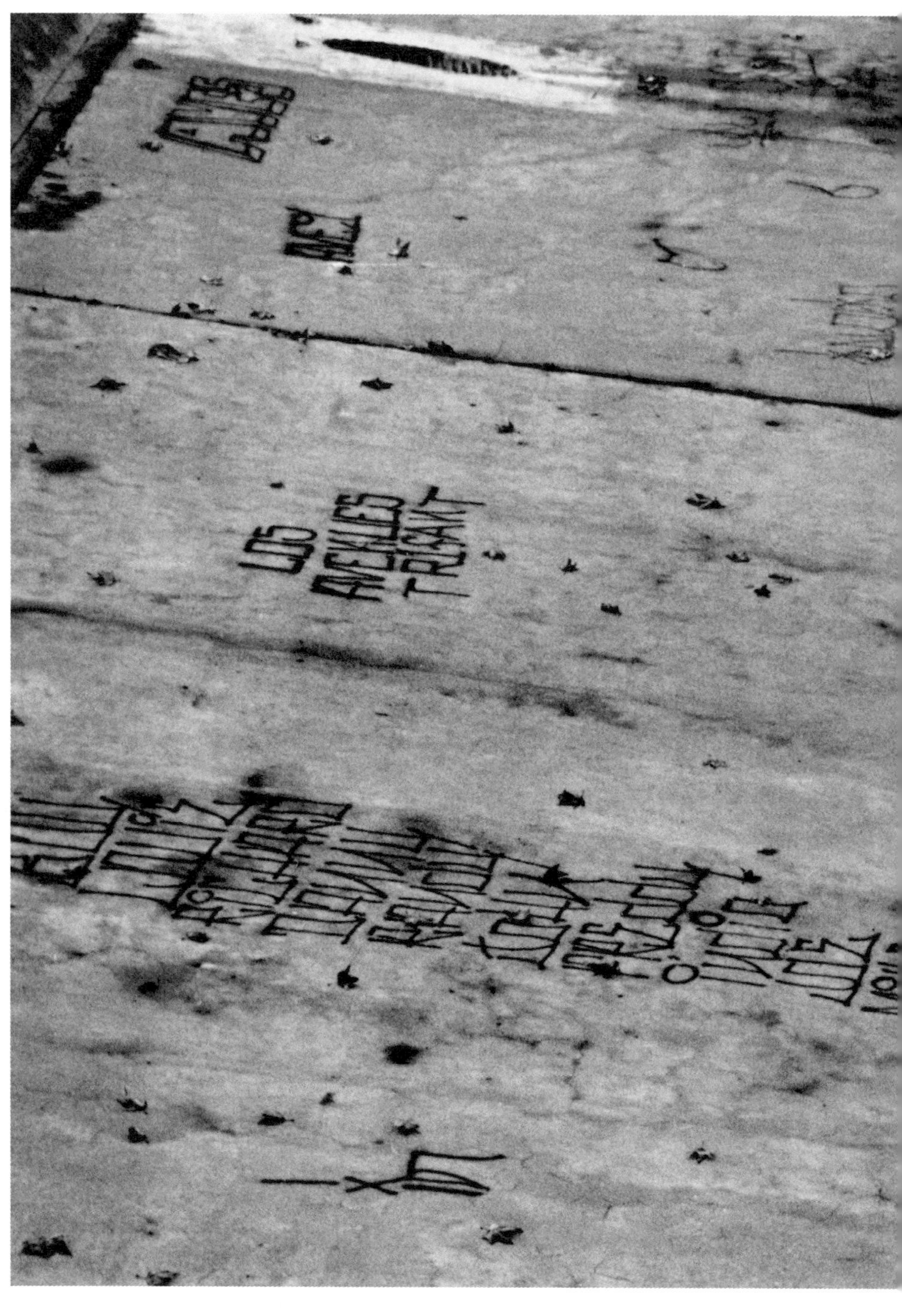

[BOY]
LOUIE
RICHARD
DANNY
RANDY
JOHN /

/ FREDDY
INDIO
JOE
MIKE
HERSHEY
VINCE /

/ TONY
CURLY
AVENUES
RIFANDO
AÑO LOCO
1970

LOS
AVENUES
— RIFAN —

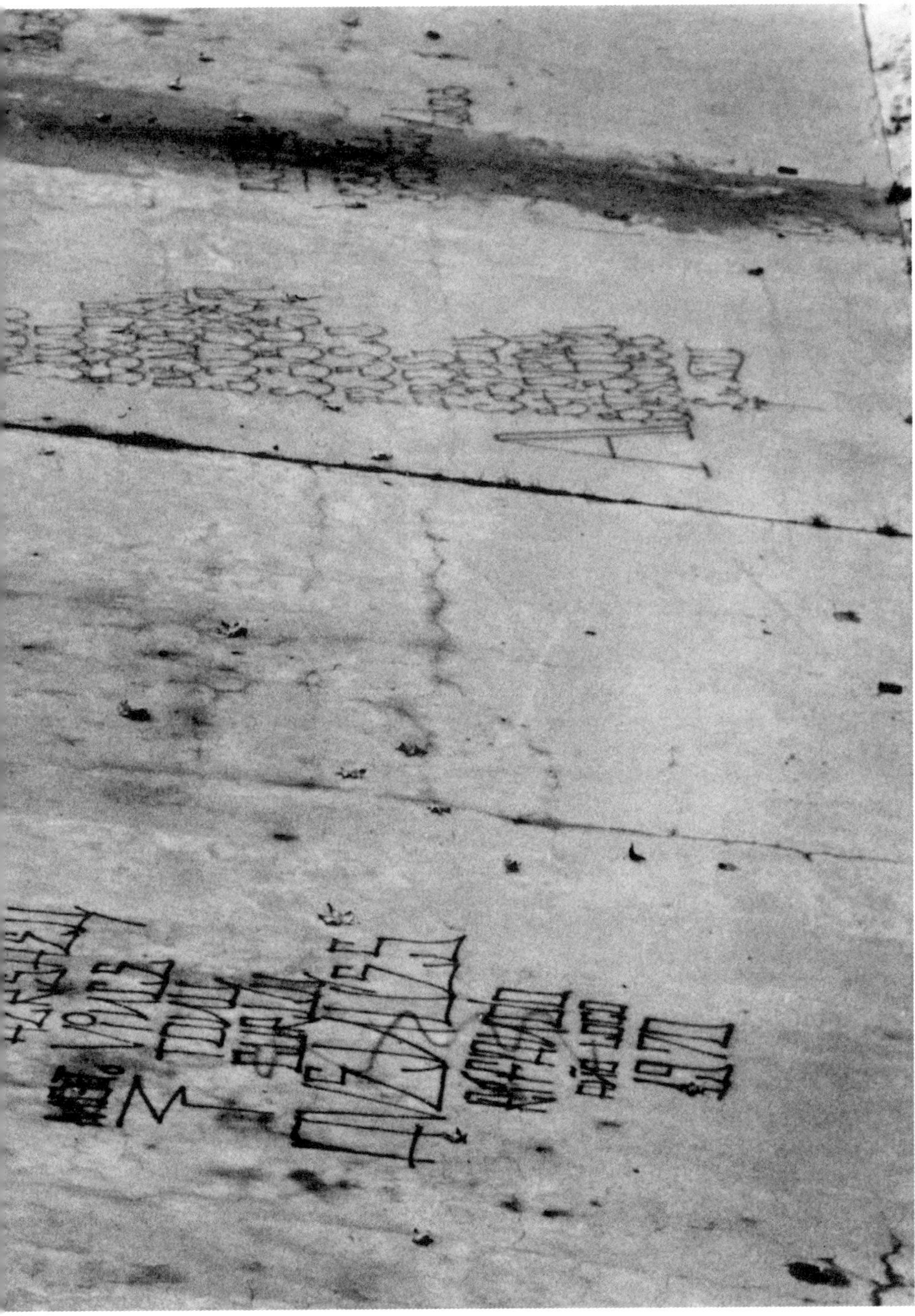

INDIO   /SOLDIER   /SHADOW   AVES   AVES
PUPPET   CASPER   AVENUES   (AVENUES)   (AVENUES)
REBEL   F LACO   L XIII
LOCO   FROG
SAILOR   CAPPY
PINGUIN /   SHORTY /

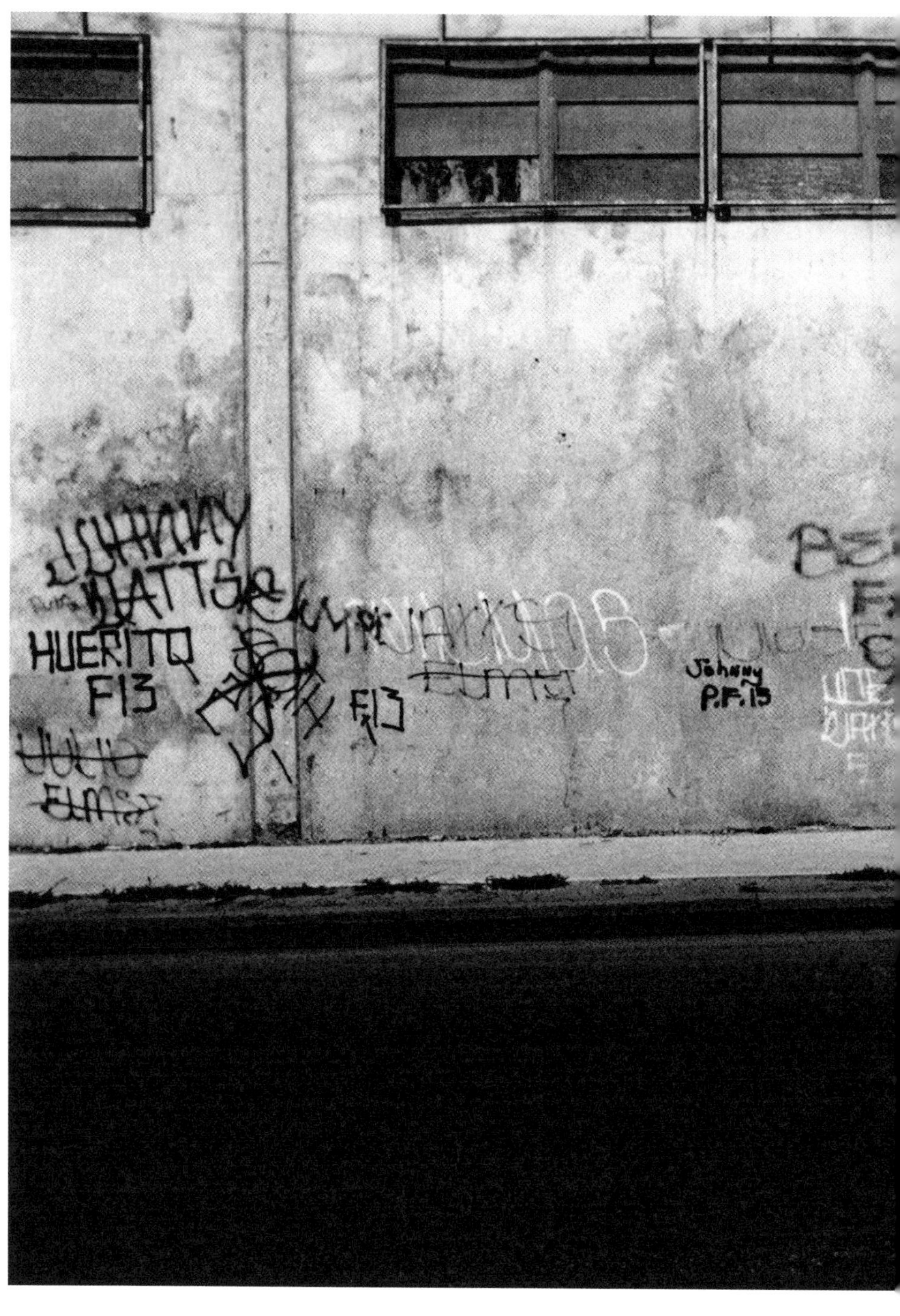

JULIO   JOHNNY   WILMAS   JOHNNY   MOSCA
ELM ST   WATTS ELM ST   WATTS   P.F.13
                        ELM ST   (PRIMERA FLATS)   JOE
         HUERITO   WATTS
         F13
         (FLORENCIA)

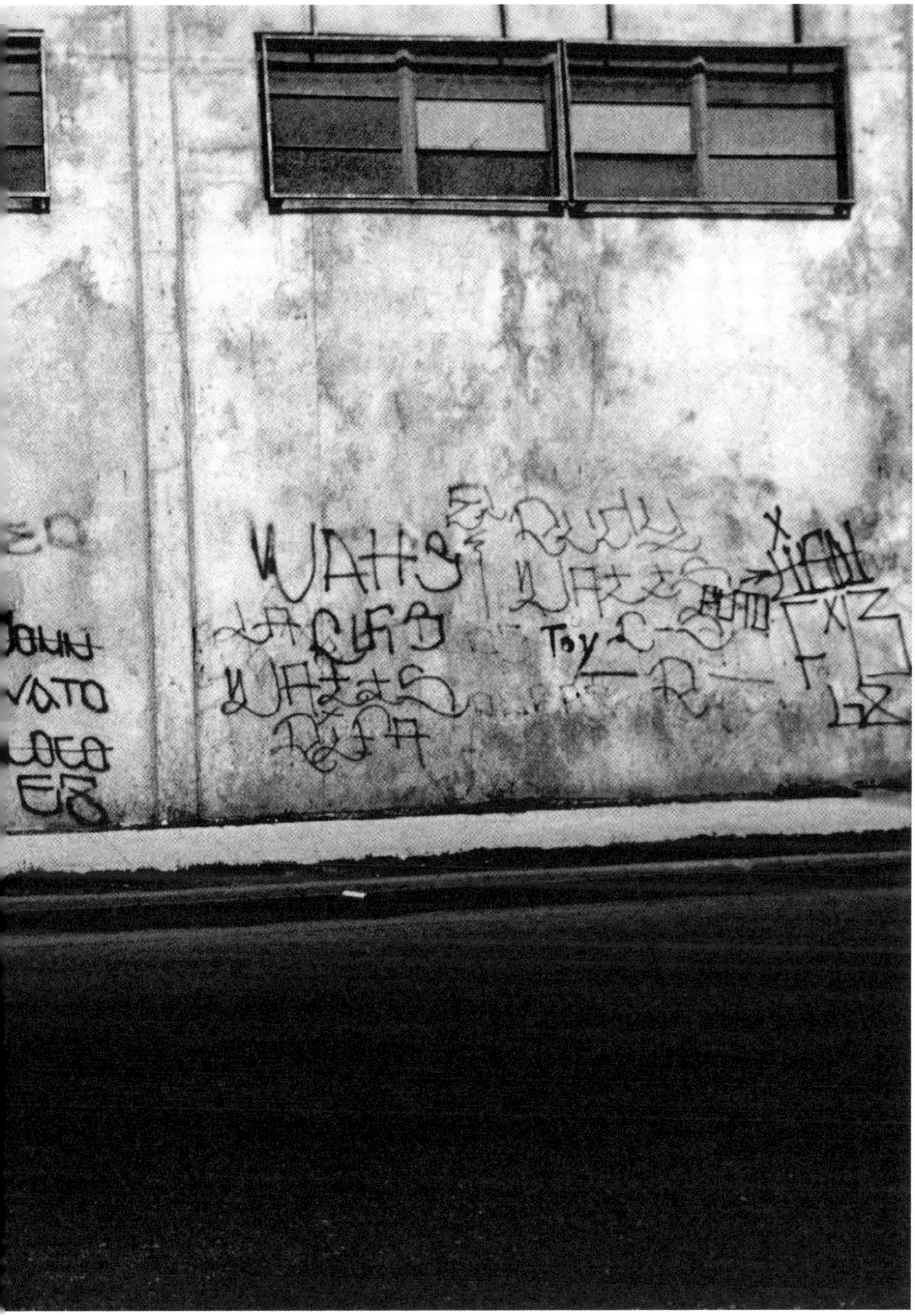

BEAVER	EL	WATTS	EL RUDY	(PUTO →)
F×13	JOHN	LA (LOS ANGELES)	WATTS	JON
C/S	VATO	C*S	C-S	F×13
(CON SAFOS)	LOCO	(CON SAFOS)	(CON SAFOS)	68
	68	LA	— R —	
		WATTS		
		RIFA		

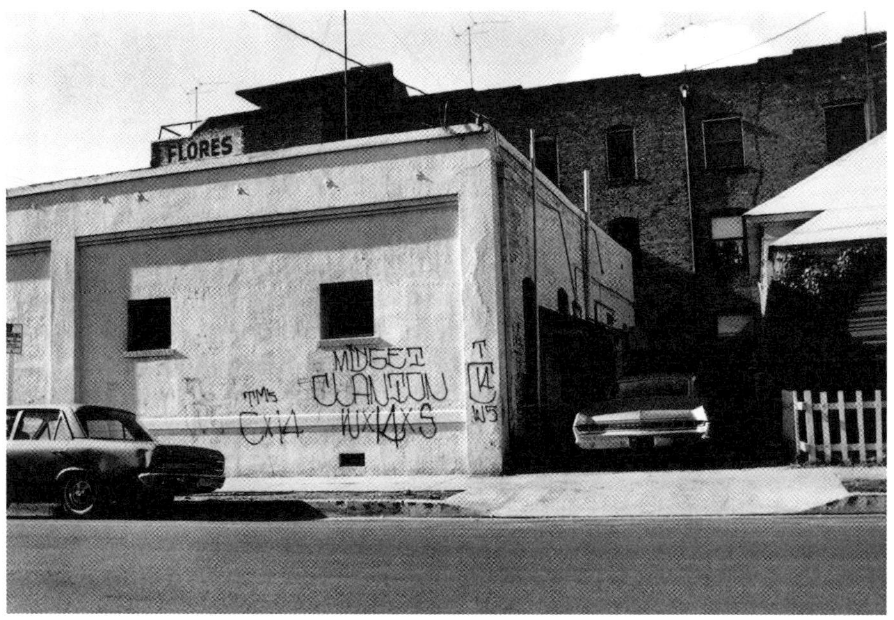

TM'S	MIDGET	T
(TINY MALOS)	CLANTON	(TINY'S)
C×14	W×14×S	C14
(CLANTON 14)	(WEST SIDE	(CLANTON 14)
	14TH STREET)	WS
		(WEST SIDE)

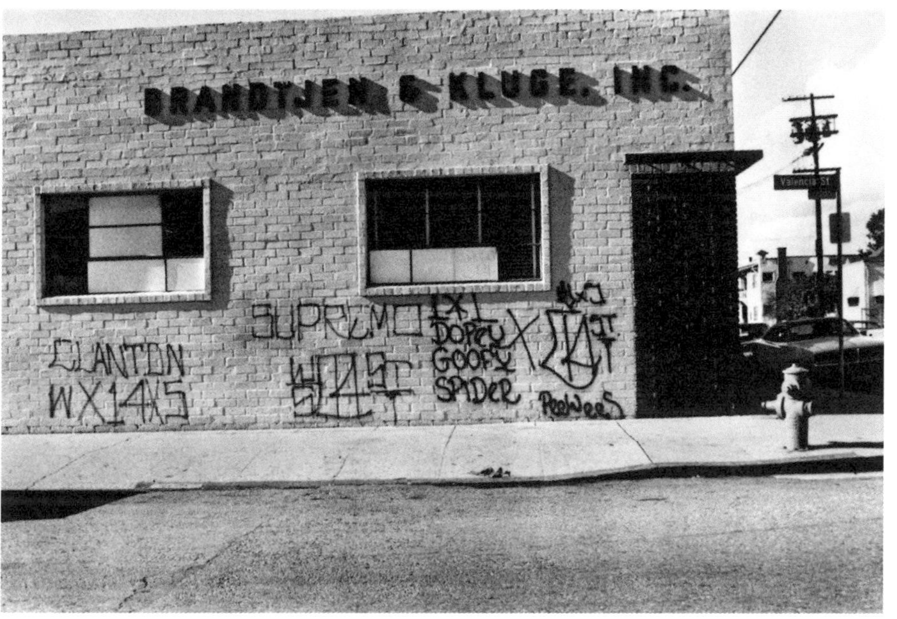

CLANTON	SUPREMO	LIL	WS
W × 14 × S	WS C 14 ST	DOPEY	(WEST SIDE)
(WEST SIDE	(WESTSIDE	GOOFY	C 14 ST
14 TH STREET)	CLANTON	SPIDER	(CLANTON
	14 TH STREET)		14 TH STREET)
			PEEWEES

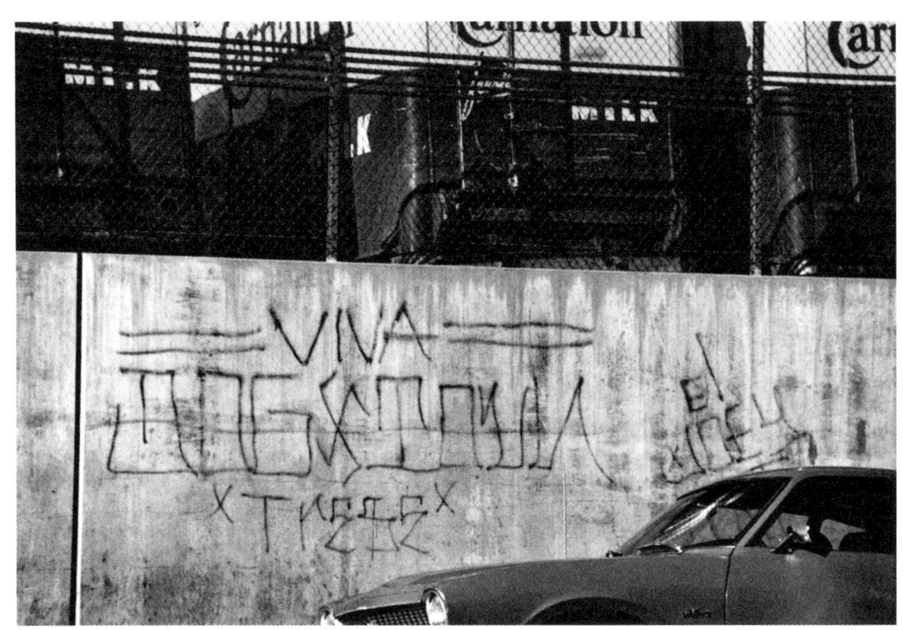

=VIVA=
DOG＊TOWN
×TRESE×

EL
JOEY

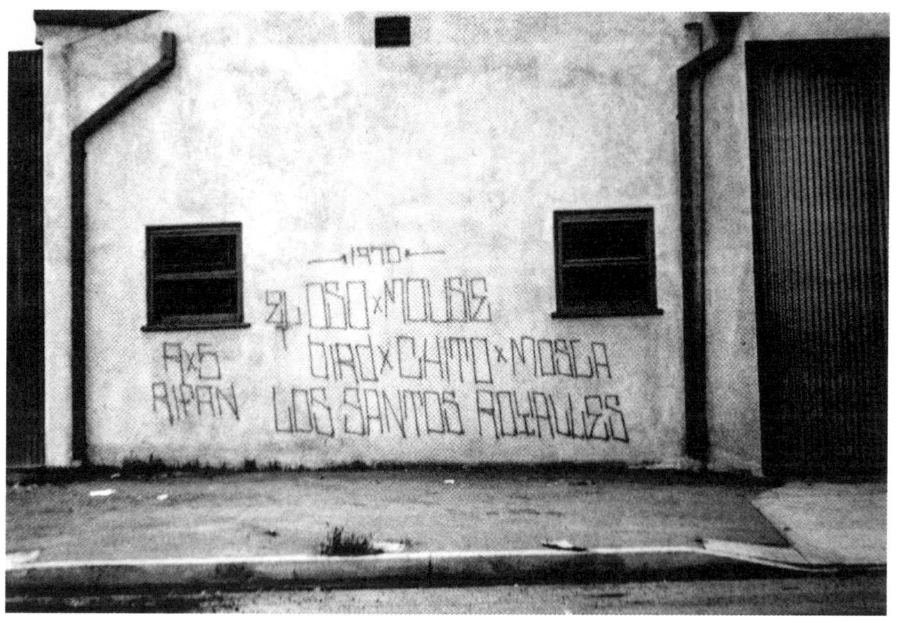

33

R × S
(ROYAL SAINTS)
RIFAN

– 1970 –
EL OSO × MOUSE
BIRD × CHITO × MOSCA
LOS SANTOS ROYALES

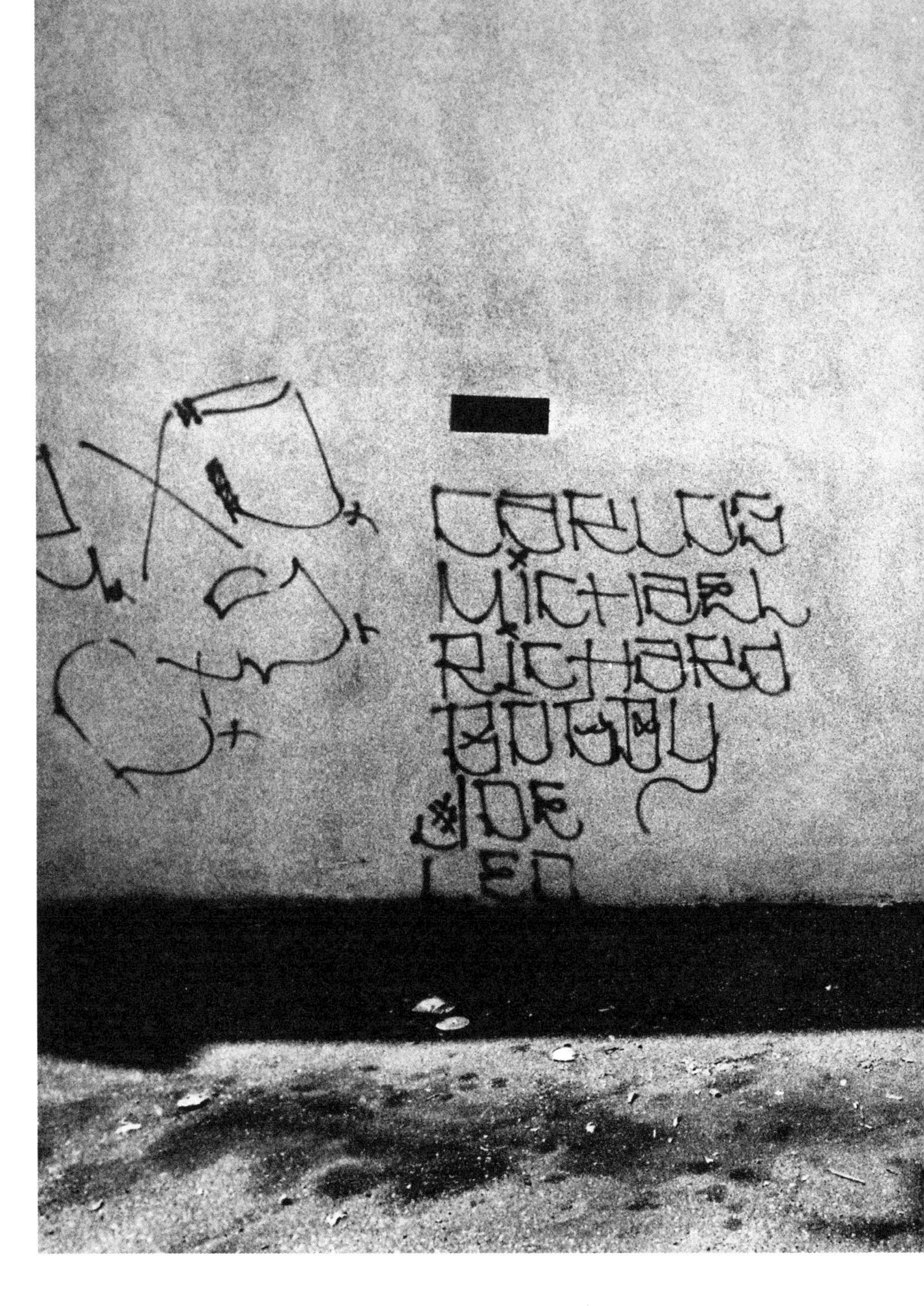

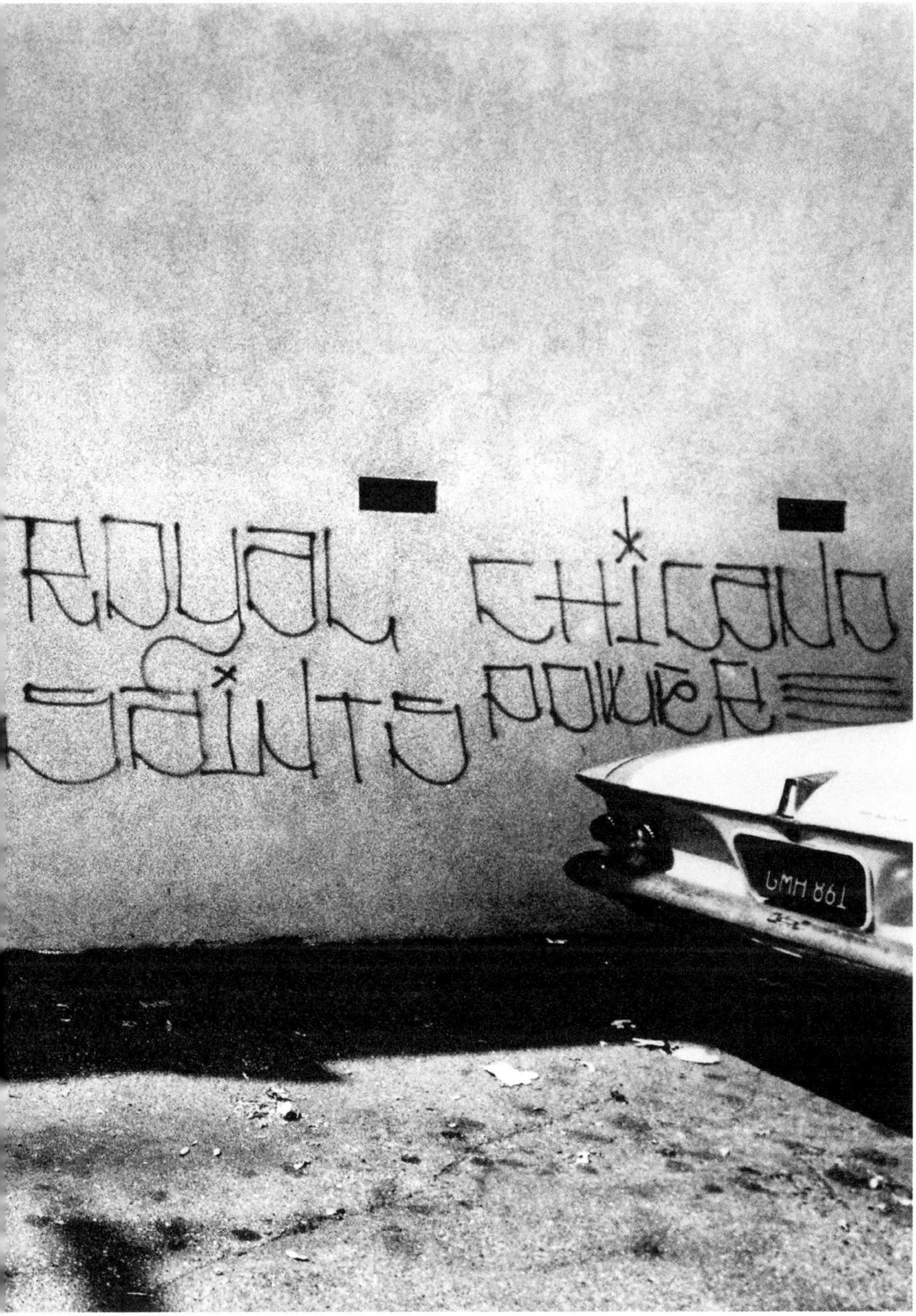

[R]×S CARLOS ROYAL CHICANO
(ROYAL SAINTS) MICHAEL SAINTS POWER—
C×S RICHARD
(CON SAFOS) BOBBY
  JOE
  LEO

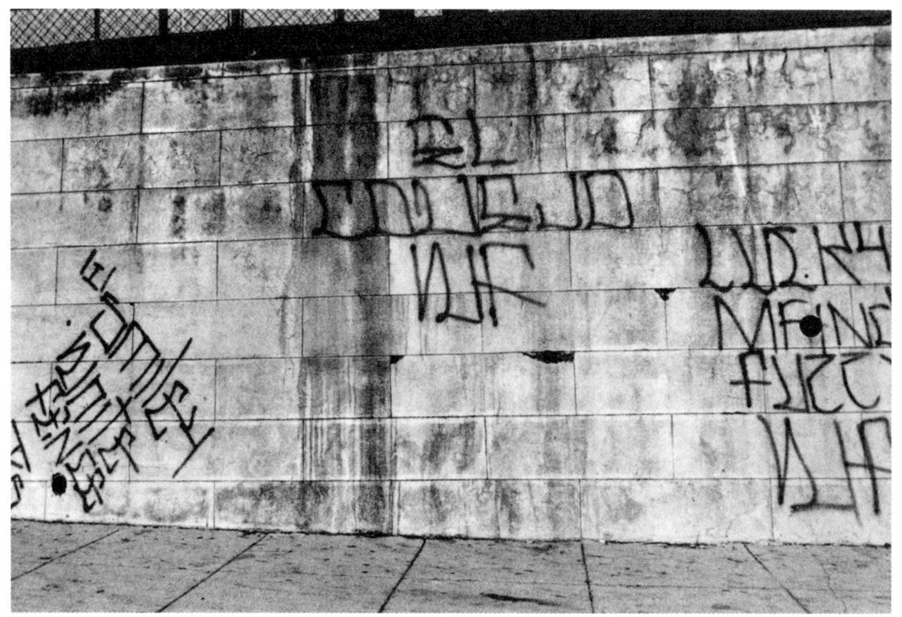

LIL SMILEY   EL   LUCKY

WHITE   CONEJO   MAND[O]

FENCE   WF   FUZZ[Y]

(WHITE FENCE)   WF

CHAPOLIN
JOHNNY
× LOCO ×
RSP
(RANCHO
SAN PEDRO)

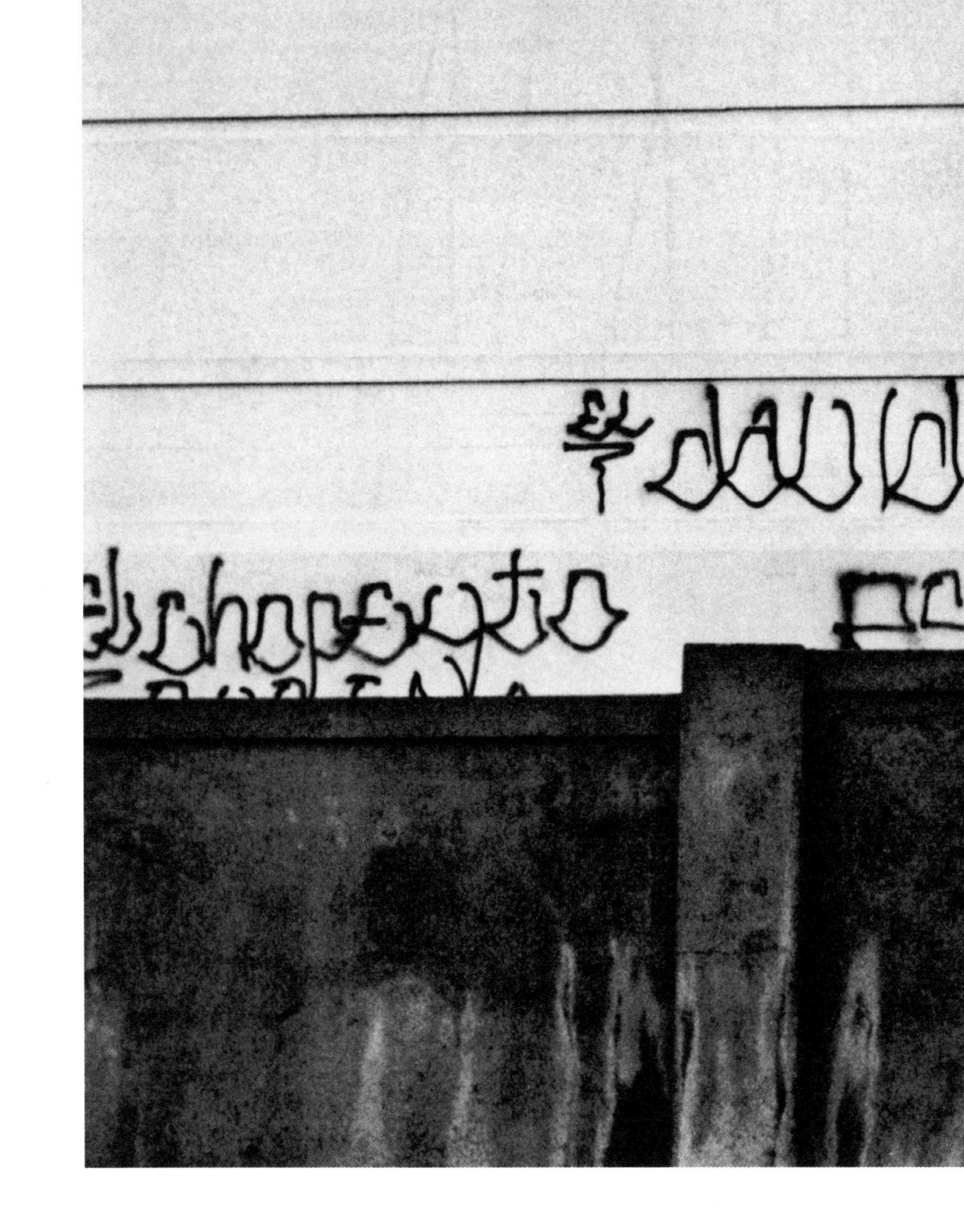

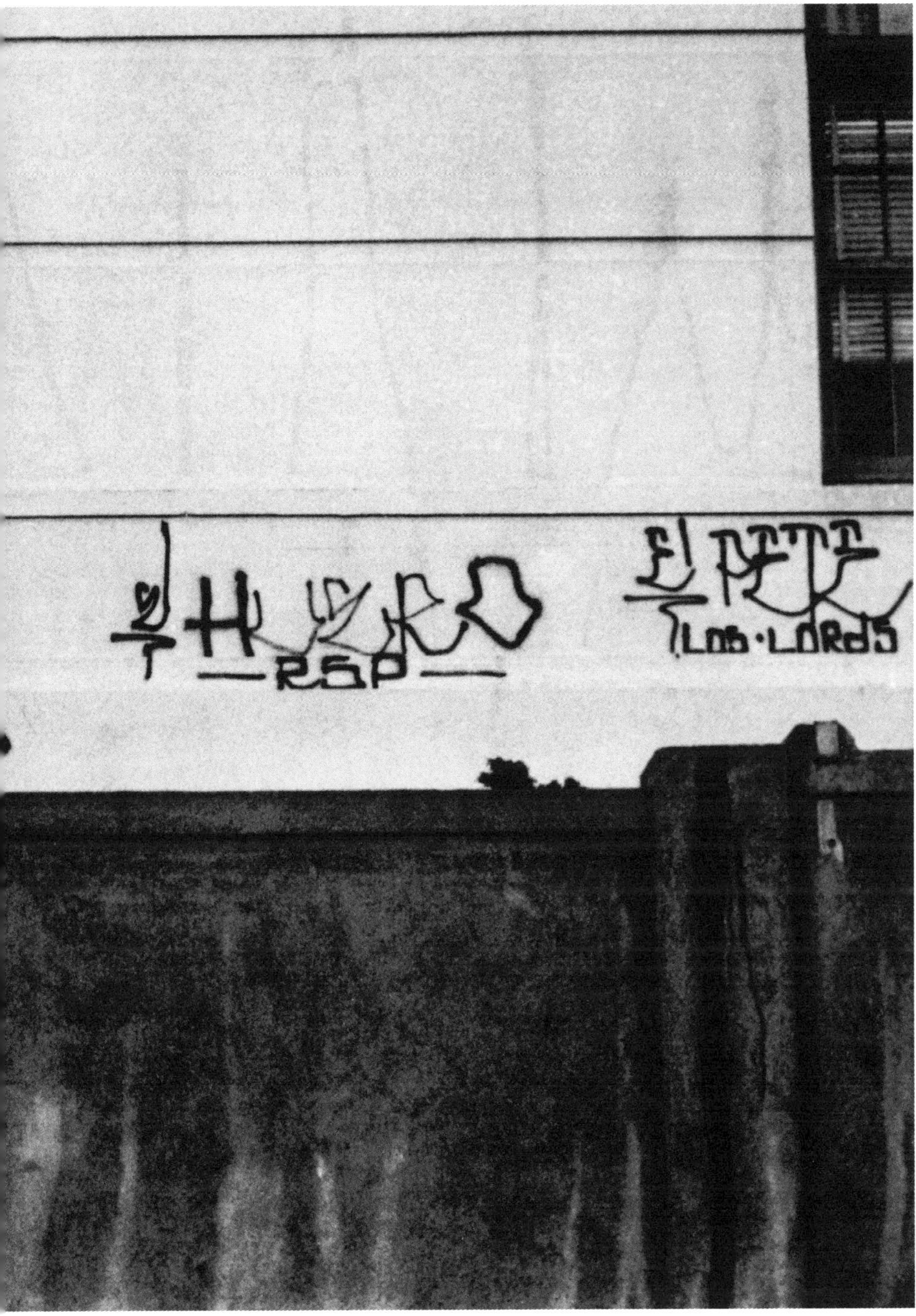

EL chopeyto

EL david

RSP
(RANCHO
SAN PEDRO)

EL HUERO
— RSP —

EL PETE
LOS·LORDS

CHATO × GATO × FISH × PATO 72
CROW × L (LIL) LARGO × TOPO × BOY
VNE × CHICO[S]
(VARRIO NUEVO ESTRADA BOYS)

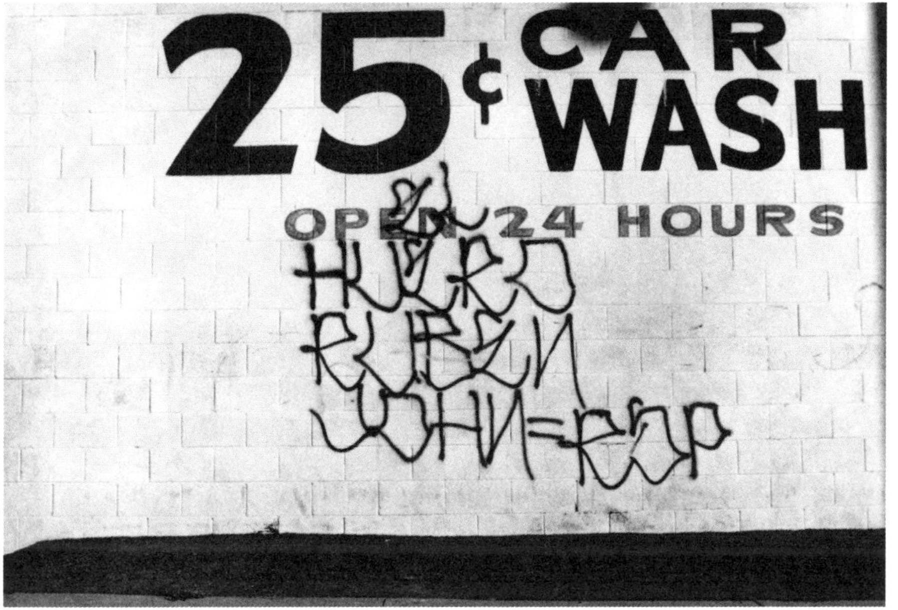

EL
HUERO
RUBEN
JOHN=RSP
(RANCHO
SAN PEDRO)

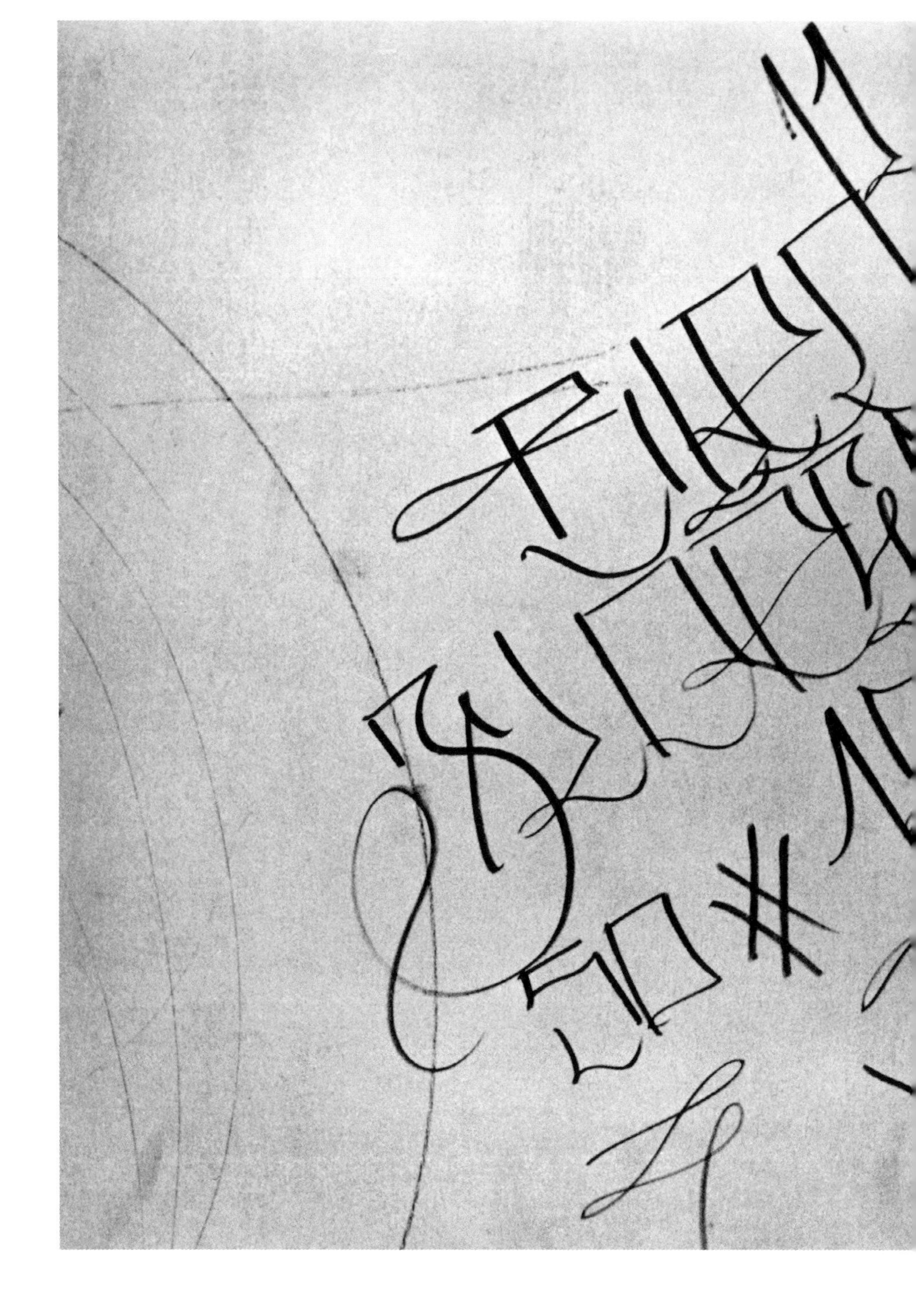

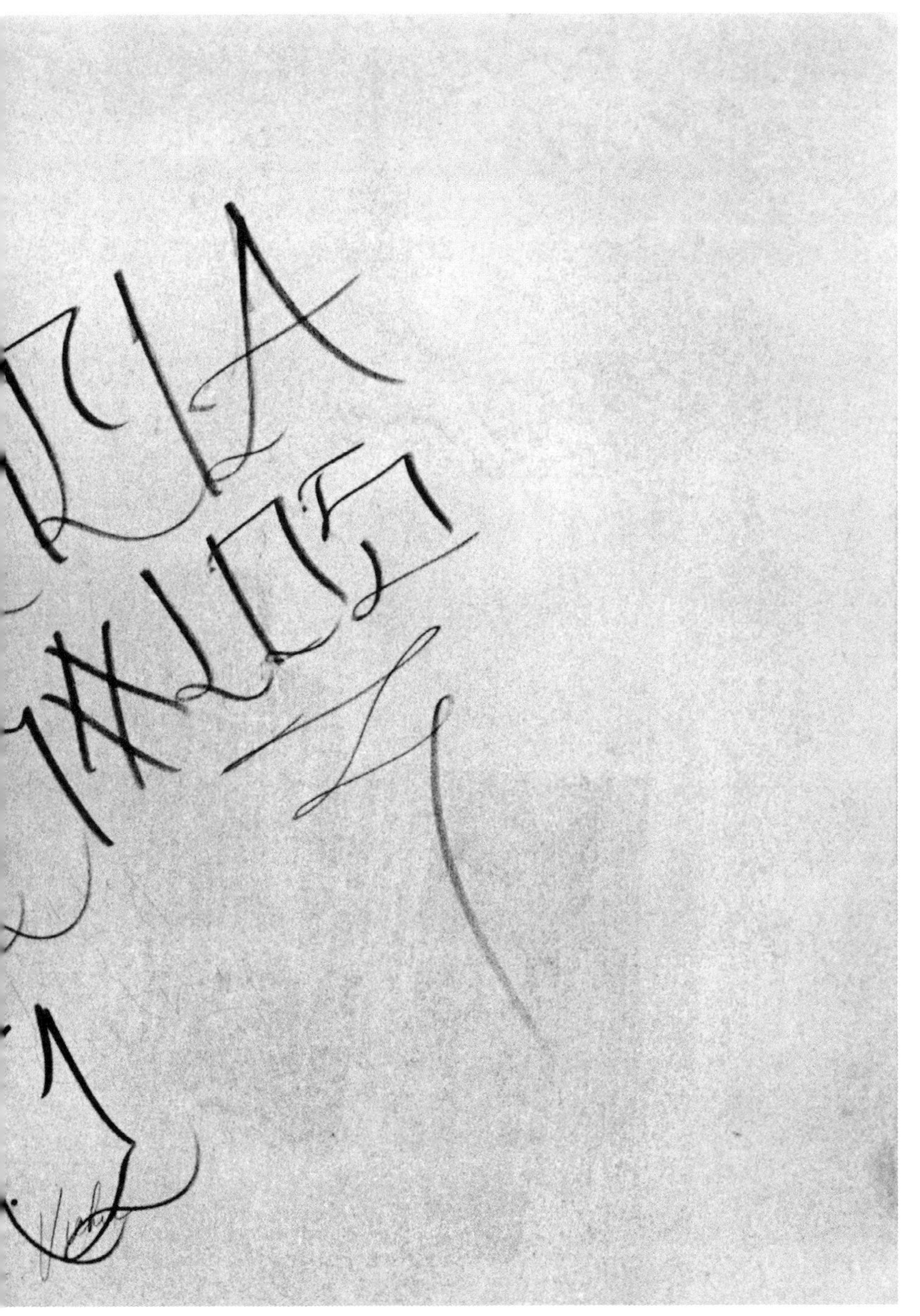

BIRD 1
FLORENCIA
SO # 13 # LOS
(SOUTH LOS ANGELES TRECE)
'71

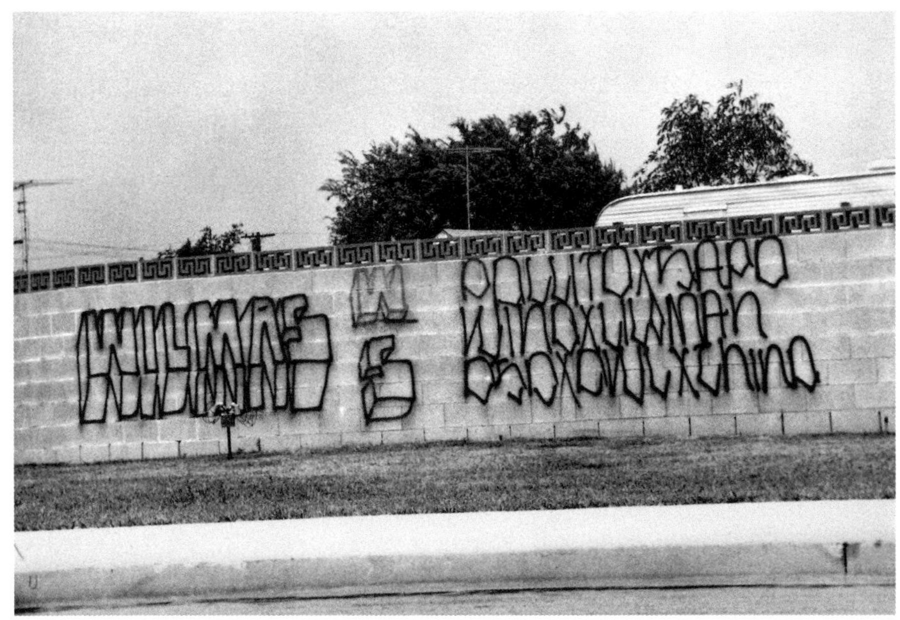

WILMAS   W   POLLITO×SAPO
                S   WINO×LIL◇MAN
                (WEST   OSO×OWL×CHINO
                SIDE)

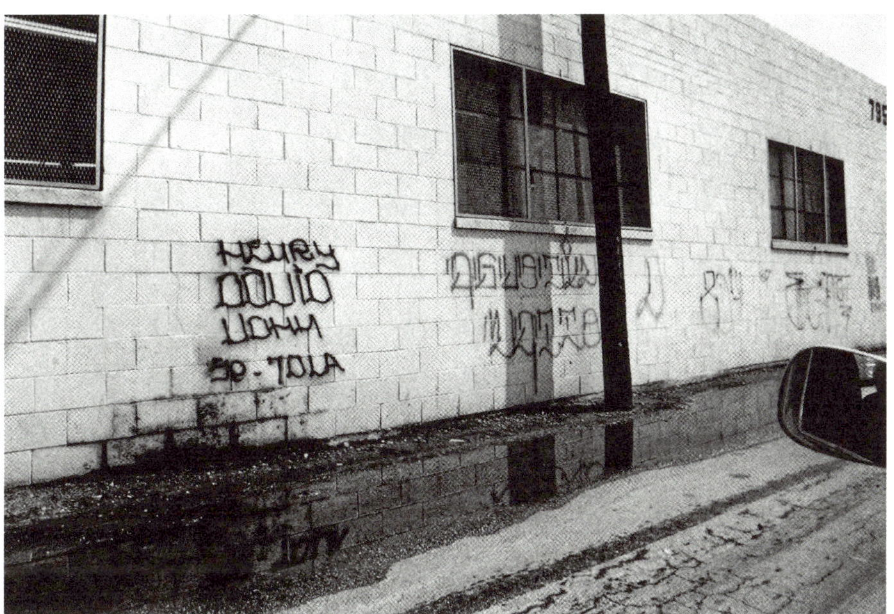

HENRY   AGUSTIN   80TH   ELM ST.
DAVID   WATTS
JOHN
SO-70 LA
(SOUTH 1970 LOS ANGELES)

The basic strokes of the Chicano style alphabet had been a fixture on public surfaces in Southern California long before I took notice. They were popularly and correctly associated with a gang culture that had been widely reported on since the so-called Zoot Suit Riots of the World War II era. Like many, I was intrigued by real and imagined images of bands of lawless youth from areas with cryptic names located in far flung corners of the city and county of Los Angeles. In high school I observed the culture on a limited basis and later, after acquiring an automobile, I set out to satisfy my curiosity by exploring a much larger area of the community.

Chicano graffiti was only a small part of a culture that was unique to Southern California. Lifestyles associated with drag racing, custom cars, surfing and the beginnings of the Hippie movement presented an even higher profile and I was also attracted to these on some level, especially as it related to the artistic aspect of each. I began to document the visual side of what I was seeing with photography, and continued to dabble in painting. Because I was attracted to a realistic interpretation, I came to rely on the photographic image as the inspiration and an aid for my paintings. At some point I decided that gang graffiti would be a basis for some of my art.

By 1970 I was becoming heavily involved with photographing the Southern California car culture and decided to get serious about it. At considerable expense, I purchased two Nikon F bodies and an array of lenses that would allow me accomplish what I figured I needed to do. Early on, I also photographed a few graffiti placas with the intention of using them as reference, and came to realize that the Cholo letterforms had a variety and style that made them interesting and unique in their own right. At this point I began to want to accumulate as many representative examples as possible. Rather than continue to snap pictures at random, I decided to map out photographic expeditions that would cover as large an area as possible. It had now become a project and I began to apply myself to it as such.

Having decided on a systematic approach, it was time to head out into the field. While this would not involve a great deal in the way of logistics, there were several considerations that needed to be taken into account. Having grown up around and personally known dozens of «gang members» I had more than a little understanding of their lifestyle and habits. In the early 1970s the Chicano gang was more of a social club than the drug dealing criminal enterprise that the popular media sensationalizes today. Even then, a neighborhood's roots could often be traced back several generations; most members were US born and spoke English, often as their first language. There was a great deal of pride in their style, as expressed by the clothes they wore, the music they listened to, the cars they drove and the way they carried themselves. The impression, carefully cultivated, was definitely that of a bad ass. This Cholo image was not really out there in your face – but it was there and those that failed to recognize it sometimes did so at their own peril.

The center of the Cholo's social life was the neighborhood or «barrio». Usually located in an area of the community that was considered less than desirable, these small enclaves nevertheless inspired great pride in the residents, and gang members in particular. It is not surprising then that these insular attitudes naturally brought individual gangs into conflict with one another and ultimately engendered mistrust of all outsiders. And the very essence of the graffiti I would be photographing was all about the neighborhood and its residents. This was serious stuff to them and so it was with some trepidation that I contemplated my project.

To approach gang members or others in each community and try to outline my objectives in hopes of gaining their understanding and cooperation seemed cumbersome. The fact was that few would be likely to grasp the concept of a photo essay depicting images that many felt were controversial and a blight on the community. And there was the perception that graffiti is illegal so perhaps the photographer would ultimately prove to be working for law enforcement. More than likely, no one thought much of it as art. So after some consideration I decided I would just drive into the areas and take my photos as discreetly as possible and get out.

A typical photo mission would involve driving the main streets, with glances down the crossing side streets often revealing promising material. Industrial areas featured buildings with large, windowless walls that provided a perfect canvas for the graffiti writer. And of course bridge abutments, retaining walls and the concrete walls of flood

control channels were likely to display graffiti.
Most could be easily photographed with
standard focal length or wide angle lenses.
Telephoto lenses of the period were large and
somewhat clumsy for use from a car window.
When approaching a subject my attention
would be everywhere except on the subject.
I wanted to be aware of the entire surrounding
situation and have a plan to egress the area
once the shutter clicked. If there was any
doubt, I would abort the attempt, perhaps
returning later. Frame the shot and get out
– occasionally the car did not even come to
a complete stop. On a handful of occasions
(such as the pictures from the Arroyo Seco
flood control channel) I did alight from the
car briefly. But for the most part my activities
were apparently unobserved.

There came a point when other interests
caused me to stop seeking out pictures
of graffiti. My intention to use the collected
examples as reference for paintings never
got going, as I moved in other directions.
Vague plans to publish a book featuring the
placas also went nowhere. When Gusmano
Cesaretti's *Street Writers: A guided tour
of Chicano Graffiti* was published (Acrobat
Books, 1975) it featured not only Cholo
graffiti but interviews and stories about
the writers and the community as well.
I felt I had nothing to add to the subject
and put the collection away.

In 2006 I became part of the Flickr online
photo sharing scene and began to put up
a large variety of photographs that I'd taken
and collected over the years. A few months
later, I thought of the graffiti collection and
decided to display those as well. Though
I didn't expect a lot of interest, I was greatly
surprised to find that these photographs,
heretofore seen by perhaps a half dozen
individuals, were an instant hit with viewers
from all over the world. They remain from
day to day the most viewed and commented
on images on my Flickr account and I am
pleased that they are now featured in this
present book. Maybe photographing graffiti
all those years ago wasn't such a crazy idea
after all.

—

[page 9] The piece on the left is dated '62 and
is the oldest observed date in the collection.
Dates are occasionally included in gang
graffiti but are not the norm. The style
and execution of the lettering, with mostly
squared strokes, is consistent with the earliest
forms of Chicano graffiti, dating from the
1940s and 1950s. To the right is a fresher
placa identifying the FLORENCIA gang.

They are not from the area and it has
been crossed out, though not very forcefully.
Photographed in East Los Angeles, near
General Hospital.

[page 11] A strange mixture of styles.
As Torrance was a predominately white
community at the time, this may be the work
of an individual with a limited understanding
of Chicano graffiti letter forms. The highly
visible nature of gang graffiti and its culture
caught the attention of suburban youth and
sometimes led to imitators. Photographed
in North Torrance and dated '69.

[page 13] This large placa is remarkable
for the inclusion of the Star of David on
the left. A Pachuco style cross is seen at
right and both symbols include sun ray
emanating from them. Gang members, being
neither particularly religious or political, are
nevertheless quick to note symbols (especially
controversial ones) and incorporate them into
graffiti. Photographed in North Torrance.

[page 14] Unlike the beach resort
atmosphere of the Southern part of the city,
North Redondo had an active gang scene until
fairly recently. These placas are obviously
the work of a skilled writer. Photographed
in North Redondo Beach in the early 1970s.

[page 15] NSR stands for NORTH SIDE
REDONDO. Photographed in North Redondo
Beach in the early 1970s.

[page 16] Wooden fence photographed in
a Harbor City alley in the early 1970s, a crisp
example of a mastered Cholo hand based on
a wireframe rendering of Old English letters.

[page 17] Placas of the HARBOR CITY gang
from the early to mid-1970s. HARBOR CITY
borders WILMINGTON and SAN PEDRO,
its two main rivals.

[page 19] An excellent example of a gang
roll call, listing nearly thirty names. Most
gangs had a particularly skilled writer who
handled the more «official» stuff like the
roster seen here. Such a list would usually
be preceded by the gang name, in the fashion
of a headline, and ended with a tag that
amounted to a signature at the bottom. Here
we see LOS VATOS LOCOS or «the crazy guys»
to the right along with H×C×R for HARBOR
CITY RIFA. Photographed on Vermont Avenue
in Harbor City in the early to mid-1970s.

[page 21] The DIAMOND STREET gang is
from a nearby area and is seen here using
a diamond shaped symbol between the letters
C and S (meaning *Con Safos*). Photographed
on Bunker Hill near Downtown Los Angeles.

[page 22] Los Angeles lies on a semi-arid
plain and the rivers of the area are usually
dry or nearly so. However winter storms

can bring considerable rain to inland areas, turning these normally benign washes into raging rivers. In the 1920s an ambitious project got underway that resulted in the banks of the major tributaries within the city being paved with concrete. Graffiti writers long ago began to use this great expanse as their canvas. The area shown here is adjacent to the Pasadena Freeway and on the turf of the AVENUES gang. The scale of the writing is quite large and was executed while working at a precipitous angle. Today the agency responsible keeps these river banks free of graffiti, probably because it is visible from the nearby freeway. Photographed in the Arroyo Seco flood control channel in the early 1970s.

[page 23] Placas of the AVENUES gang photographed in the early 1970s. This piece is dated 1967 and is among the earliest observed. At the time, communities did not aggressively act to remove graffiti as soon as it went up. If on private property it was up to the landlord to take care of the removal and many simply didn't bother. The assumption, probably correct, was that the writers would quickly mark the buffed wall again. Later, as gangs became a high profile urban problem, it became more politically expeditious to attack the graffiti than the gangs themselves.

[page 25] Here, in the early 1970s, the AVENUES gang has marked the concrete banks of the Arroyo Seco River. This area was photographed in the early 1970s by Gusmano Cesaretti for *Street Writers: A guided tour of Chicano Graffiti.*

[page 27] The concrete lining of the Arroyo Seco river provided ample space for elaborate pieces such as this lengthy roll call listing members of the local AVENUES gang.

[page 29] Watts was best known at the time as a predominantly Black community, but the graffiti here has all the earmarks of the Chicano gang style. Several placas are crossed out, the work of rival gangs who usually added their gang moniker alongside as a form of challenge. Seen here are a variety of placas in several styles by writers with varying degrees of artist ability. Included is one from a Harbor Area gang known as WILMAS. It has been overwritten by WATTS ELM ST, which has in turn been crossed as well by a third party. While seemingly a childish activity, this manner of insult can become deadly serious business in the gang culture. Photographed in South Central Los Angeles in the early 1970s.

[page 30] The CLANTON 14 gang dates from before World War II and was originally centered around 14th Street, later moving a few blocks away when the original neighborhood was redeveloped. It is not unusual for gang members to take the name of their organization with them when they relocate. Needless to say, this practice can be a source of friction with rivals. While the use of 14 here designates a street number, later in the 1970s prison gangs from Northern California adopted 14 as a representation of their Northern turf, as opposed the Southern California gangs that had long used the number 13 in their graffiti. Photographed in the early 1970s in the vicinity of Pico Boulevard, near Downtown Los Angeles.

[page 31] Gangs located West of the Harbor Freeway (or, some would argue, the Los Angeles River) define their presence as WEST SIDE, represented here the initials WS. Seen at right, the term PEEWEES defines a set in the gang staffed by junior members. Photographed in the early 1970s on the CLANTON 14 gang's turf near Downtown Los Angeles.

[page 32] The DOGTOWN gang originated before World War II and takes its name from the city animal shelter (known in those less politically correct times as the «dog pound») that was located nearby. A well known line of skateboards and apparel later adopted the name *Dogtown* and it is claimed that the term refers to an area across town near Santa Monica. Be that as it may, the Dogtown logo pays obvious homage to old school Cholo graffiti letter forms. The word TRESE is Spanish for 13. Chicano graffiti of the 1970s often used the swastika as a decorative element. This was more an attempt to attract attention to the placa than an indication of Nazi sympathies. It is unlikely that most gang members then, or now, have much appreciation for world history. Photographed in the early 1970s just North of Downtown Los Angeles.

[page 33] The ROYAL SAINTS apparently wrote their name in Spanish too. Such translations of English words are rare, possibly because most gang graffiti writers of this period were US born Mexican-Americans and spoke fluent English. Photographed on the West side of Los Angeles (Venice, Palms or Culver City) in the early 1970s.

[page 35] Several unusual features are seen here. The CHICANO POWER on the right was a popular slogan of the late 1960s and early 1970s and often seen in graffiti, but not so much so in gang graffiti. Writers of this period and before often included the letters CS at or near the end of a placa. This stands for *Con Safos.* Definitions of the term vary but it is usually taken to mean that the

placa is «protected by God» and should not be removed or defaced. This warning has gradually ceased to be used in more recent times. Also of interest here is the roll call of given names rather than usual gang monikers. Photographed in the Venice / Palms / Culver City area early 1970s.

[page 36] The WHITE FENCE gang was established in East Los Angeles well before World War II and remains active to this day. There are many individuals today willing to offer up detailed histories of the gangs and their members, and most major gangs have their own websites. However, such information is mostly hearsay and folklore, often colored by the historian's allegiance to a particular group. Nevertheless, gang roots run deep and are taken very seriously. Photographed in East Los Angeles early 1970s.

[page 37] RSP stands for RANCHO SAN PEDRO gang. Historically, Rancho San Pedro was the name of a large Spanish land grant but in the early 1940s a public housing project was given the name. The local gang has adopted the name as their own. LOCO, seen at right, is Spanish for «crazy». This term is often used in conjunction with gangs and their members. Rather than an insult or deficiency, gang members see it as a badge of honor and apply it to their own. Photographed in the Harbor Area community of San Pedro.

[page 39] Seen at right, LOS LORDS would be an individual set or clique under the larger umbrella of what would be considered the RANCHO SAN PEDRO gang. Having the Spanish article EL (or LA in the case of females) before Chicano gangster nicknames is a widespread recurrent usage. Photographed in San Pedro in the early to mid-1970s.

[page 40] VNE or the VARRIO NUEVO ESTRADA gang, came out of the Estrada Courts public housing project in East Los Angeles. With older gangs already established in the area, the original members decided to insert the Spanish word NUEVO (meaning «new») into the title. Like many Chicano gangs, VNE has a presence in other far flung areas of Southern California. Presumably, gang members have moved from the old neighborhood and «colonized» outlying communities. It is interesting to note that gang monikers have a certain commonality and there are some that will be found duplicated in almost every neighborhood. Photographed in the early to mid-1970s in East Los Angeles.

[page 41] RSP is the RANCHO SAN PEDRO gang from the Harbor Area. Photographed in San Pedro in the early to mid-1970s.

[page 43] Traced with a chisel tip marker, this exquisite piece of calligraphy was rendered by BIRD 1. This work is also remarkable in that the writer was a black man at a time when Cholo gang members were almost exclusively Mexican/American. He was rather prolific at the time and usually wrote just his name and FLORENCIA, or F13. Operating over a wide geographic area, he might be considered an early tagger and had either studied calligraphy or had a tremendous talent for innovation. Other examples of his work with spray cans were equally impressive but more in the traditional Chicano style. The FLORENCIA gang was from the area of Florence Avenue in South Central Los Angeles. Photographed near the Long Beach Pike amusement park.

[page 44] Wilmington is a community near the Port of Los Angeles. Local residents and gangs long ago informally modified the name to WILMAS. The West side and East side of WILMAS are long time rivals so the prominent WS seen here is an important distinction.

[page 45] SO LA indicates South Los Angeles, an area that would also include Watts. Behind the post, AGUSTIN / WATTS is a rare lettering example with doubled vertical ornamental strokes in a simple tag, exactly like in Old English uppercases, dated 1970.

[page 51] Far left, note EL LOBO handstyle dated 1962. See the broken line evolution in the early 1970s with BOSCO or PATO from the EAST SIDE 18TH STREET gang. Location is near Los Angeles General Hospital in East Los Angeles.

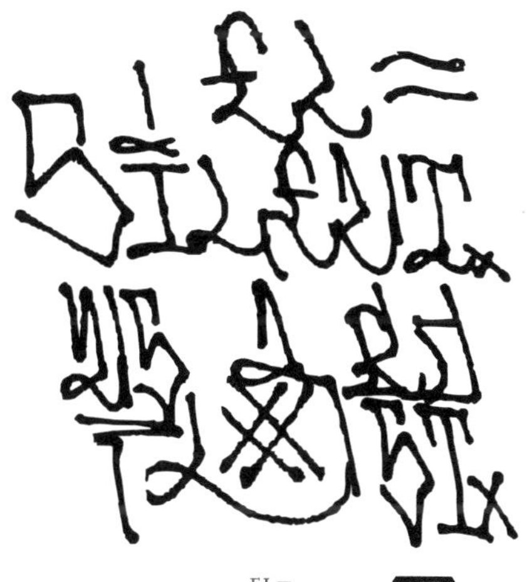

EL=
SILENT ×
WS #3RD ST ×
(WEST SIDE
THIRD STREET
GANG)

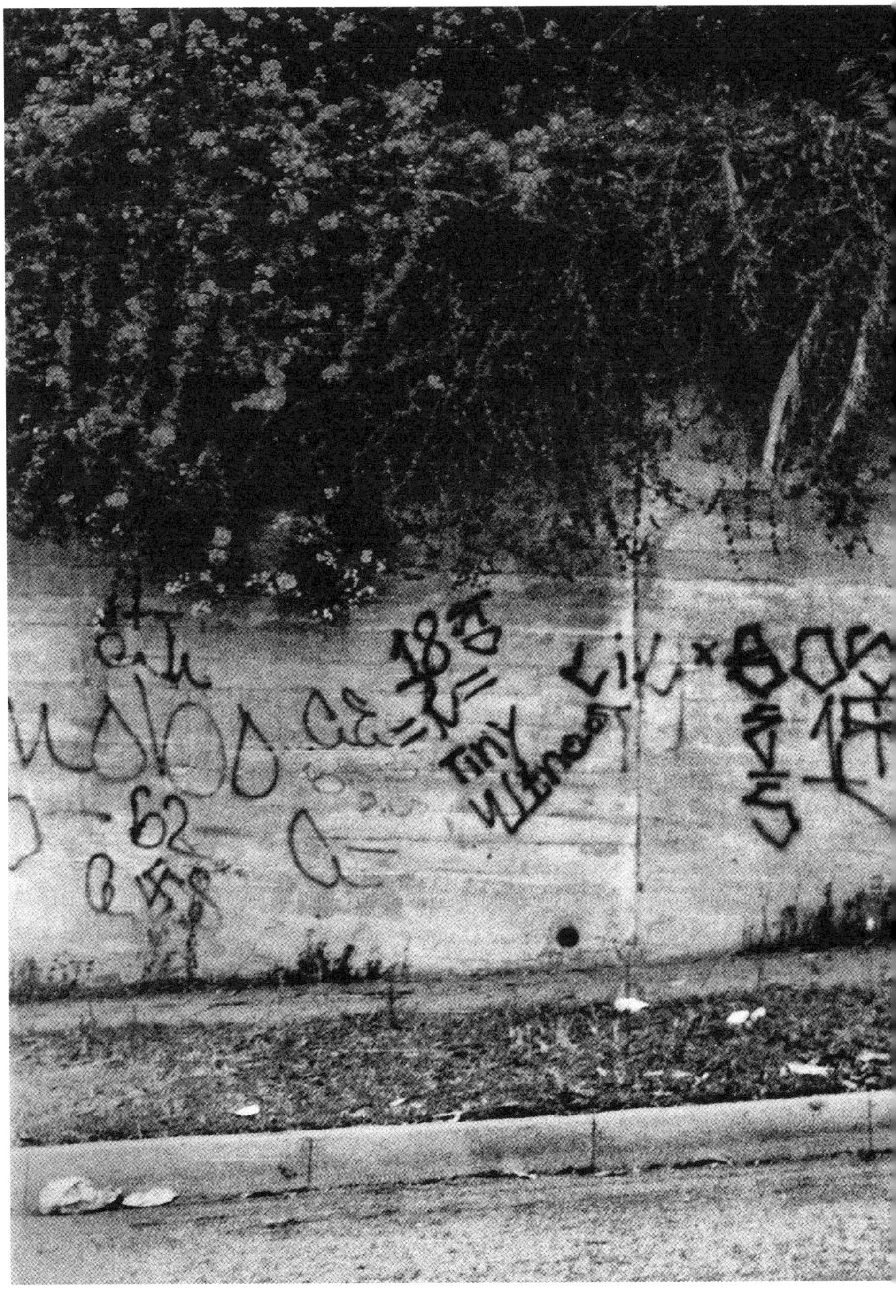

†   …   18 ST   LIL × BOSCO

EL   =R=   E/S (EAST SIDE)

LOBO   (RIFAN)   18 ST

−62−   TINY

C◇S   WINO

(CON SAFOS)

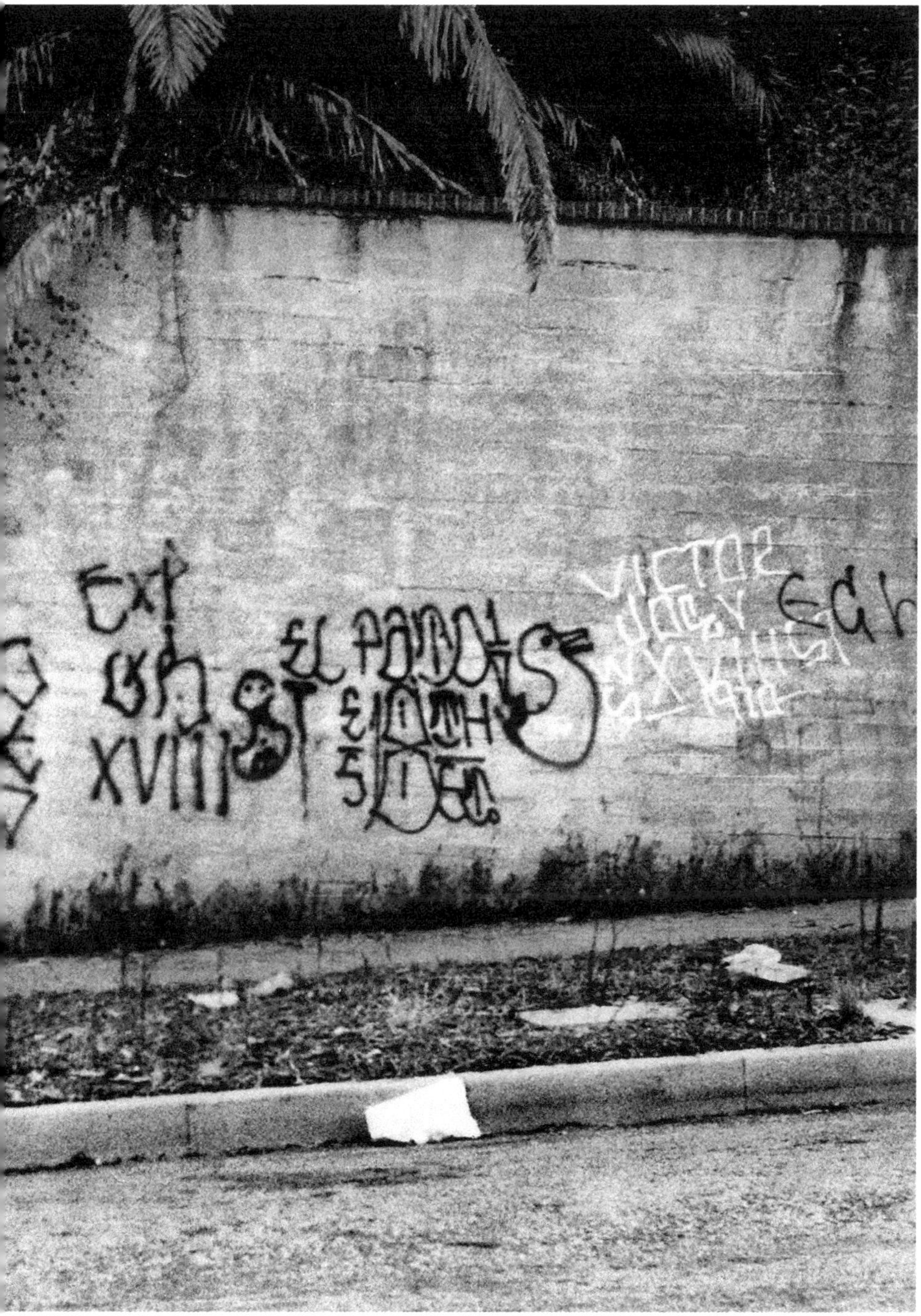

E×P

L×B

XVIII

(18 TH STREET GANG)

EL PATO 1

E/S (EAST SIDE)

18 TH/ST

VICTOR

JOEY

W/S (WEST SIDE)

XVIII ST STREET

−1970−

essay
The Gangster £
François Chastanet

Written language is part of the daily experience of life in any metropolis that has reached a certain degree of urban «maturity». Competing signals dominate the landscape, from commercial neon signs to different types of graffiti; the relentless pursuit of visibility has become the norm. The massive serial signatures known as tags are familiar both as an element of the worldwide image of the metropolis, and as a symbol of Western urbanity. Their main purpose is to invade public spaces or transport networks, and thus be seen all-city or even transnationally. Such street letterings, based on the aesthetic conventions of the gestural signature, are now a worldwide youth practice – almost a new conformity, based on the New York style of graffiti letterforms and augmented by local stylistic variations.

Cholo writing, originally the handwritten letters drawn by the Mexican gangs of Los Angeles, is a distinct phenomenon, with a very specific place in the history of urban graffiti in the Western world. It is probably the 20th century's oldest form of «styled name», with a unique aesthetic that developed long before the East Coast movement began in Philadelphia and New York City in the late 1960s. *Placas* or *placazos* («plaques» in English) are names – prestigious signs of invisible territorial frontiers and pledges of loyalty to a specific neighborhood. The visual control of symbolic space is accompanied by the gang's active physical control of the barrio («neighborhood» in English). These wall-writings, intended primarily to define the area of a gang's influence, seem to emerge in the 1930s, with the Latino Zoot Suiters / Pachucos gangs.

The word *xolotl* (pronounced «cholotl») is originally an Aztec word which means «dog». It is from this meaning that the word *cholo* developed its negative connotation. Cholo as an English-language term dates at least to the early 1900s; in modern usage in the United States, the term *cholo* usually indicates a person of Mexican, Central American or Indio descent, who is associated with a particular Southwestern culture. The word has historically been used along the borderland as a derogatory term for lower class Mexican migrants, and in the rest of Latin America to mean an acculturating Indian or peasant. The term *cholo* is used in *caló* slang, but was then turned on its head and used as a symbol of pride in the context of the ethnic power movements of the 1960s. It has infiltrated mainstream American English, specifically in association with Latino youth movements following the Pachuco tradition from which emerged the idea of *La Raza* or Chicano nationalism.

The growing nationalist consciousness of the Chicano people advanced the concept of *Aztlán*, a Chicano nation. Los Angeles is often seen as Aztlán's capital in reference to the legendary ancestral home of the Nahua peoples, one of the main cultural groups in Mesoamerica (Aztec is the Nahuatl word for «people from Aztlán») and more generally Southern California as the Northern land of Aztlán. Aztlán was conceived by the Aztecs themselves as a mythic place rather than a concrete geographical location. The name Aztlán was first taken up by a group of Chicano independence activists during the Latino movement of the 1960s and 1970s (*El Plan Espiritual de Aztlán* was a manifesto adopted at the first National Chicano Youth Liberation Conference, 1969). They used the name Aztlán to refer to the lands of Northern Mexico that were annexed by the United States as a result of the Mexican-American War (Mexico in 1848 signed a treaty ceding California, Utah and Nevada along with parts of Colorado, Arizona, New Mexico and Wyoming, to the United States). Underwritten by the claim of some historical linguists and anthropologists that the original homeland of the Aztecs was located in the Southwestern United States, Aztlán became a symbol for mestizo activists who believe they have a legal and primordial right to the land – and a way of empowering young Chicanos in America who never learn about their ancestry in school. Aztlán is about more than lost land; it's about identity. The analogy of Aztlán now also reaches far northward, as a concept embracing a range of values brought by modern immigrants engaging in the vital new process of assimilation, cultural reformulation and renewal among the many communities of peoples in the US. This imagery of Aztec mythology (warriors, pyramids) is still very present in the Latino gangs' symbolism (especially in tattoos and mail art in jails) even if the political meaning and consciousness is not as clear as it was in the 1970s. Some photos by Howard Gribble show mentions of «Chicano Power» alongside gangs' names [pages 13, 35]. Drawing letterforms is a practice to which identity and questions of origin are essential. Therefore, Cholo writing or placas are all about «Brown Pride» or *La Raza de Bronce* dignity, and thus specific letterforms representing the image of the Mexican American or Chicano community in Southern California since the first half of the 20th century.

Los Angeles is frequently described as a «gangland paradise». In the popular imagination, LA's main gangs are the Bloods and Crips, Black gangs whose wars in the 1990s were confined to the South Central LA area. This is due to strong national (and international) media coverage, but it belies the real situation. Some of the active Chicano gangs in Los Angeles have existed since the 1920–30s (like HOYO MARAVILLA, PRIMERA FLATS, FROGTOWN, LINCOLN HEIGHTS, CLANTON, TEMPLE ST., DOGTOWN, DIAMOND ST.), with East LA and the Boyle Heights area as the main birthplace of the gangs. South Central neighborhoods like Florence and Watts also had original *colonias* of immigrants. Boyle Heights was once called *Paredón Blanco* or «White Walls» when California was part of Mexico, maybe explaining the origins of the name of one original historic local gang called WHITE FENCE [pages 36, 59, 75–79] also originally known as LA PURISSIMA CROWD (associated with a local church's name). Latino gangs have their own traditions and codes – from oral language and styles of dressing to hand signs and letterforms. Their aesthetic has influenced many of California's underground cultures, including the outlaw bikers of the 1960s, the Los Angeles punk scene in the 1970s and 1980s, and the Crips and Bloods of the 1980s and 1990s. Hispanic gangs originally «talked the talk & walked the walk», i.e. invented the local gang culture and styles. Black gangs took from it to create their own identity, then pioneered their own aesthetic.

Nowadays, a large body of literature is focused on gang activities, and since the mid-1990s much has been said about *la vida loca* or «the crazy life». We will note here the work of the photographer Joseph Rodríguez, whose *East Side Stories: Gang Life in East LA* (PowerHouse Books, 1998), is a photographic essay documenting «the core of violence in America, not just the physical violence against one another, but the quiet violence of letting families fall apart, the violence of segregation and isolation». Similarly, the movie *American Me* (1992) directed by Edward James Olmos, depicts a fictionalized account of gang structure, chronicling the emergence of the MEXICAN MAFIA in the California prison system from the 1950s to the 1980s and the identity crisis faced by Chicanos living in the US (the film starts with the famous Zoot Suiters Riots in 1943). The fact that gangs of the same ethnic origins fight each other seems to be mainly a question of clannish violence linked with a strong territorial mentality now mainly due to the control of drug trafficking areas; apparently a behaviour far less present back in the days. The situation changed dramatically in the 1980s because of the massive boom in the drug market and the huge rise in the number of gangs in LA County. Without ignoring the violence and self-destruction inherent to *la vida loca*, i.e the banality of everyday murdered people of the same ethnic community, it is vital to document the visual strategies of Latino gangs attempting to survive as visible entities in an environment comprising a never-ending sprawl of warehouses, freeways, wood framed houses, fences and back alleys.

Name writing has always been closely linked to death and memory. Writing a group name on a wall makes it immortal. The image remains, even as the carnage between gangs continues. Few books concentrate on Cholo graffiti practices themselves; one of the most complete work on the subject is *Wallbangin' Graffiti and Gangs in LA* by the anthropologist Susan Phillips (University of Chicago Press, 1999). Observers describe blackletter typography as one of the main influences in the appearance of Cholo writing, but none of them traces the presence of the blackletter skeleton throughout Cholo scripts from various periods. The work of Howard Gribble – frontal visual recordings of various placas of the early 1970s – constituted a unique opportunity to try to push forward the calligraphic analysis of Cholo writing, its origins and formal evolution.

Cholo writing conveys territorial delineation. It is mainly graffiti «by the neighborhood, for the neighborhood», and gang members usually write within their own territory only. Reading the walls tells you which neighborhood (or «hood») you're in, and also who's controlling it. These territorial signs are sometimes called the «newspaper of the streets»; by observing which gang is getting crossed out, you can be aware of the current gang wars. Los Angeles is a sprawling city, mainly composed of individual houses and condominiums. Large public walls are offered by the freeways, the real monument of that city [pages 88, 107] or warehouses [pages 109, 111, 115]. The main spots for inscriptions are small fences in back alleys [page 16], and neighborhood groceries or liquor stores at intersections are a target of choice [page 80].

Ideally, the writings had to be visible from passing cars; in order to resist to the massive presence of huge billboards and commercial signage, placas tend to develop a (sub)urban efficiency in lettering, i.e. drawing letterforms visually effective in this specific flat urban landscape. But for some years, the different municipal authorities of Los Angeles County have had strong erasing campaigns, especially against gang graffiti, so Cholo writers have had to develop other tactics in order to maintain their constant visual presence: almost hidden «low visibility» inscriptions that last over time – on thin pillars of metal fences, pavement edges [pages 92, 93, 98] – since most of the larger prints painted with spray cans are removed within 12 hours.

Placas are public announcements of names that are always visually structured in the same manner. Gang names are related to their immediate surroundings, and very often the name of the street where they live is the most common choice. In Los Angeles, street names are often only numbers from a grid division, so many gang names are just numbers. Among the most famous is the 18TH ST. gang originating from Pico Union, but you can also find the 38TH ST. gang in South Central, etc.

In Cholo writing, the image of the name is traditionally composed in a recurrent visual manner, a mixture of English and Spanish: first comes the letter V or, more rarely, B, to abbreviate the term BARRIO (which has been expressed in the vulgar and grammatically incorrect term VARRIO, the letters V and B having a very similar pronounciation in Spanish). Then comes the geographical zone or «side», expressed in cardinal points of the neighborhood in relation to a hypothetical central location in the city (Downtown LA), always marked with two letters and as an acronym (ES for EAST SIDE, WS for WEST SIDE and SS for SOUTH SIDE). This is followed by the name of the gang itself, which is a repetition of the street or neighborhood name, then the letter R or the word RIFA, a recurring verb signifying that the gang rules the place. Then follows the number 13, which represents the underground administrative code of *Sureños*, i.e. gangs of Southern California and stands for M (the 13th letter of the alphabet), showing allegiance to the MEXICAN MAFIA also known as *La Eme*. The *Norteños* or NUESTRA FAMILIA / NF affiliated groups, i.e. Latino gangs of Northern California (mainly in the San Francisco / Oakland areas) use the number 14, representing the letter N in the latin alphabet, considered as rivals. Then

come other acronyms such as LS (for LOCOS or «mad guys»), TLS (for TINY LOCOS), MLS (MALOS or «the bad guys») or DVS (for DEVILS), expressing the different «cliques» in a gang, sub-groups mainly based on generational hierarchy. This basic form of the group signature is very often completed by the name of the individual who actually drew the inscription, and also by «roll calls» [pages 19, 27, 40, 63, 95, etc.], i.e. the complete list of active members of a gang and their different nicknames.

Many times, we also note the presence in the inscriptions of arrows pointing to the ground, signifying the idea of the «here-and-now», a symbol of the will to control the public space of a given neighborhood. Quotation marks are often added around the gang name, visually presenting the name as an oral announcement in the public space. These wall-writings constitute an efficient parallel signage system (for example, in South Central you can observe 36TH ST. gang inscriptions next to official street signage plaques indicating 36th St.), entirely composed of encrypted names, that can be truly used as a means to orientate yourself in this Southern Californian landscape of banal suburban continuity. It can, however, get confusing when a gang and its members change locations, but continue to write their original neighborhood name origins, i.e. a street number in a new and different context.

Beneath functional issues of territory and representation lie questions of identity. How do we make things, how do we represent ourselves, how we display our names? It is style that tells us who we are. These street signatures may constitute collective identity practices encouraging gang strength, but they are also executed by individual gang members skilled in graffiti mastery, whose function within the group is to design the image of the gang's name within strict conventions. Some can be considered highly skilled calligraphers [pages 27, 43, 63, 129]. Typically, one «writer» writes for the whole gang – even the long roll calls displaying individual nicknames, which have to be as straight and clean as possible in order to lend regularity to the different inscriptions.

Each Latino gang, each neighborhood, has a slightly distinct style, but visual conventions in letterforms are clearly shared, defining a kind of «geographic homogeneity» in wall handwriting, i.e. a lettering identity on a metropolitan scale. The Los Angeles «gangster touch» in letters can be presented as a writing system of four handstyles:

• the Cholo or gangster script, mainly composed in uppercase letters, hybrid monolinear versions of mixed «Old English» (Anglo-Saxon common expression for Textura, and connoting gothic / blackletter in general for a wider audience) uppercases with roman capitals [pages 16, 27, 41, 69, 76, 83, 102, 117, 130, etc.] • the outlined block letter, with sometimes additional tridimensional cross-hatching fill-in shadings [pages 77, 99, 115, 123] • the strict and precise typographical outlined renderings, essentially from gothics or more rarely of heavy slab-serif romans, almost exclusively composed in uppercase and sometimes filled in [pages 59, 88, 125] • the cursive script, close to an «English Roundhand» or pointed pen calligraphy (rarely observed in the streets, but used extensively in skin tattoos of Latino gang members). Aside from the block letters introduced in the 1980s for greater street visibility, which have their own dynamics and formal development, the other three styles are all more or less mastered experiments in letterforms made on the basis of fixed typographic shapes executed through gestural «monolinear» stroke interpretations. One of the main historic models for these LA gangster letterers seems to be various blackletter fonts uppercases, especially in the classic Cholo writing and in the sharply outlined typographic letterings, where the spacing is carefully worked, with no ligatures observed. This relation to typographical writing pace and classic epigraphy practices is one of the main features of Latino gang writing as opposed to individual tags.

Through this process of copying typography, the main objective seems to be to give an image of «officialdom» to your name. Chicano gangs wanted to build an aura of prestige around their street names, to represent them with maximum dignity and pride. At least throughout the first half of the 20th century, the greatest image possible for a word, the most official or extraordinary letter was the so-called Old English genre as shown by various examples in everyday life – printed objects such as administrative forms, diplomas, certificates and newspaper headings (such as *The Los Angeles Times*). Fonts like *Engravers Old English* or *Wedding Text* from American Type Founders designed by Morris Fuller Benton in 1901 and based on rather decorative English "Texturas" that were probably brought to the US through printing material acquisitions (such as the 1785 Double Pica Black by William Caslon I and influenced by older Dutch types) proved

to be excessively popular. Other influences can be found in sports teams' logos (such as the recurrent use of the LA Dodgers monogram) and shop letterings. This choice of Old English as the main model is also probably related to the fact that the Cholo scene is directly connected with Mexican culture, where non-verbal significance in the chosen aesthetic of letters is omnipresent: in Mexico, the use and recurrent presence of handpainted blackletters in unorthodox and baroque interpretations is a commonplace practice, from transport and commercial signage to churches and religious paintings (especially around the various representations of the *Virgen de Guadalupe*, patron saint of Mexico, a very important Catholic figure of the American continent, an icon omnipresent in Mexican gangs' tattoos that can be seen from a socio-historical point of view as the Catholic continuation of the fecundity goddess *Tonantzín* from the Aztec religion). There are probably some cross-influences: Rotunda typefaces coming from Spain through Mexico City's first typographical press established in the New World in the early 16th century on one side, and Old English-Textura calligraphic models, for example observable in American lettering manuals like *The SpeedBall Textbook* (distributed since the early 20th century in both the US and Mexico and heavily influential for signpainters and lettering amateurs) on the other.

Cholo writing can be seen as an indirect consequence of the popularity of gothic calligraphy among sign painters in Mexico. There are strong circulating and shared stereotypes through letterforms in all societies, and blackletters for the Mexican community consciously communicate tradition, taking the written message to an almost religious level, or at least a certain degree of importance or transcendence.

In all calligraphic manuals it is clear that the gothic / blackletter alphabets are not suitable for setting words in uppercases only (also called initials), as this solution provides a highly illegible image of the word. Writing a word with only blackletter initials is an error made by calligraphers with an approximate historical background, a typical solution that you can observe in Mexican sign painting and in Latino gang graffiti in Los Angeles. In the Western world, everybody learns the universal Roman capital letters in school and uses them widely – in handmade basic architectural titling and demonstration banners, for example. Some commercial signs in Mexico and Cholo writing hybrid styles

56

can be described as a consequence of this universal way of writing / thinking in capital letters on which is simply pasted a gothic aesthetic, where expressiveness, and not legibility, is the primary goal. It is impossible to precisely date the first use of blackletters in Cholo writing, but it is obvious that they influenced the whole genre, which has evolved from generation to generation: the persistence of the historical gothic-blackletter «skeleton» is still perceivable in a majority of letters of the basic Cholo script in the streets today, even if the hybrid combination with Roman capitals gained importance over the years. The fact that placas originate from blackletters is not clear at first sight. Cholo writing has now existed for more than eighty years – a relatively long period that favored the development of its own dynamic of letterforms. To become fully aware of this blackletter affiliation, one needs to study in detail some landmark letters of the Cholo hand, specific signs actually presenting clear formal borrowings from the gothic *ductus* (i.e. number, order and direction of strokes).

One of the letters, the so-called «gangster E», an uppercase that looks like the figure 3 rotated 180 degrees, encapsulates the whole Los Angeles Cholo identity in letterforms [figure 1]. This sign influenced all the other local types of graffiti, mainly the versions of New York tags that started to appear in Los Angeles in the early 1980s. The similarity of this Los Angeles identitarian landmark sign with variants of the calligraphic Textura initial E from the 13th and 14th centuries is astonishing [figures 2.1 and 2.2]. But the borrowing may not be so direct: the current gangster E is an obvious monolinear interpretation of the common uppercase E of more classic typographical Texturas that went through a process of simplification [figure 2.3], a cursive evolution of a sign made of several distinct strokes (separate moments of tracing) into a monolinear unique gesture. One can find clear evidences of this idea when carefully observing the photographic archive of Howard Gribble from the 1970s and chronologically comparing the glyph E in different inscriptions [figure 1]. A similar rhythmic pattern is observable in the construction of the L, a shape that can also be found in the drawing of the vertical stem of the T [figure 2.8] and other letters.

The seemingly reversed Roman uppercase N is also a landmark letter of the Cholo script. In fact, this sign is not reversed but a simplified central-line interpretation of an uppercase blackletter N [figure 2.4]

COMPARISONS OF
BLACKLETTER INITIALS
AND ROMAN CAPITALS
WITH TYPICAL CHOLO LETTERS

[pages 27, 32, 65, 72, 113, etc.] which looks like a lowercase n (some gothic uppercases being formed on the strucure of the lowercases, with a larger, rounder and more ornamental aspect). The Cholo letter N also shows the triangular backward and forward movement at the bottom of the vertical strokes, typical of some blackletter calligraphies (notably in cursive Frakturs). Other letters, such as the broken S, or the B, R, M, O, T, or Y represent signs with the distinctive features of the placas [figures 2.5, 2.6 and 2.7]. However, the pedigrees of letters like T or I are not absolutely clear, and seem to have possible typographical origins in uppercase Roman letterforms. Here also, we may be seeing a monolinear interpretation of a printed letter [figures 2.9 and 2.10], or maybe original creations to fit with the main typical Cholo letters to better fill space – T and I always being problematic letters for spacing and visual balance in a word-image. Placas can truly be understood as hybrid uppercase blackletters, the gangster E representing the summarization of identity of Cholo letterforms.

On web forums and blogs, *vatos* (Chicano «homies») write all their messages in capitals, like in classic Cholo writing. They use the 3 or £ (British pound) to replace the E, the 1 to replace the I when using system fonts for screen; but they haven't found (yet) a solution to represent the supposedly reversed gangster N. All these tricks are coming straight out of graffiti street practices and radically change the texture of a text online.

From what can be observed when comparing Howard Gribble's photographs from the early 1970s with ones from the late 2000s, especially illustrations concerning the very same vne gang (varrio nuevo estrada) signatures [pages 40, 64–73], it seems obvious that Cholo writing has singularly constant letterforms, close to the logic of headline printing. The origin in typographic mimicry is probably the reason for this stability. It also seems manifest that Cholo handstyles of that time were more diverse and more mastered in their spatial presentation, from simple and basic letter systems inscribed in a rectangular frame with an almost monospace spacing [pages 33, 37], to more complex and ornamented letterforms with clear blackletter influences [pages 15, 22, 27, 39, 41, 43]. Moreover, an older style from the 1950s and 1960s that was about an aesthetic of squarish letters softened by diagonals or diamond shaped corners [pages 21, 23], seems to have completely

57

disappeared from the formal range
of Cholo writers. One can also observe
that in the 1970s the signatures were
apparently designed to last longer, contrary
to handlettered prints and block letters of
the early 21st century that are deliberately
designed for ephemeral existence and
immediate efficiency [pages 87, 113, 115,
121, 123], with less care in stroke execution.

Cholo inscriptions have then a speficic
written aesthetic, a kind of «standardized»
handstyle based on a monolinear adaptation
of gothic printed letters for street writing in
(mainly) capital letters. Placas are built up
of clear and shared letterforms conventions
representing the Chicano community.

For example, a bit after the birth
of the Chicano movement *La Causa* and
the appeerence of the Brown Berets in Los
Angeles (a Chicano political defense group
based on the model of the Black Panthers),
a Chicano artists' group called *Asco*
(signifying «nausea») did a guerilla
performance in 1972 entitled *Spray Paint
LACMA*. Three Asco members signed their
names on the Los Angeles County Museum
of Art walls, using the barrio turf-staking
practice of Cholo gang graffiti as a conceptual
critique, converting the museum into a work
of Chicano art. This intervention was a protest
against racist comments by that institution's
curator about the possibility of including
Chicano art in museum exhibitions.

Seen from a distance, the image of
the Cholo letter that explodes from suburban
Los Angeles can be understood as a possible
visual identity representing the very essence
of this city without limits marked by banality.
Placas paradoxically gave an original visual
identity to the young metropolis constituted
by an infinite suburbia, even if this culture
was (and still partly is) denied. Cholo writing
spread out of its original geographical
community limits and represents Los
Angeles' identity in a broader sense,
in a kind of process that can be described
as «franchising a metropolitan identity».

The first expression of that idea was
the worldwide visibility and spreading of the
placas lettering aesthetic through different
graphic design pieces produced for various
skateboard companies, with their first
commercial explosion at the end of the 1980s
(remember the «Rat Bones» Powell-Peralta
logo in 1983, a direct borrowing of placas of
that time) [page 15]. The skateboard itself is a
pure Los Angeles invention, and the Dogtown
neighborhood is considered the birthplace
of progressive skateboarding. Some of these

now «old school» skateboard companies,
such as *Alva Skates* or *Dogtown Skateboards*
(original logo designed by Craig R. Stecyk),
naturally took the Cholo writing style from
their everyday environment [page 32] for
their home-made corporate identities and
decorations of decks, and still use it today,
marketing a worldwide recognizable hardcore
Venice «skate mystique». Wes Humpston
aka «Bulldog», skater and illustrator, designed
the original drawings for the first hand-made
Dogtown decks around 1976 using the
«Dogtown Cross» logo created by Craig
R. Stecyk with multiple variations during
the following years.

According to Chaz Bojórquez, the surf
culture was actually the first to respect Cholo
letters outside the «hood». Especially the
gothic / cholo lettering work of Rick Griffin
through posters and cover designs was
a foundation of «modern-hippie-cholo» kind
of graffiti. He seems to be one of the first
artists to address the art in Cholo graffiti and
connect it to California culture in the 1960s,
creating a specific West Coast aesthetic.
Griffin has been hugely influential within
contemporary visual culture.

In 1974, the band Ruben And The Jets (led
by Rubén Ladrón de Guevara Jr.) published an
album entitled *Con Safos*, an explicit reference
to the Chicano graffiti world: the illustration
and photo montage-based cover, designed by
Cal Schenkel, shows consistent Cholo writing
from that era. Jackson Brown's album
The Pretender, published in 1976 and
designed by Gary Burden, is based on the
opposition of a stencil sans serif and Cholo
handstyle. Rank Strangers' 1977 eponymous
album designed by Rick Griffin is then not
the first record cover using Cholo writing as
sometimes stated, its use of Cholo letters is
more dramatic: the front cover is only using
a calligraphic image of the name over circular
echoes in the background centered on the
inscription. No photo nor figurative drawing
here, the letter stands for itself as a sufficient
image to fully represent Los Angeles.

The local punk rock scene of the 1980s
also used, in a similar manner, Cholo letters
to represent a typical Los Angeles image,
the most famous and internationally visible
band being Suicidal Tendencies from Venice
(see, for example, their fourth album in 1989
Controlled by Hatred / Feel Like Shit... Déjà Vu,
using extensively both Cholo script and gang
block letters). Similarly, Kid Frost's first
Hispanic rap hit single *La Raza* in 1990 was
mixing bold sans serifs with Cholo lettering
on its cover. And most of the LA-based Latin

hip hop artists are nowadays intensively using blackletters, following the worldwide success of Cypress Hill's landmark record sleeve layouts.

Nowadays, the strong eradication campaigns against gang graffiti weaken the presence and the coverage of placas on the streets, but instead of solving anything, it only hides the gang reality (most of the inscriptions in the color photographs in this book were removed with in the next 24 hours). It is only a simple displacement of the problem. That's why Cholo writing at first sight could actually seem to represent a culture more alive through tattoos in the prisons and jails of California and other southern US states than on Los Angeles walls. Since the early 1980s, the underground *Teen Angel* magazine has published «barrio art» made by prisoners, displaying various content – drawings on paper and mail art, poetry, gang obituaries and photos of gangsters – sometimes with thematic issues on specific gangs.

But the most brutal international export is the implantation of gang culture and its visual lettering conventions in Central American shantytowns, mainly in El Salvador and Guatemala (and also partly in Mexico) where placas are flourishing in a pure Los Angeles style. In the beginning of the 1990s, deported gang members from the US spread the lifestyle of two main Los Angeles rival gangs, MARA SALVATRUCHA or MS-13 (a mostly Salvadorian gang) and 18TH STREET or CALLE DIECIOCHO [page 127]. Most of local youngsters have actually never been to the United States, but live by a strict Los Angeles gang code (especially with regard to tattoos, here covering the whole body and even the face), the city of Los Angeles being considered a mythical motherland. The *maras*, or Central American gangs, are mainly groups of kids with no ideology (or purely territorial ones limited to the simple elimination of rival groups) and today constitute an international problem that is partly financed by narco-trafficking; this contemporary ultraviolence is an image of our modernity. The association *Homies Unidos*, based in both El Salvador and Los Angeles since the end of the 1990s, tries to work to diminish the violence that plagues too many lives in these communities, their members having dedicated themselves to creating alternatives to crime, drugs, and violence, providing hope and opportunities (including deportee assistance, education, job training or tattoo removal). Donna De Cesare documented this phenomenon of gang «franchise holders» in Central America in her photo essay *Deporting America's Gang Culture* in 1999, where much old school Cholo writing can be observed. Apparently, the style of placas observed there corresponds to former letterforms, compared to the current Cholo hand that has continuously changed in Los Angeles year after year. This fact is typical of exiles who suspend the evolution of language or visual culture when they leave their homeland. It seems clear that Cholo writing will continue its worldwide spread under the banner of its mythical Los Angeles origins – geographical moves that will probably bring further mutations. There has been, for example, a rapid growth of Mexican and Central American gangs in New York city these last few years, and the presence of Salvadorian maras was recently reported in Barcelona, Spain. *Placazos*, these hybrid monolinear blackletters from the Southern Californian suburban utopia, will perhaps be visible one day in Europe, the birthplace of gothic lettering, transported back from the New World.

All local identities constitute a narrative as well as variations and adaptations from a model, in this case the Latin alphabet in the Western-influenced world, from both the humanistic and gothic models (that indeed both originated in the Carolingian minuscule calligraphy of the late 8th century). As the typeface Garamond is the image of French Renaissance, as the typeface Gill Sans is the spirit of England, Cholo writing in the same manner represents the very essence of Los Angeles, Southern California.

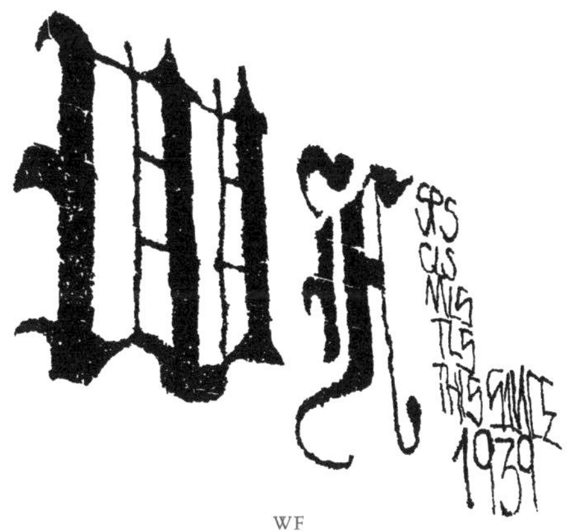

WF
(WHITE FENCE)
SPS / CLS / MLS / TLS
(CLIQUES' ACRONYMS,
SPIDERS / CRIMINALS
/ MALOS / TINY LOCOS)
THIS SINCE 1939

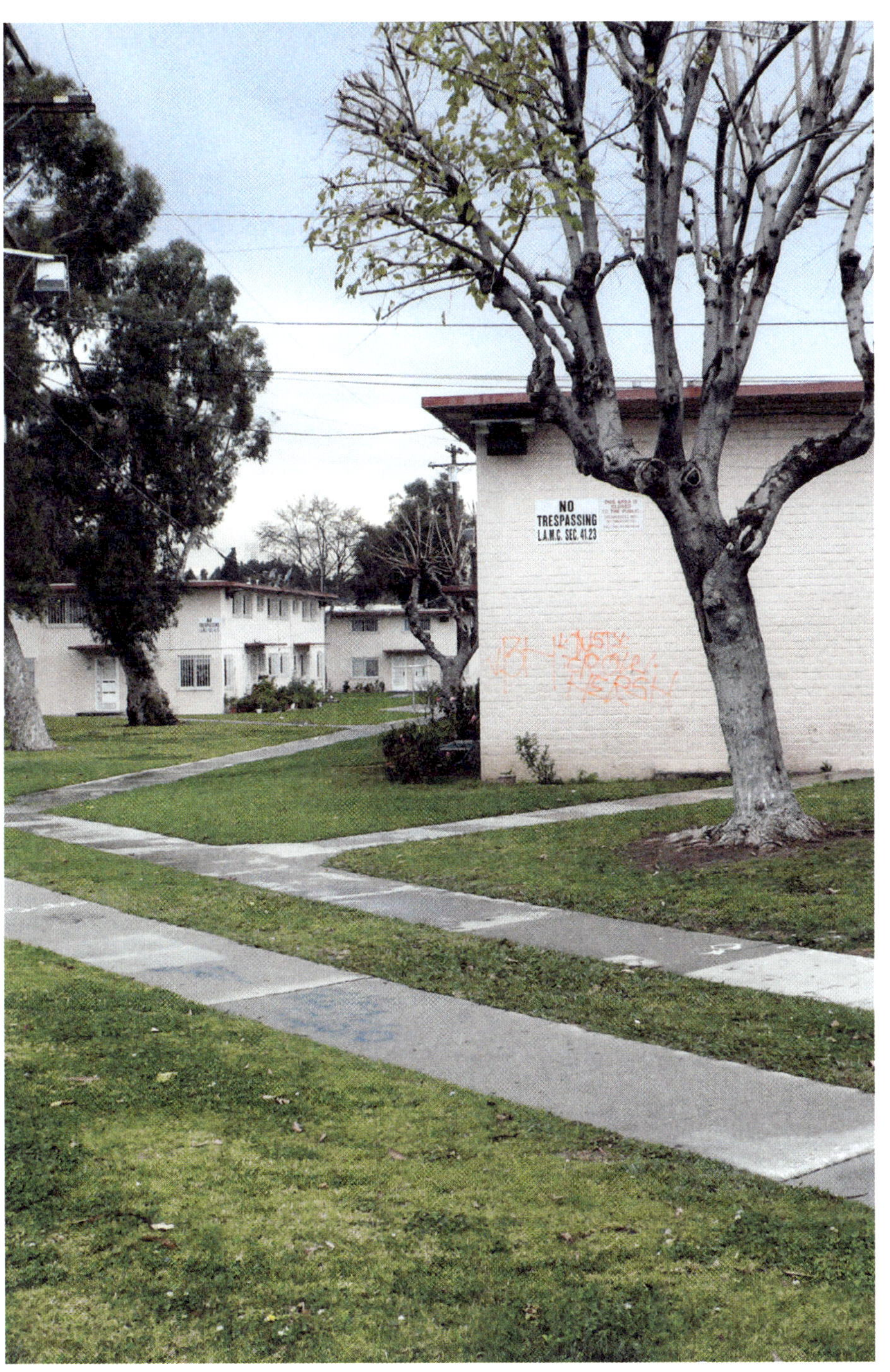

V BH
(VARRIO BIG HAZARD)
L·(LIL) DUSTY·
CROW·
HERSH

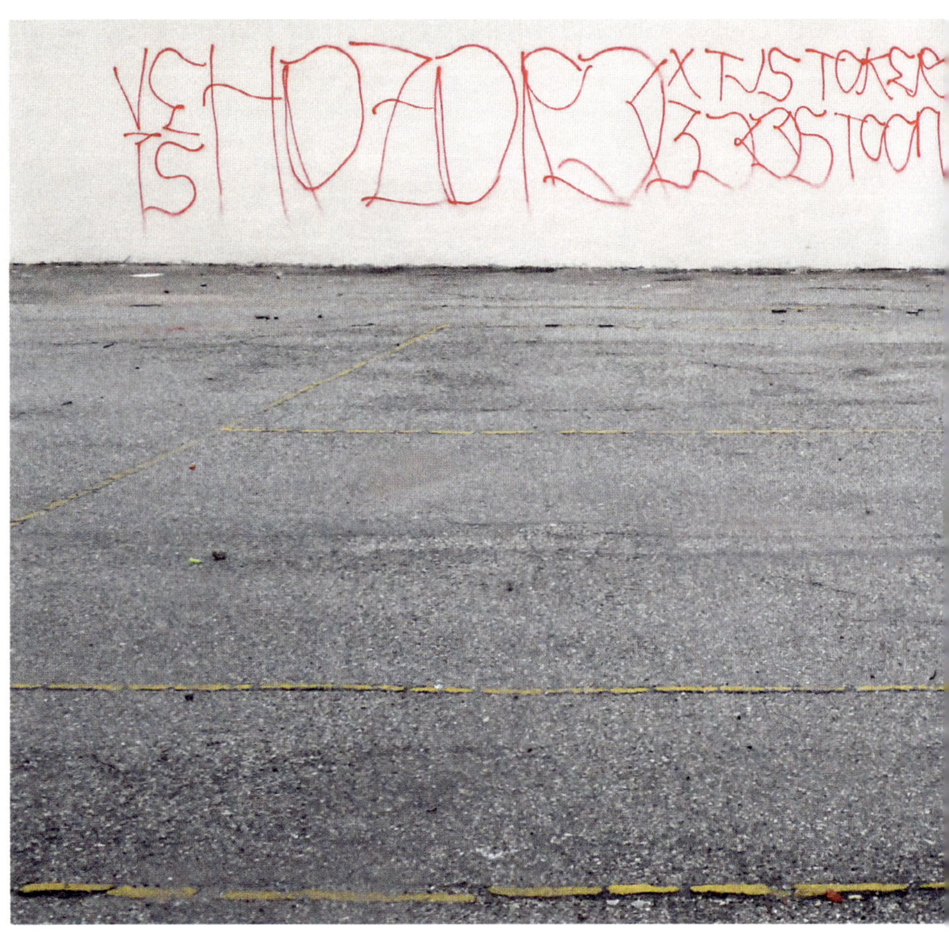

v (varrio) e (east) hazard x tls toker shorty

s (side)   3 fds toon smiley

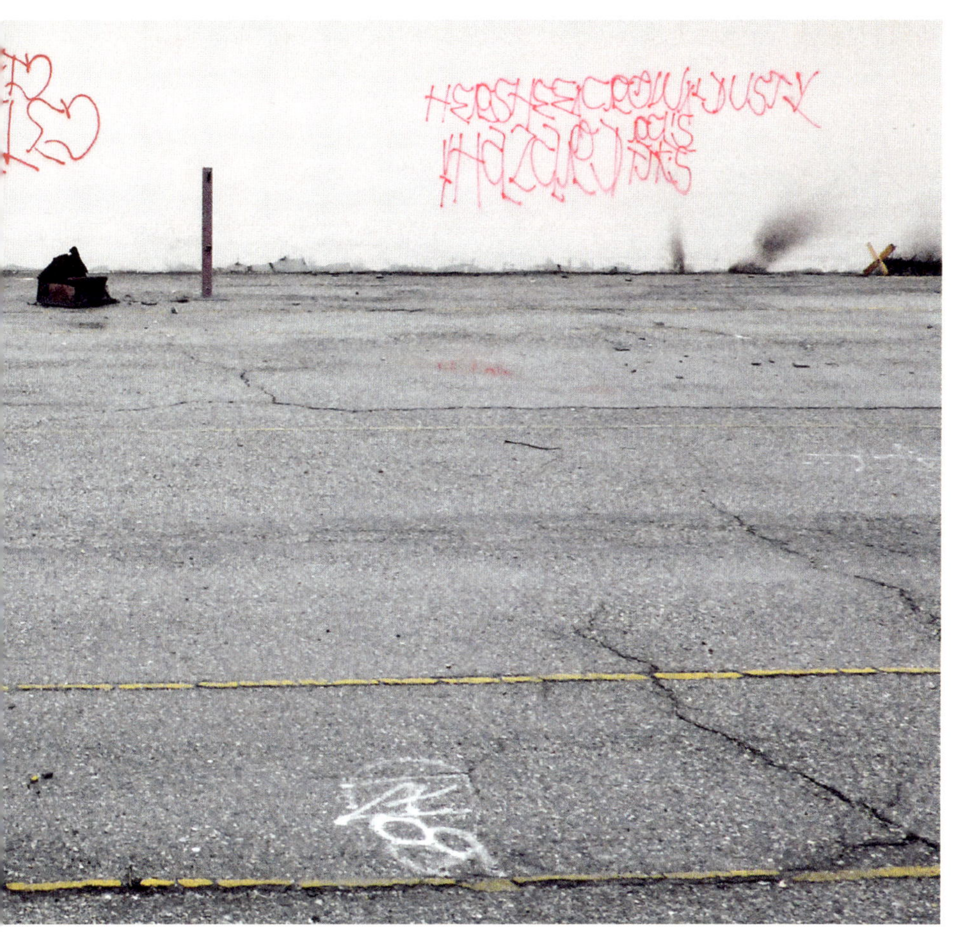

63

HERSHEE × CROW × L (LIL) DUSTY
V (VARRIO) HAZARD RCL'S TJK·S

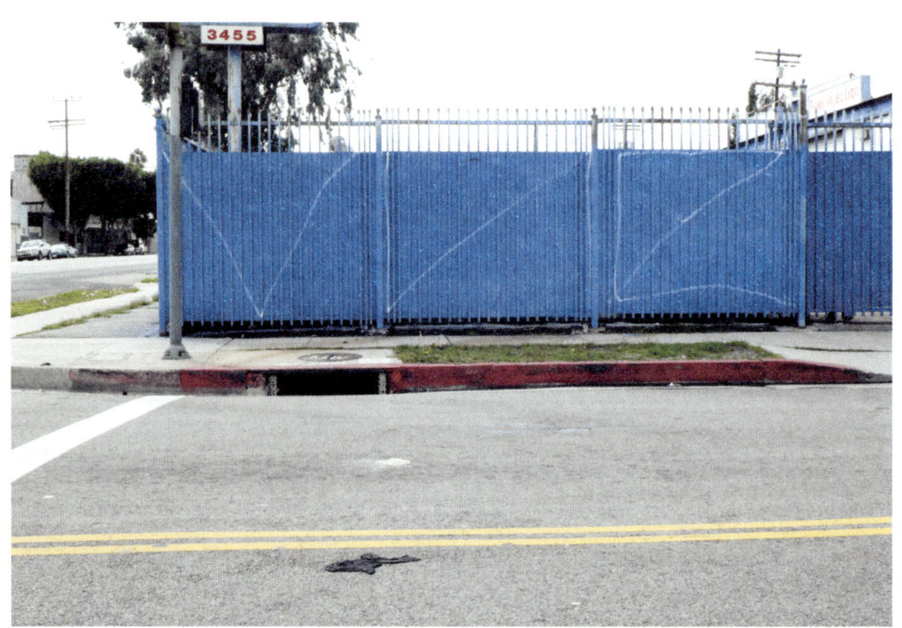

vne
(varrio
nuevo
estrada)

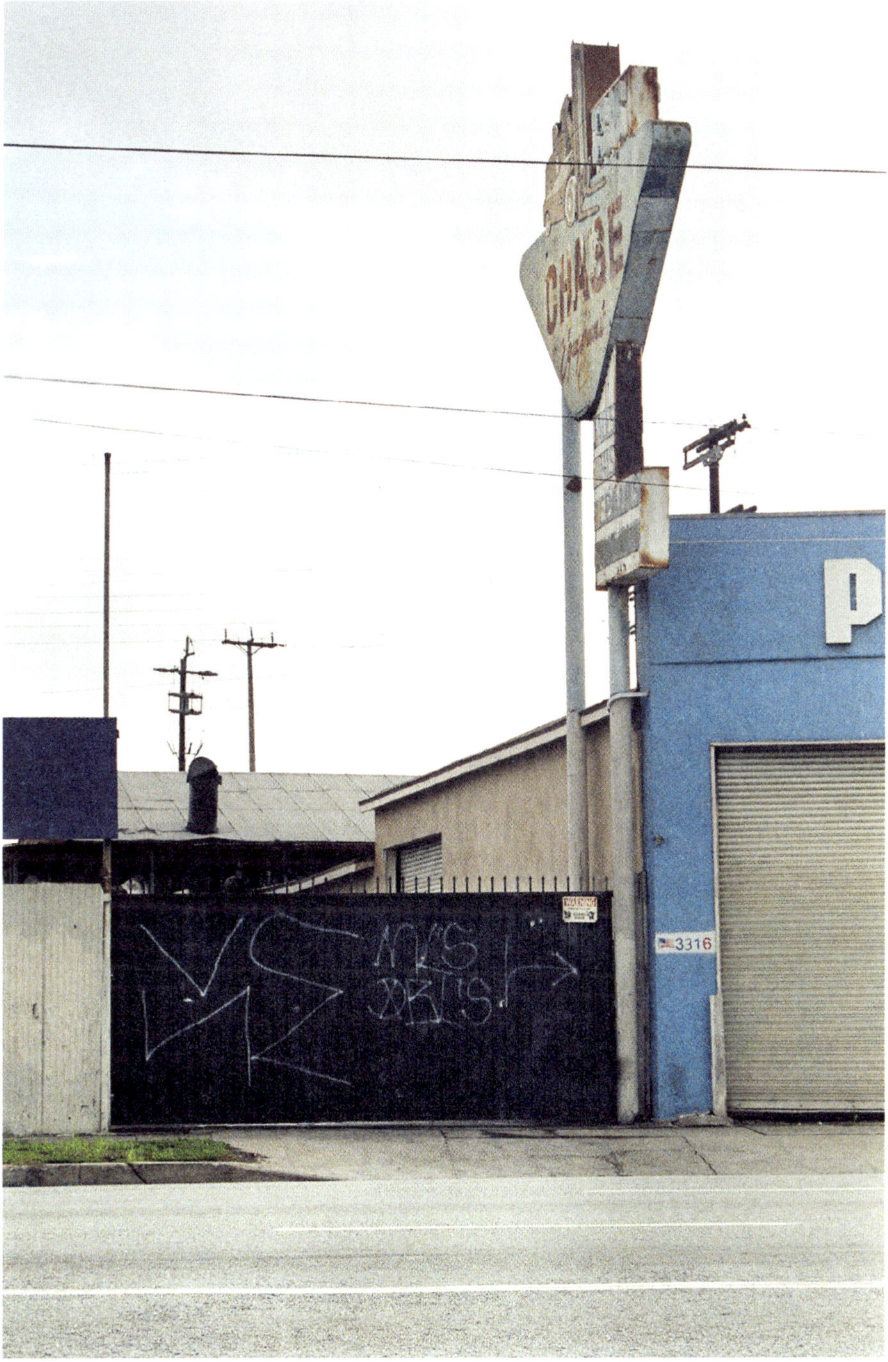

VNE   ML'S →
(VARRIO   (MALOS)
NUEVO   DBL'S
ESTRADA)   (DIABLOS)

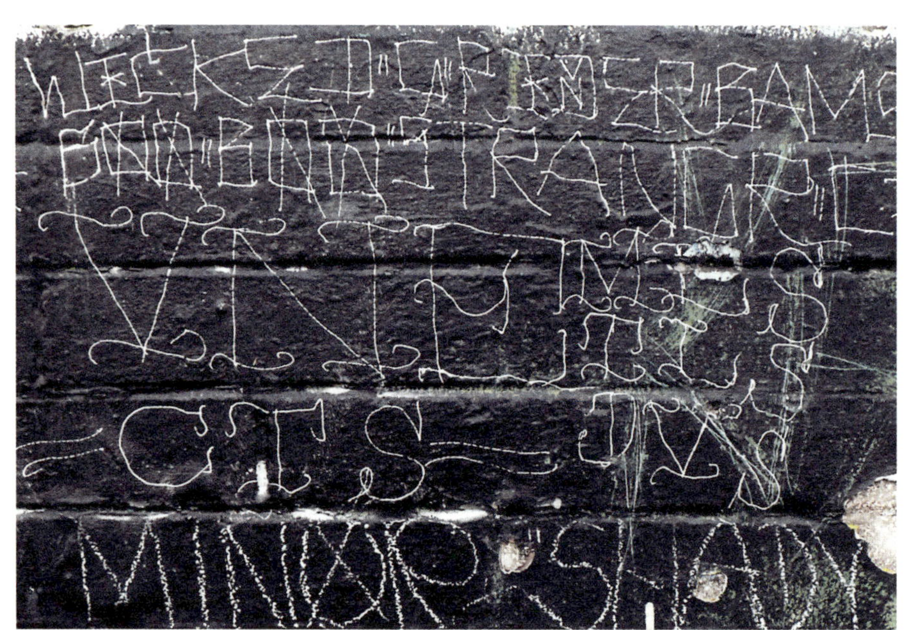

WICKED || GRIDER || BAMS
BOO || BOO || STRANGR

VNE
= CTS =
(VARRIO
NUEVO
ESTRADA
COURTS)

MLS (MALOS)
TLS (TINY LOCOS)
DV'S (DEVILS)

MINOR SHADY

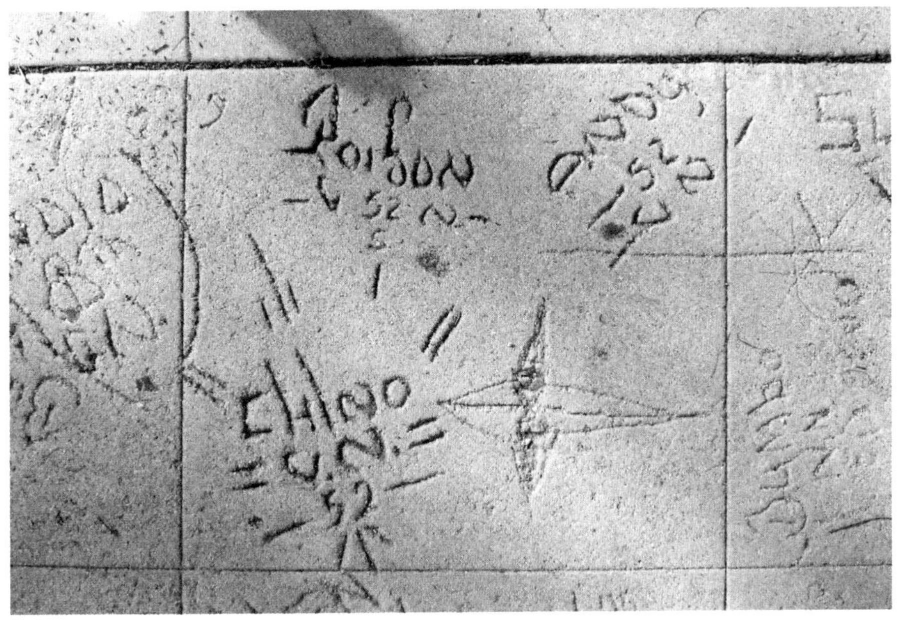

CHINO   POISON   ANDY

=V.N.=   −V 52 N−   −52−

−52−   (VARRIO   −VN−

NUEVO

1952)

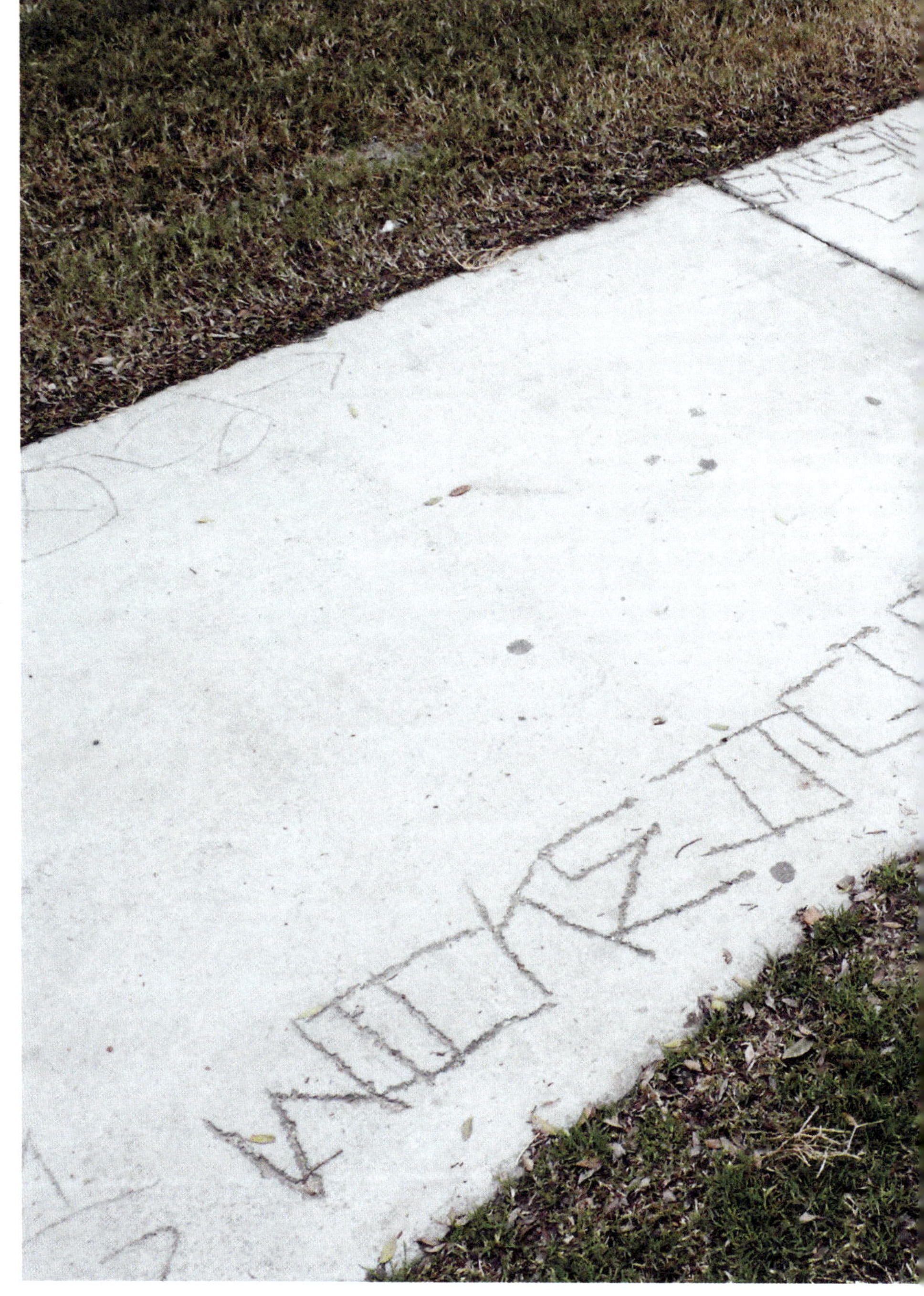

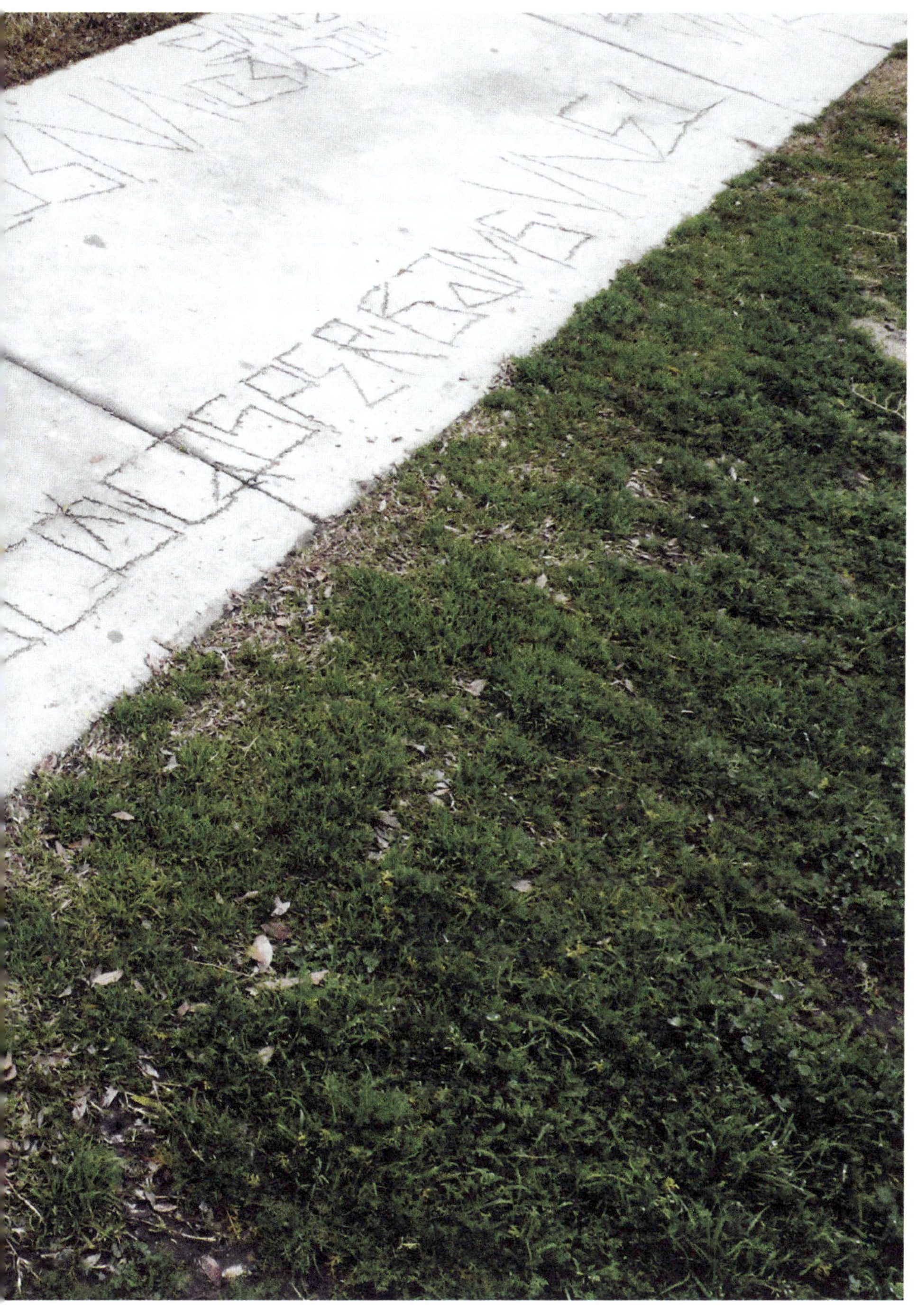

WICKED ı CISCO ı CASPER ı BAMS ı VNE1
(VARRIO NUEVO ESTRADA NUMBER ONE)

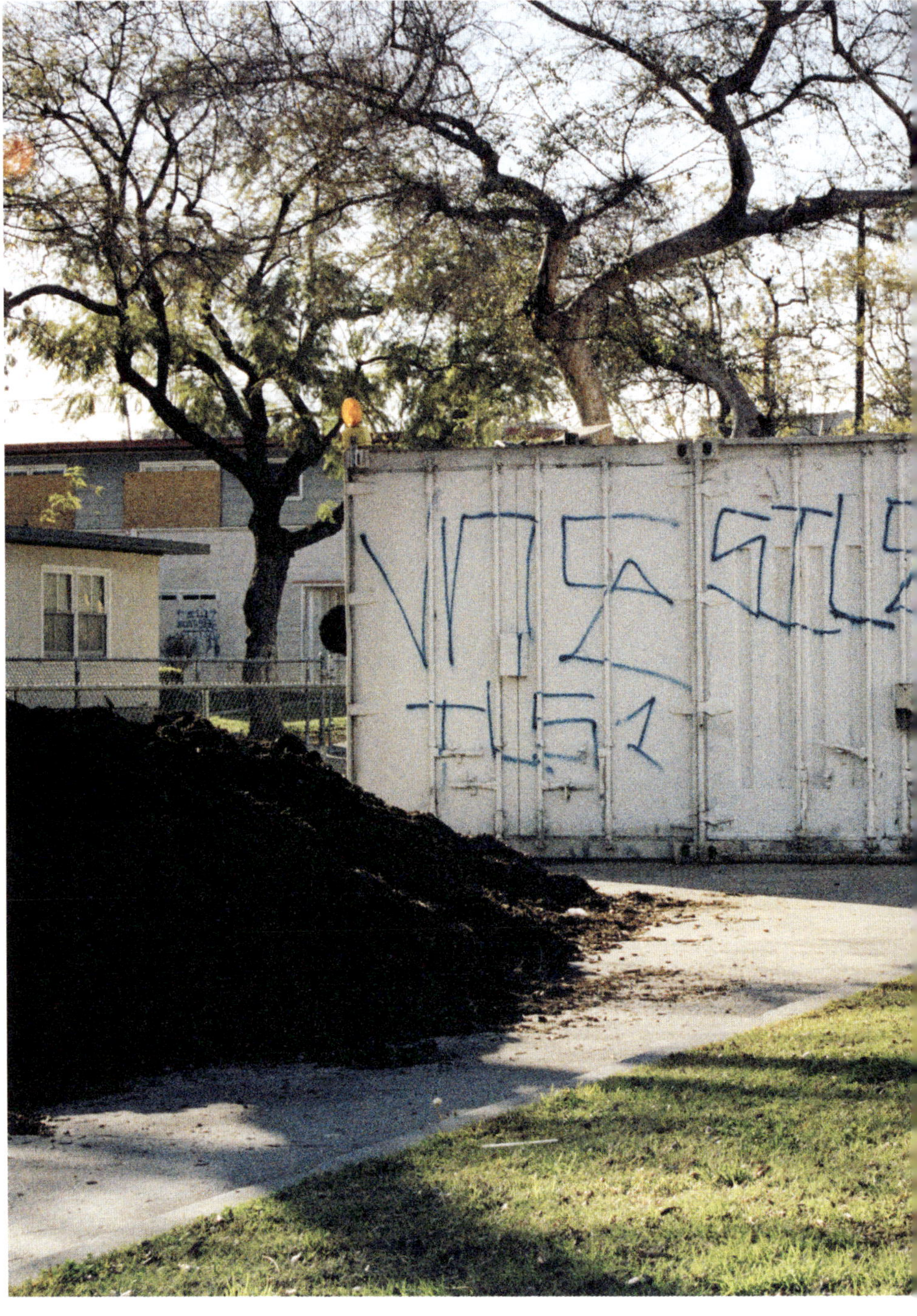

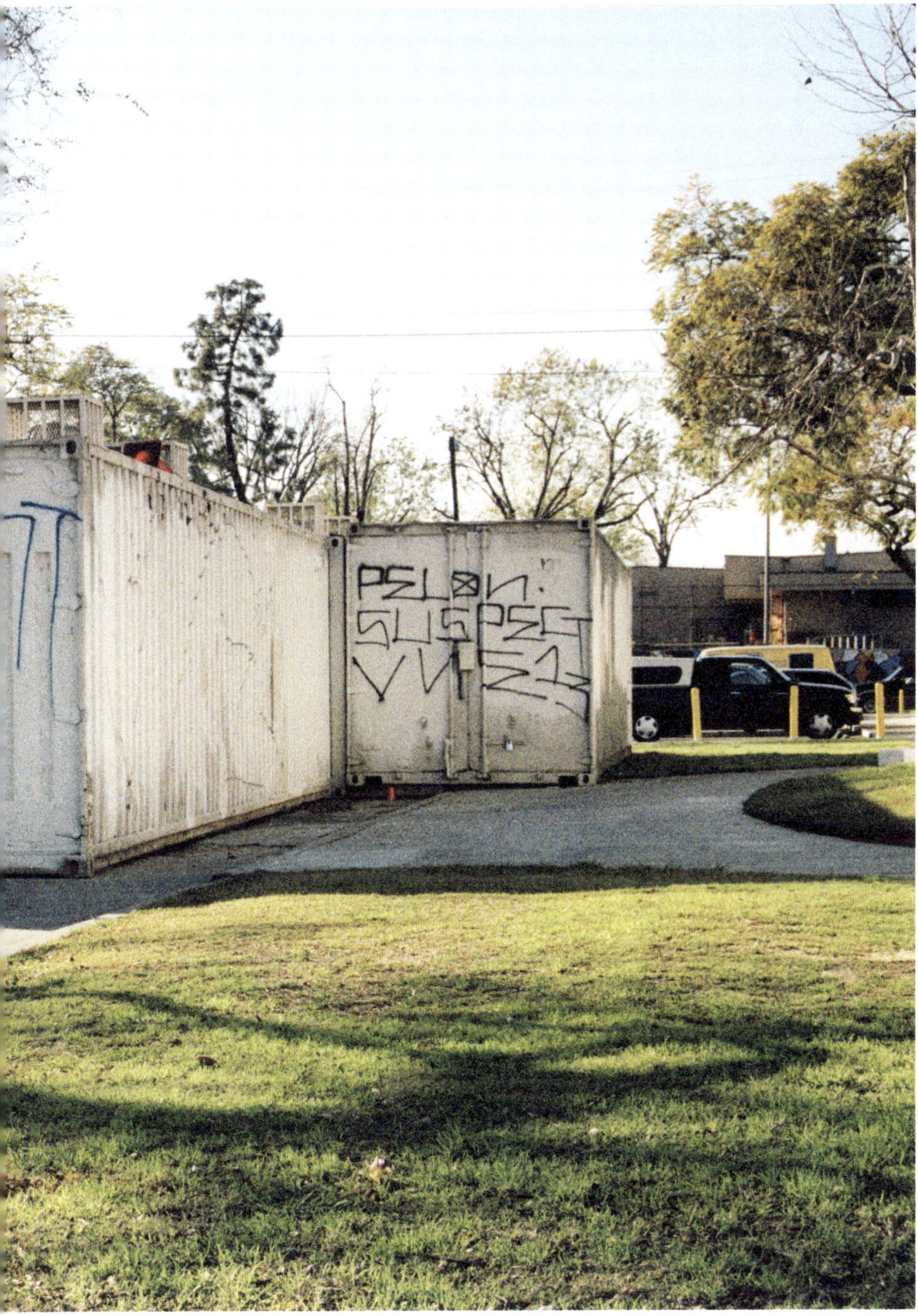

VNE
(VARRIO NUEVO
ESTRADA)
TLS 1
(TINY LOCOS)
SILENT

PELON ·
SUSPECT
VNE 13
(VARRIO NUEVO
ESTRADA TRECE)

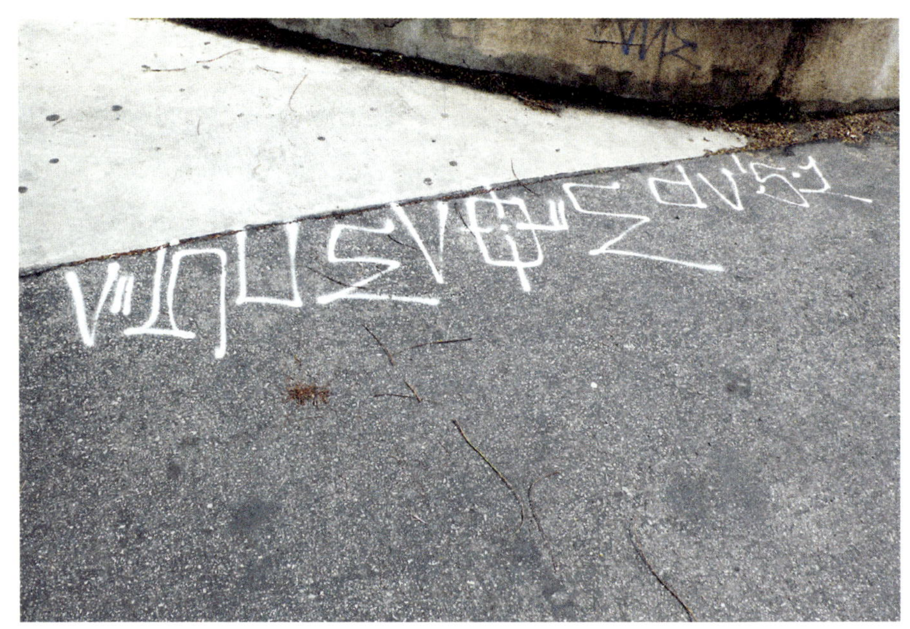

72

VꞋꞋNUEVOꞋꞋE DV'S · 1
(VARRIO NUEVO ESTRADA DEVILS)

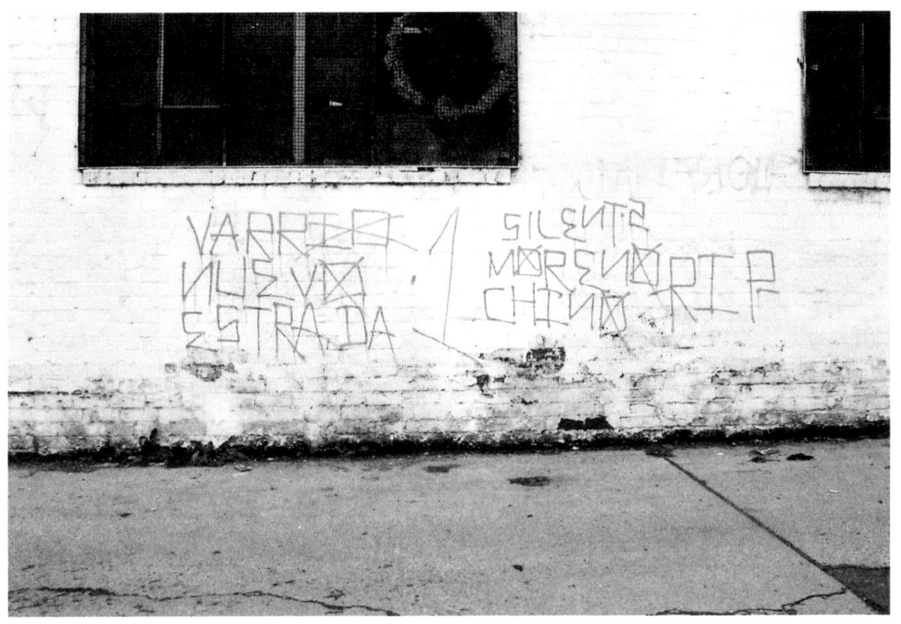

VARRIO   SILENT·2
NUEVO ·1 MORENO   — RIP —
ESTRADA   CHINO

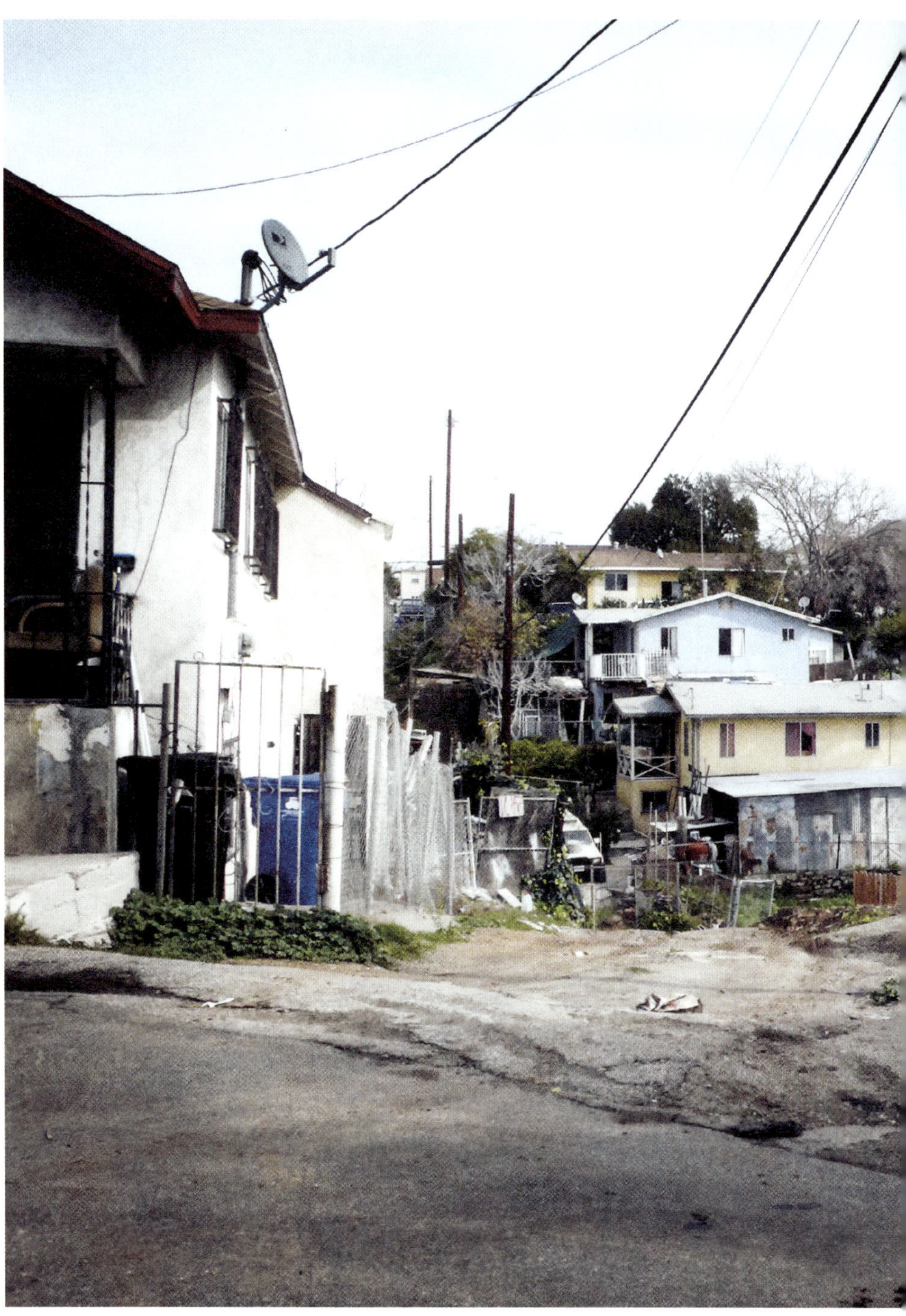

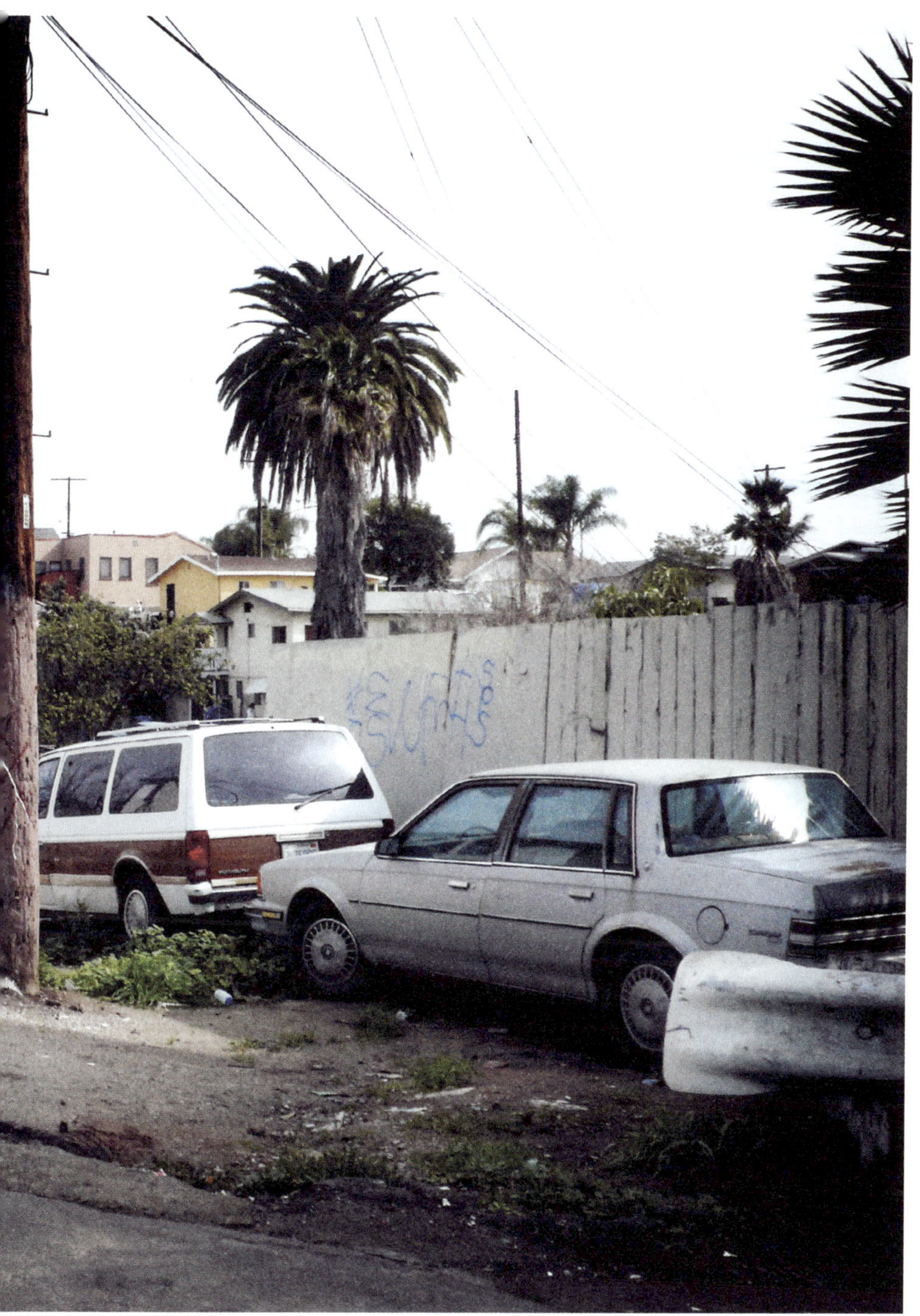

V ES WF TH SPS
(VARRIO EAST SIDE WHITE FENCE
THE HOLE SPIDERS)

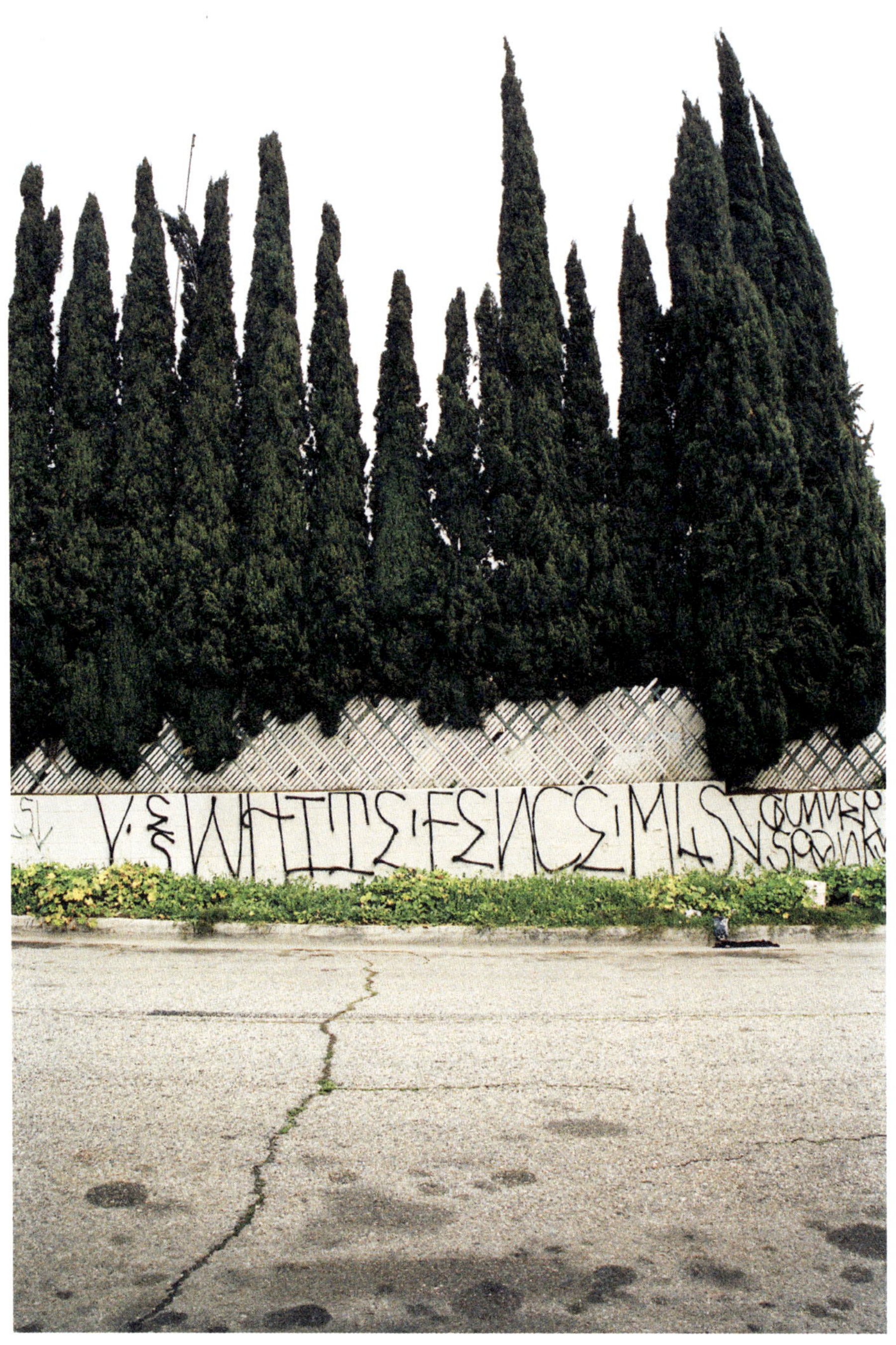

V (VARRIO) · ES (EAST SIDE)
WHITE ∙ FENCE ∙ MLS ↓
(MALOS)
GUNNER
SPANKY

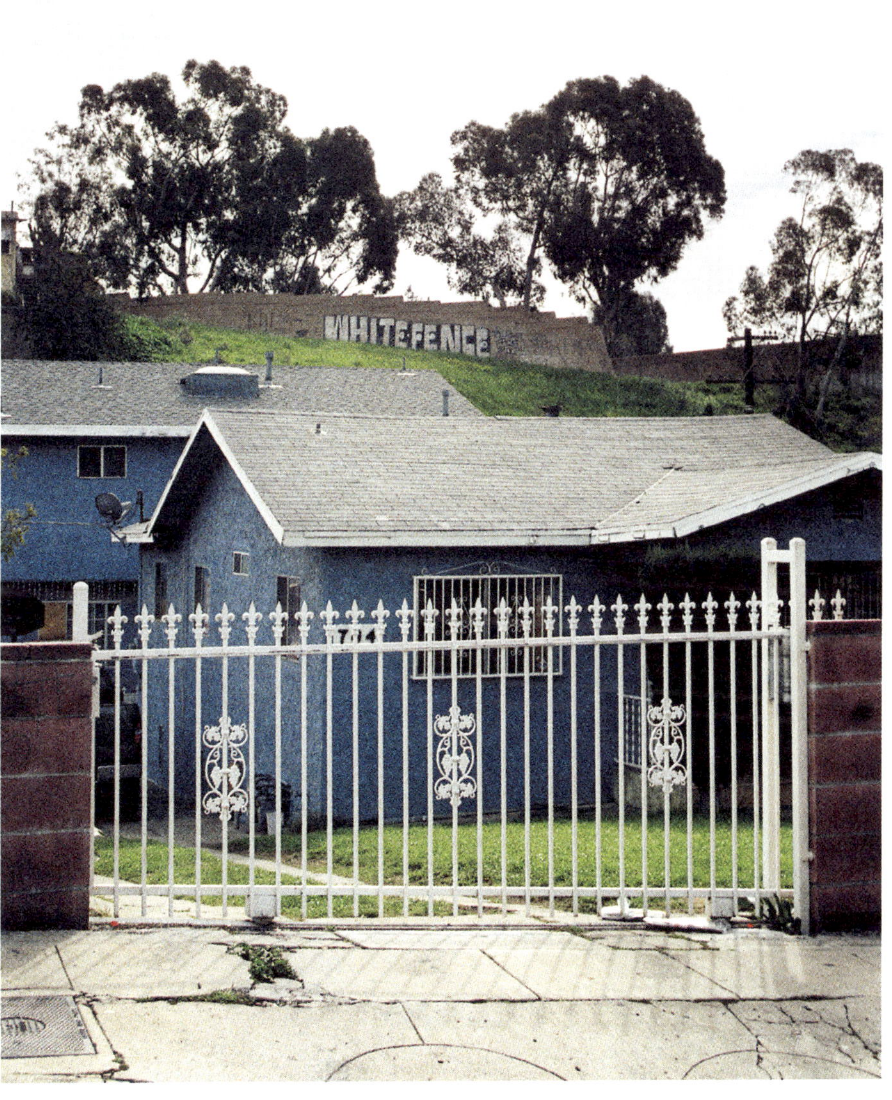

WF WHITE · FENCE

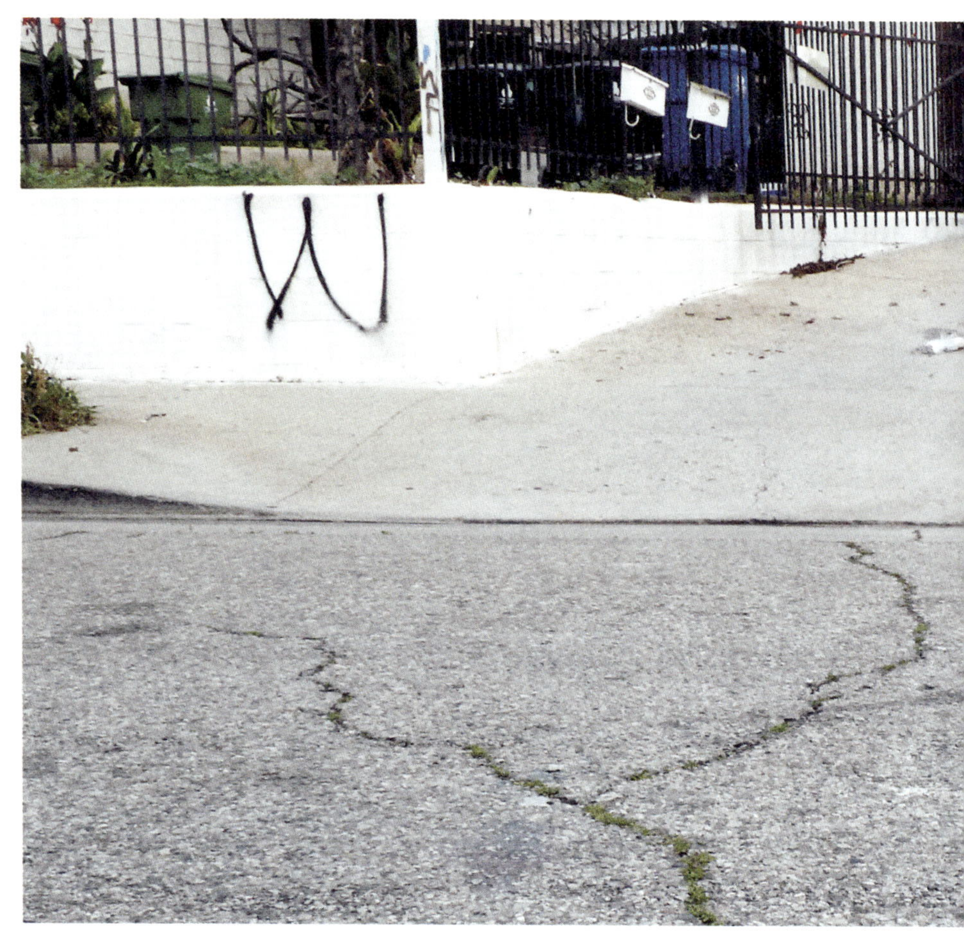

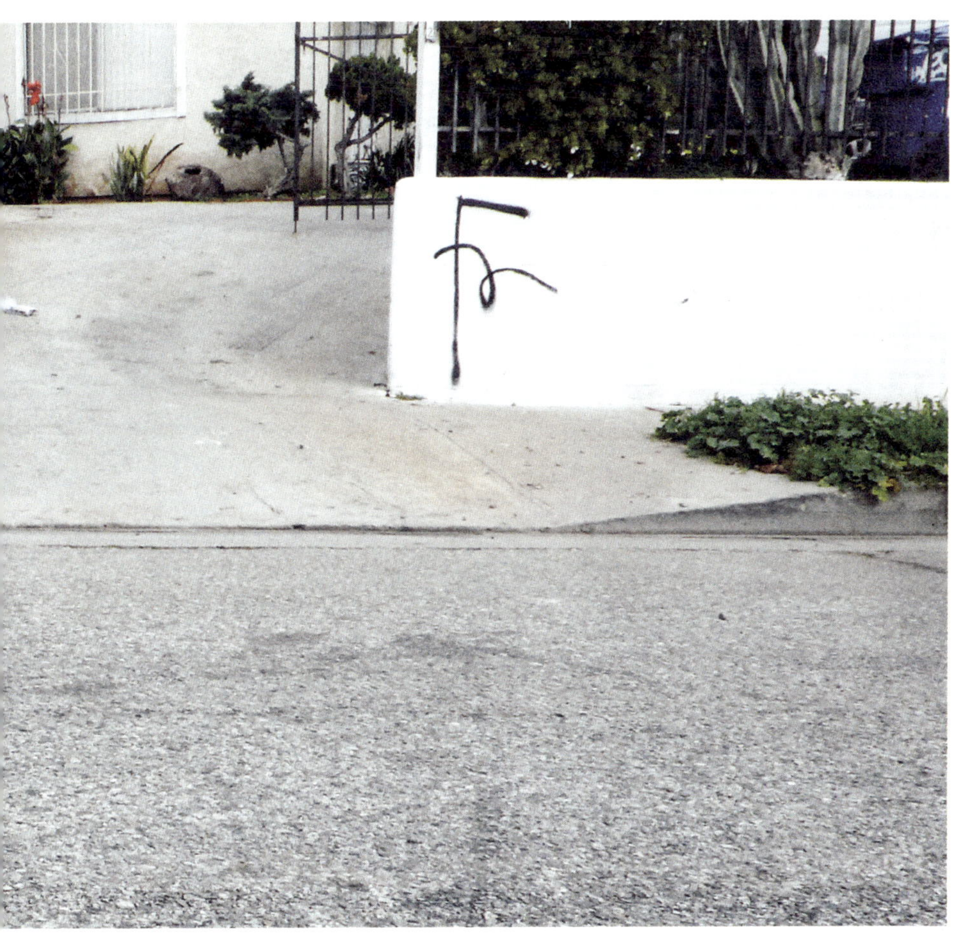

WF
(WHITE FENCE GANG)

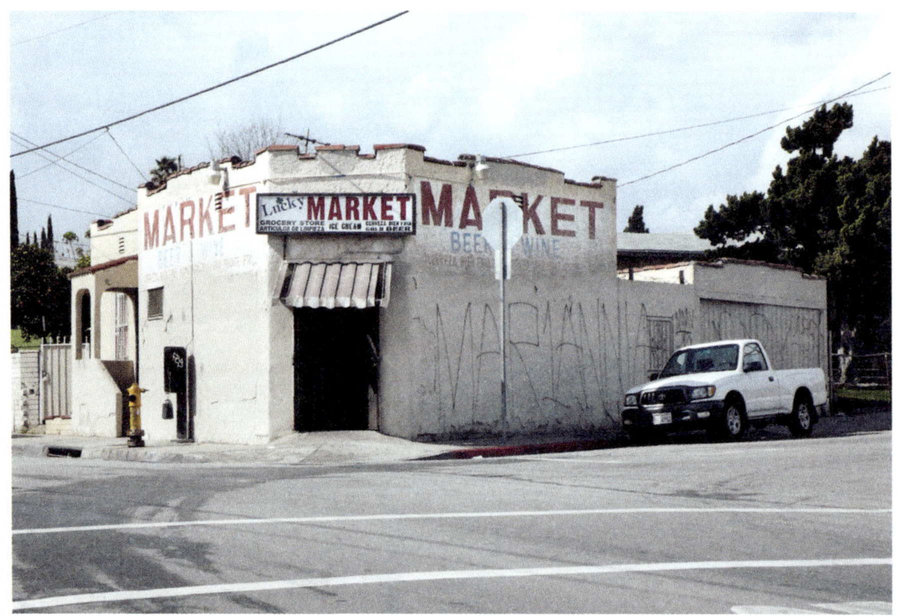

MARIANNA
(MARAVILLA)
MMV 187

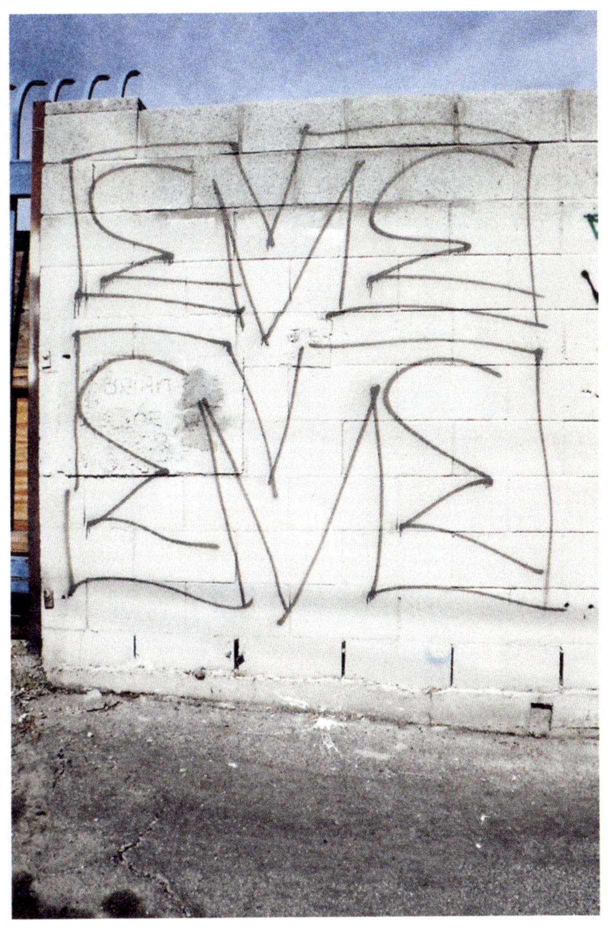

M / EME
M / EME
(MARIANNA
MARAVILLA
VARRIO)

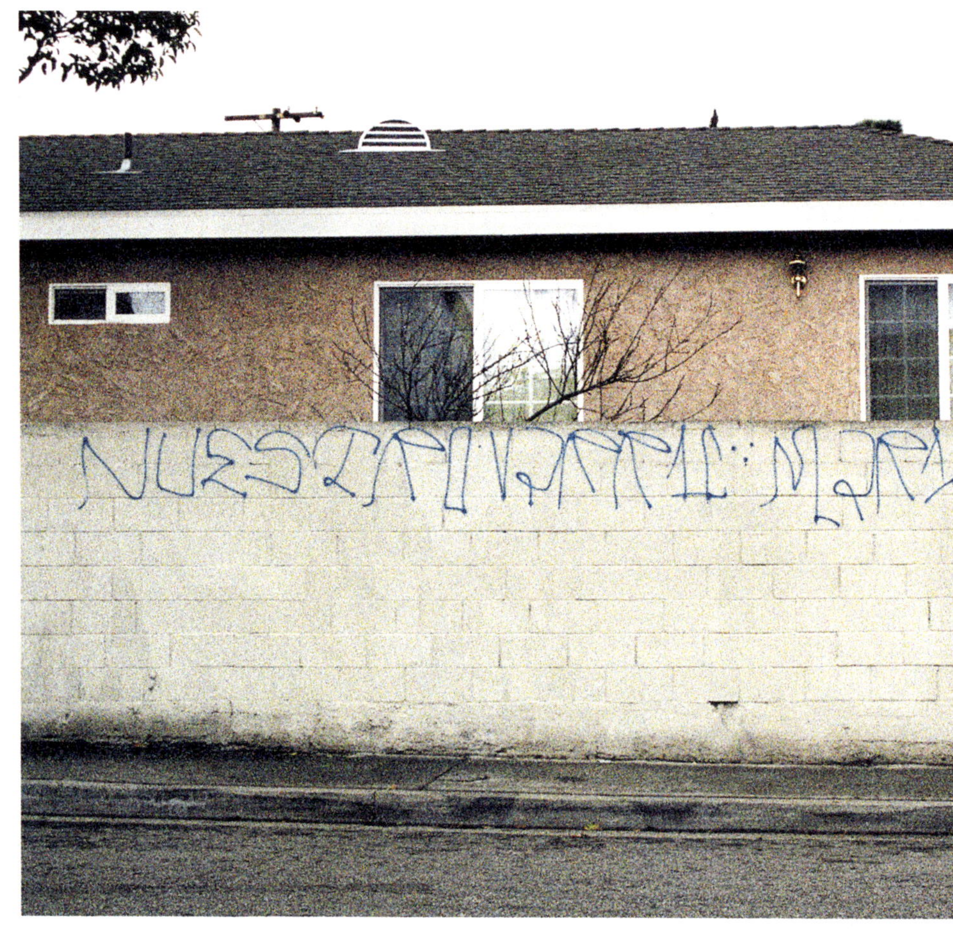

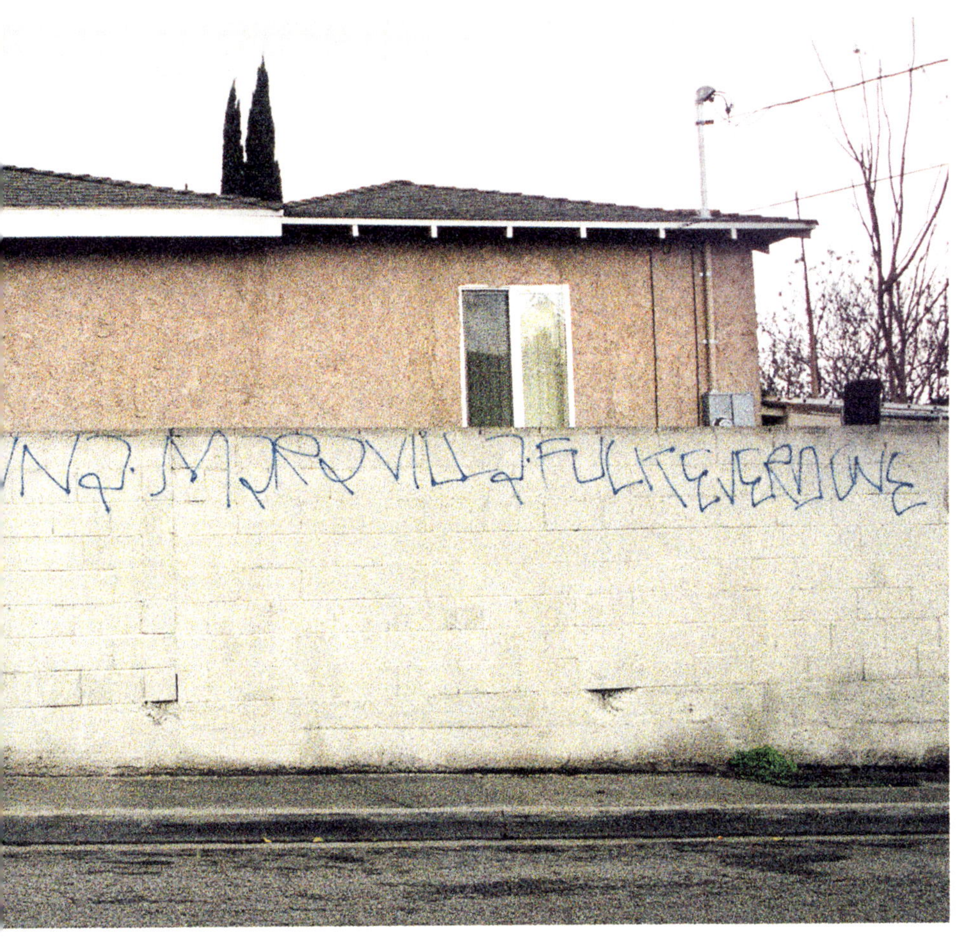

NUESTRO · VARRIO ·.· MARIANNA · MARAVILLA · FUCK EVERYONE

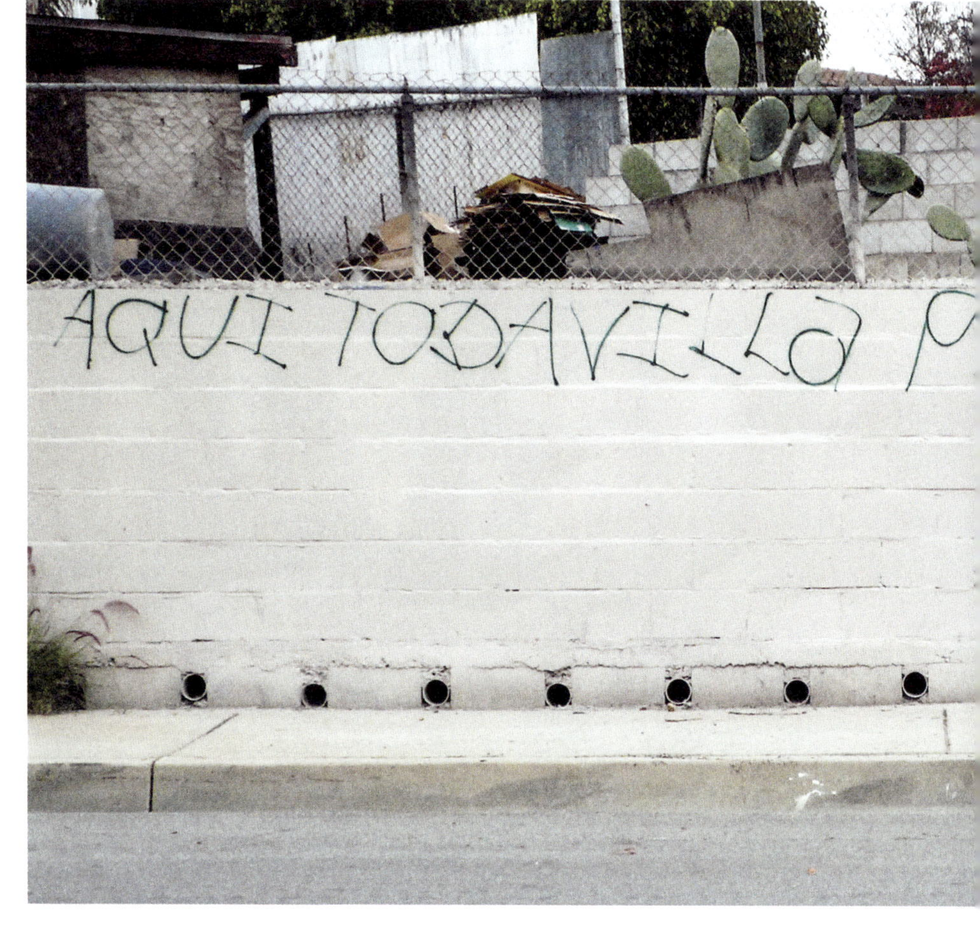
AQUI TODAVILLA P

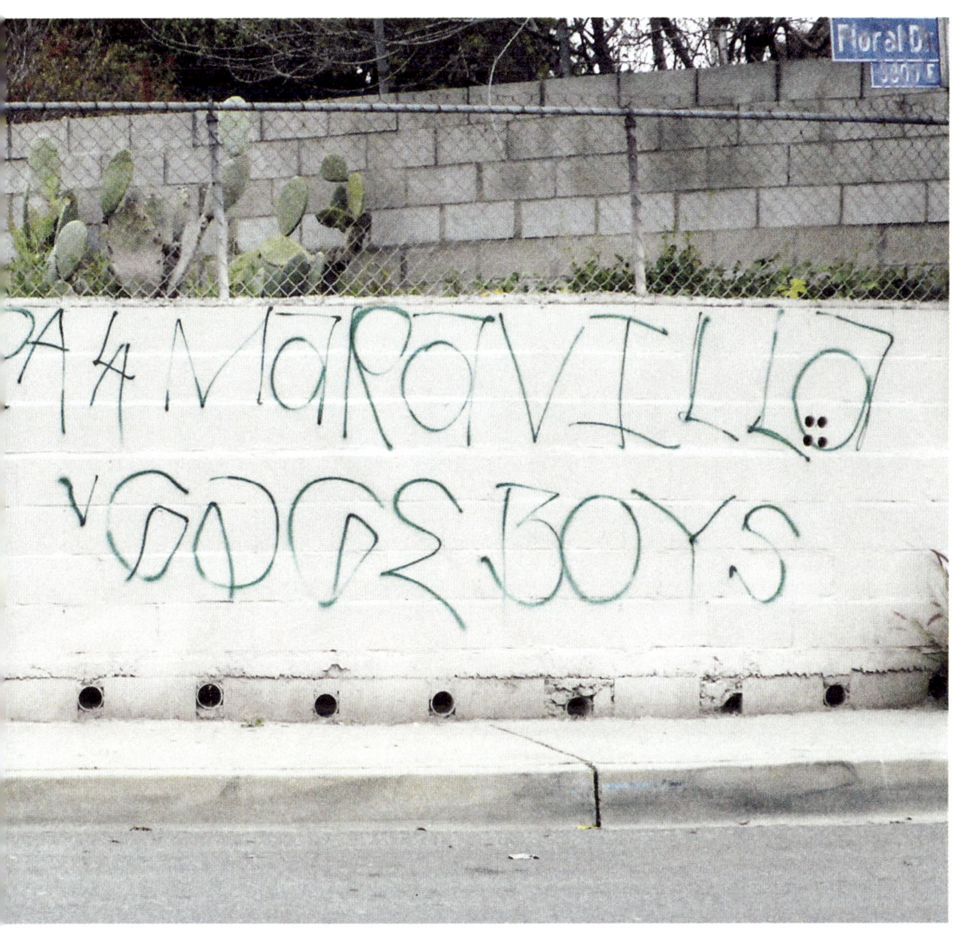

AQUI TODAVILLA PARA LA MARAVILLA
V (VARRIO) GAGE BOYS

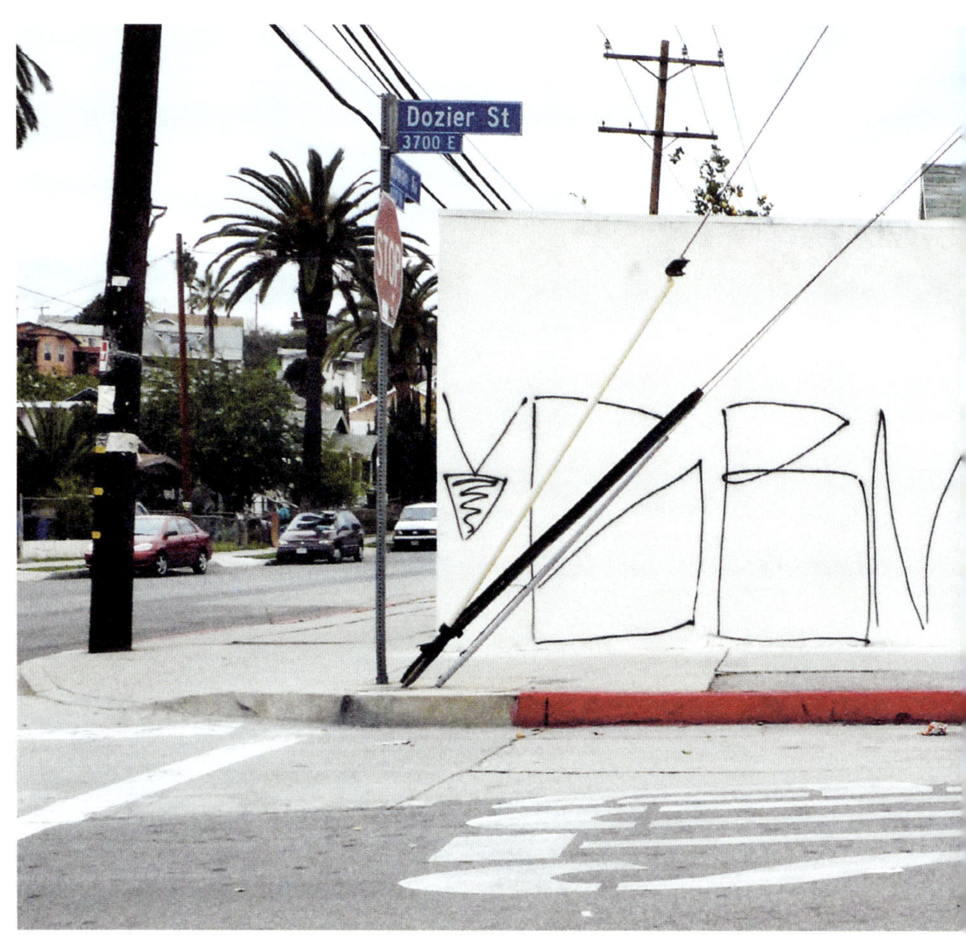

Dozier St
3700 E
STOP

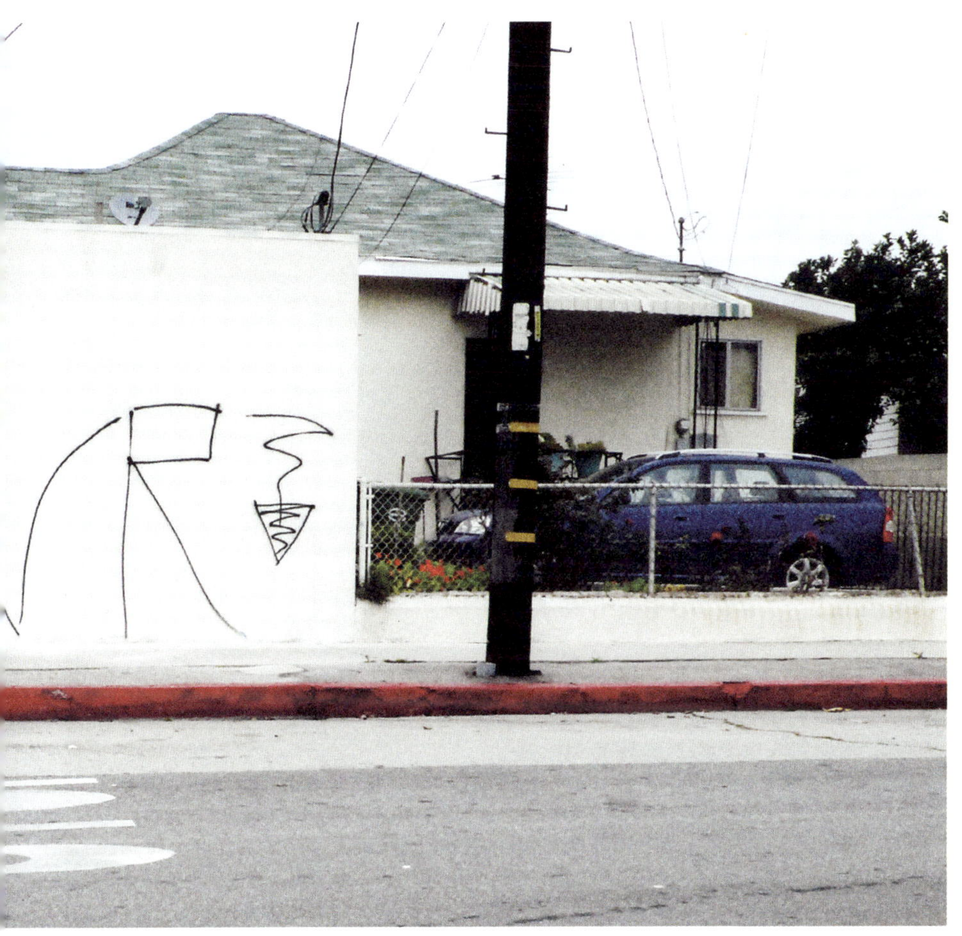

V GBMVR!
(VARRIO GAGE BOYS MARAVILLA RIFA)

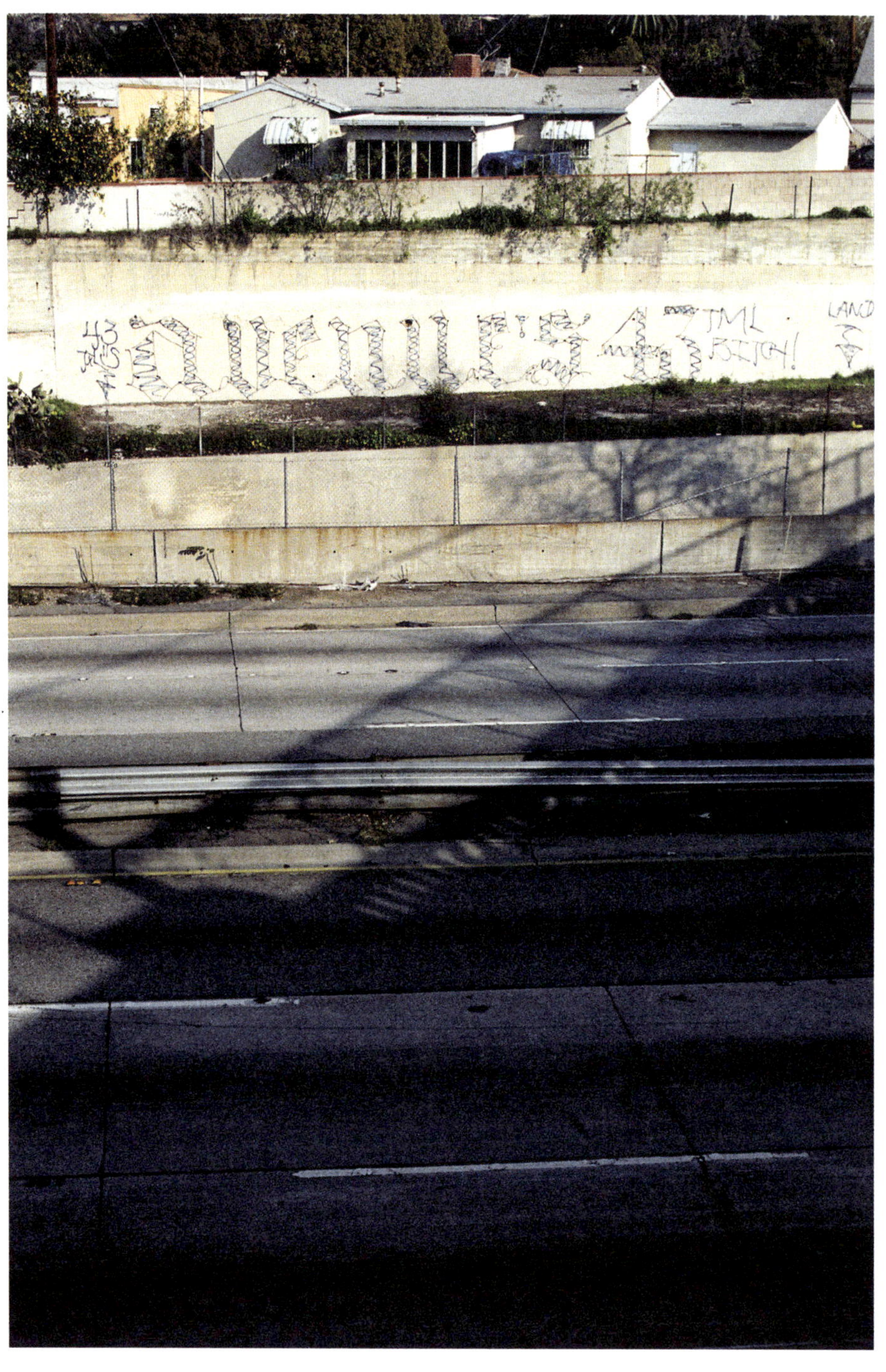

43 T×L's avenues 43 TML BITCH!
(43RD STREET TINY LOCOS)
(AVENUES GANG 43RD STREET)
(TINY MALOS)

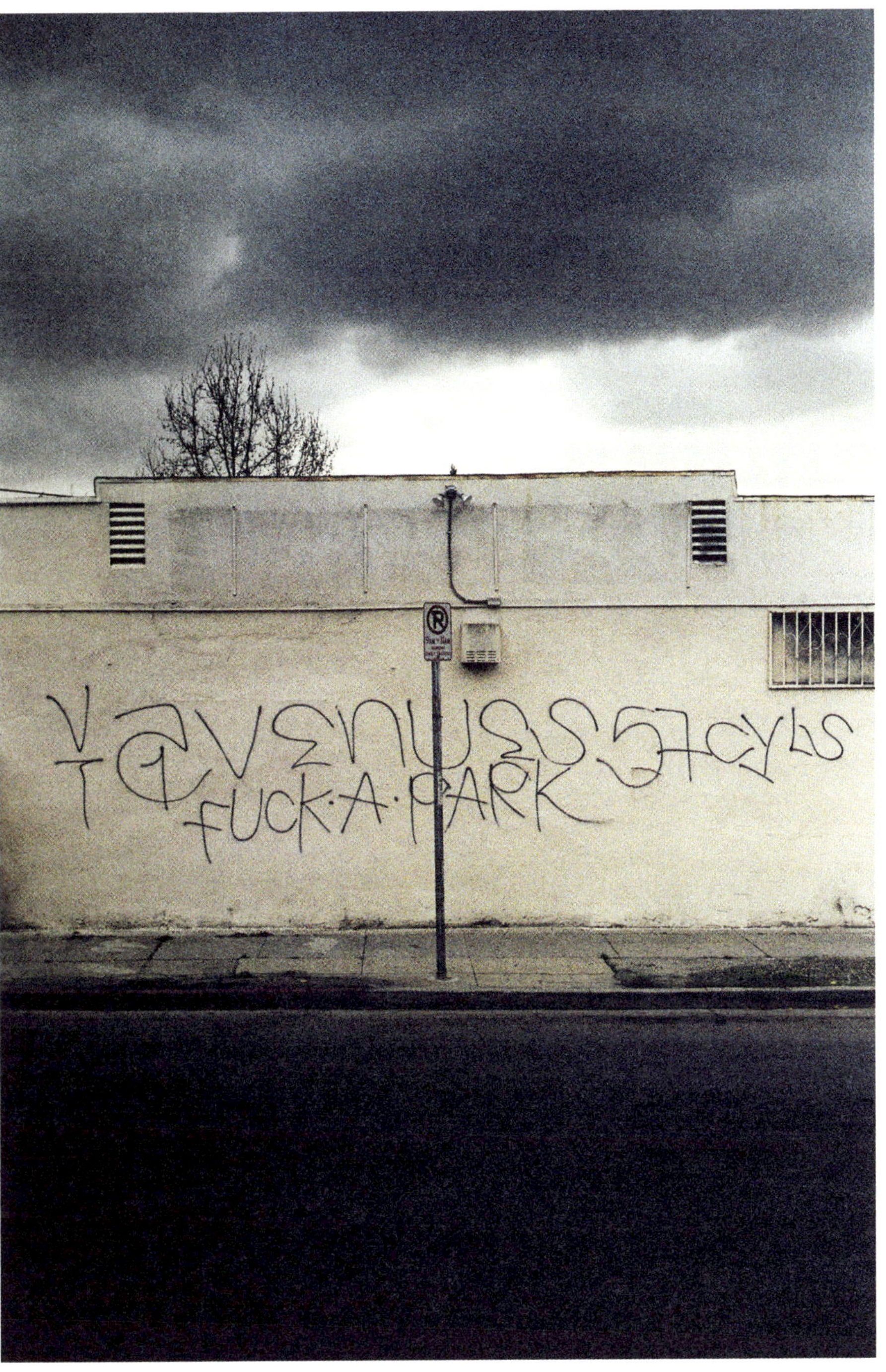

V (VARRIO) AVENUES 57 CY LS (CYPRESS LOCOS)
FUCK·A·PARK

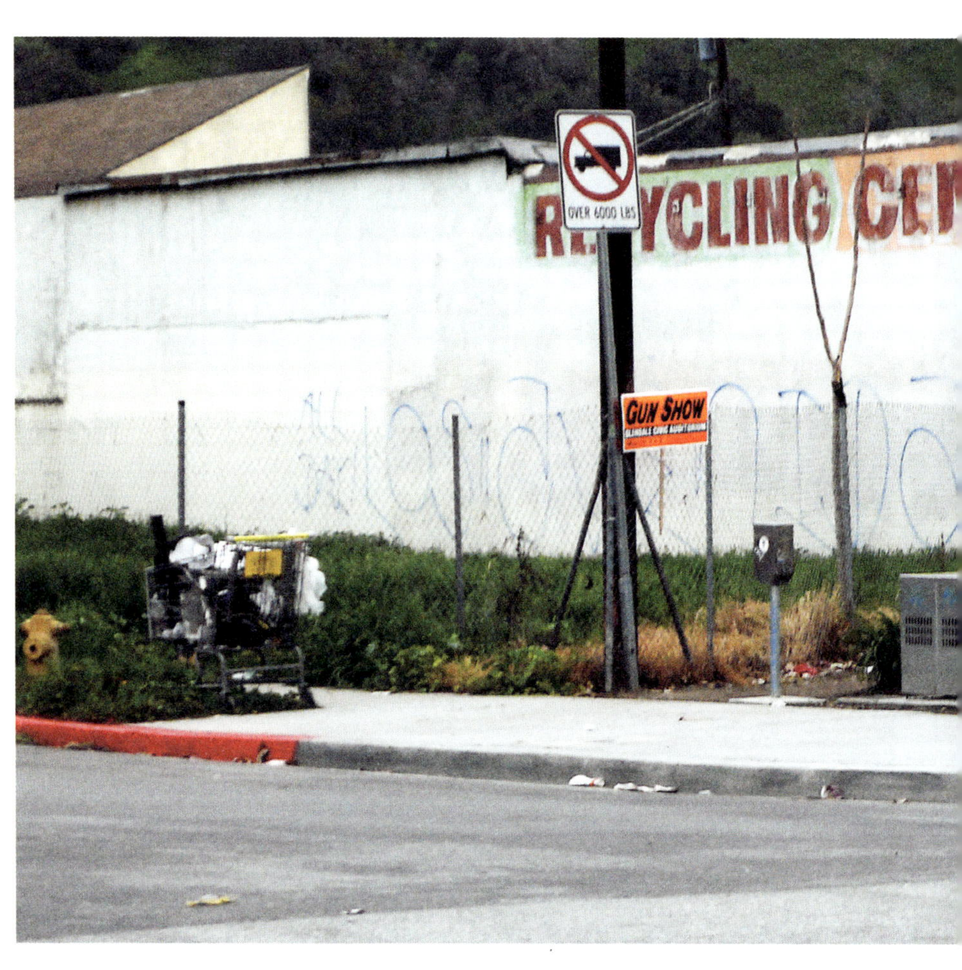
OVER 6000 LBS
RECYCLING CEN
GUN SHOW
GLENDALE CIVIC AUDITORIUM

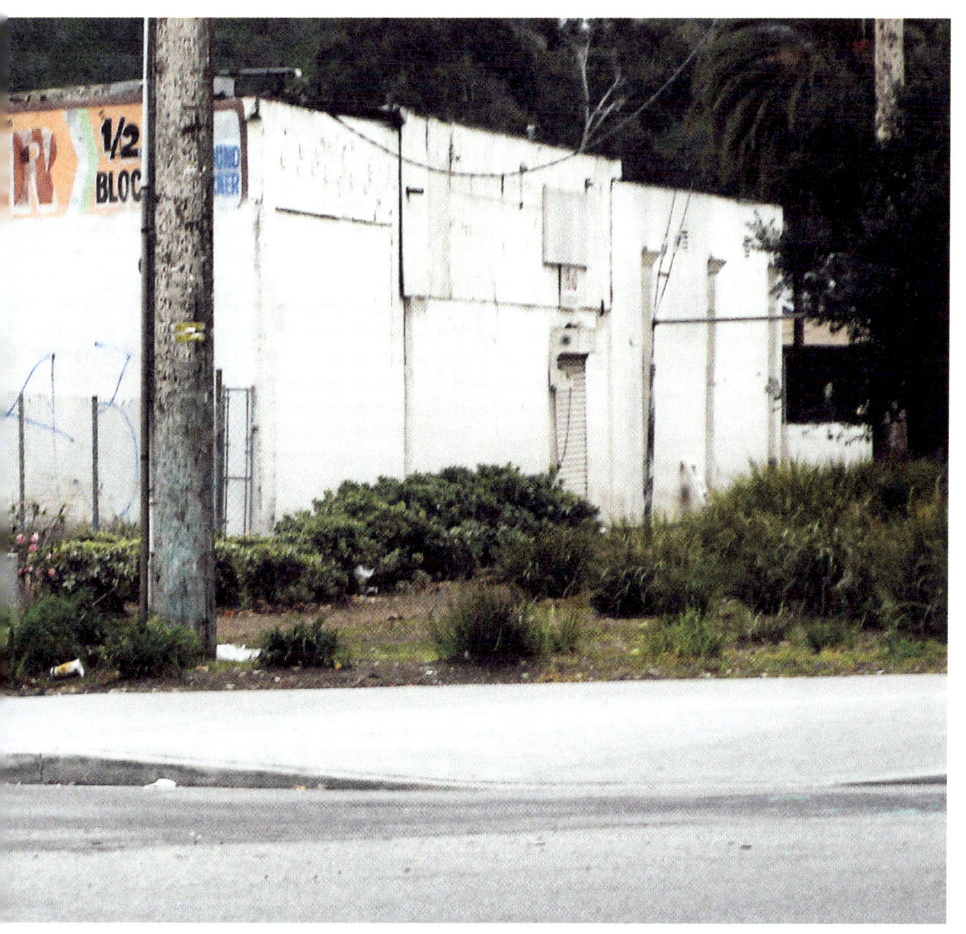

ALL DAY! LOS‖aveNIDa's 43
(AVENUES GANG 43RD STREET)

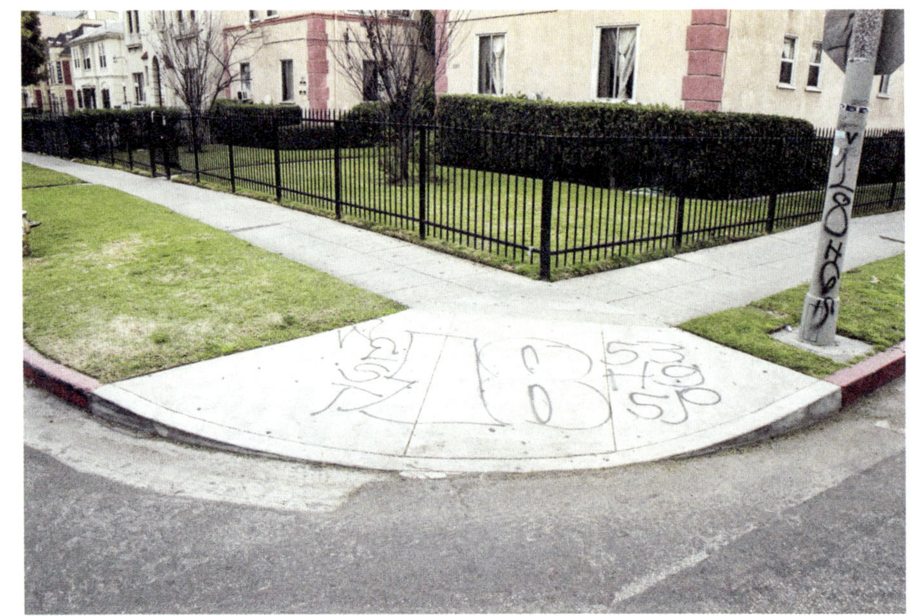

WEST 18 53HGSP
(EIGHTEEN ST. GANG)

V
1
8
H
G
S
(VARRIO DIECIOCHO
HGS—HOLLYWOOD
GANGSTERS)

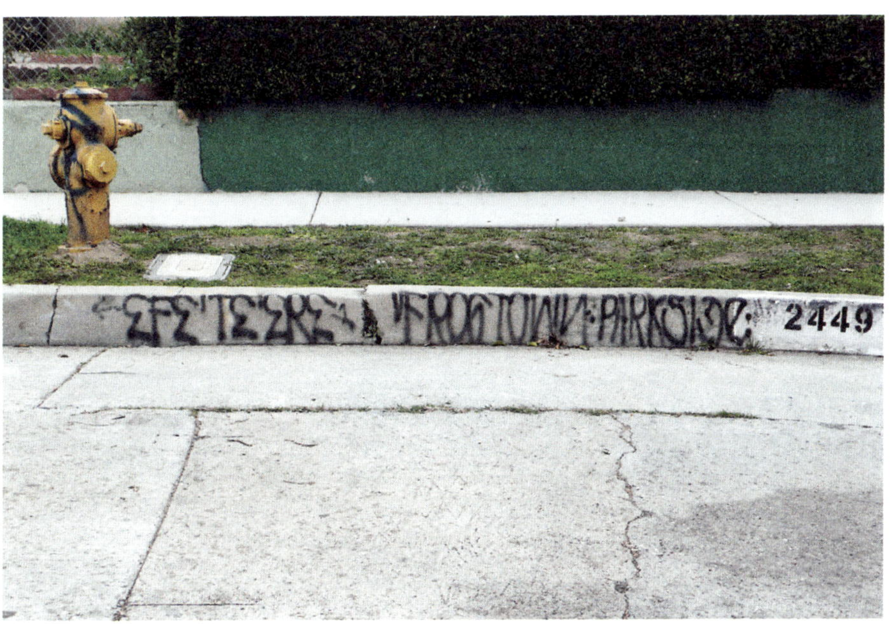

←EFE'TE'ERE'/ FTR (FROGTOWN RIFA) V (VARRIO) FROGTOWN·PARKSIDE·

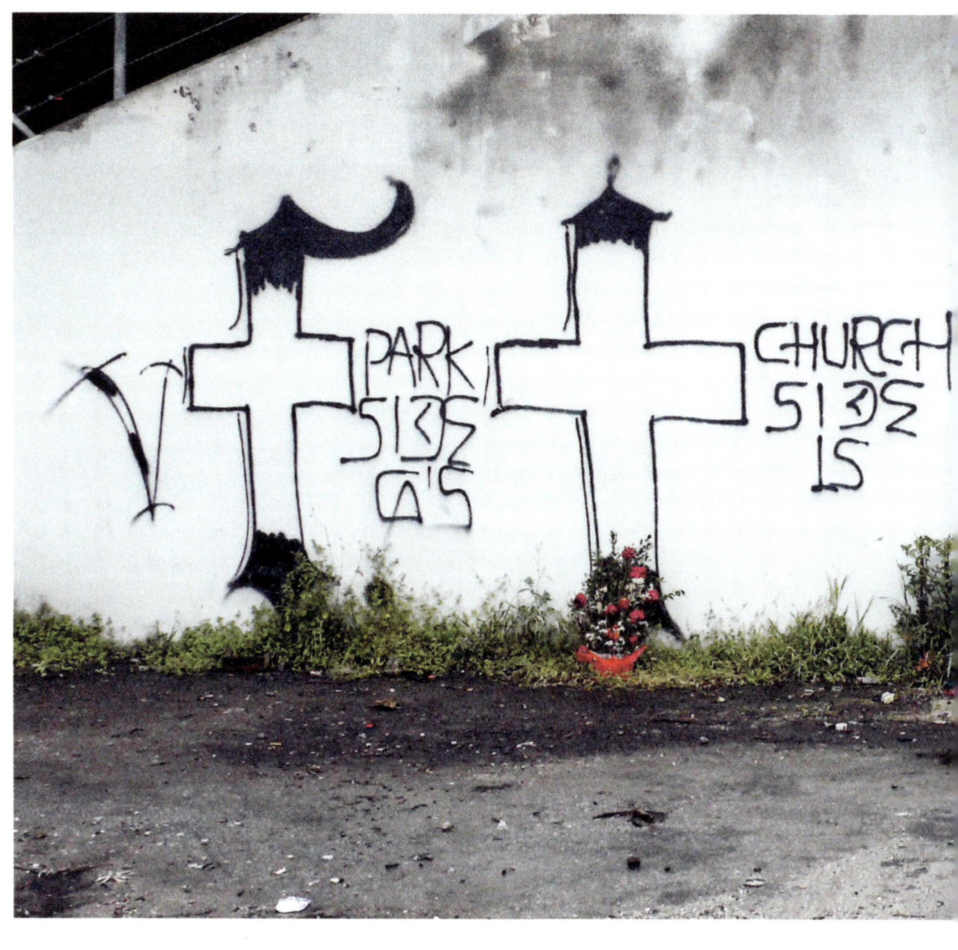#

v   f   t

(VARRIO)   (FROG)   (TOWN)

PARK   CHURCH
SIDE   SIDE
G'S   LS
(GANGSTERS)   (LOCOS)

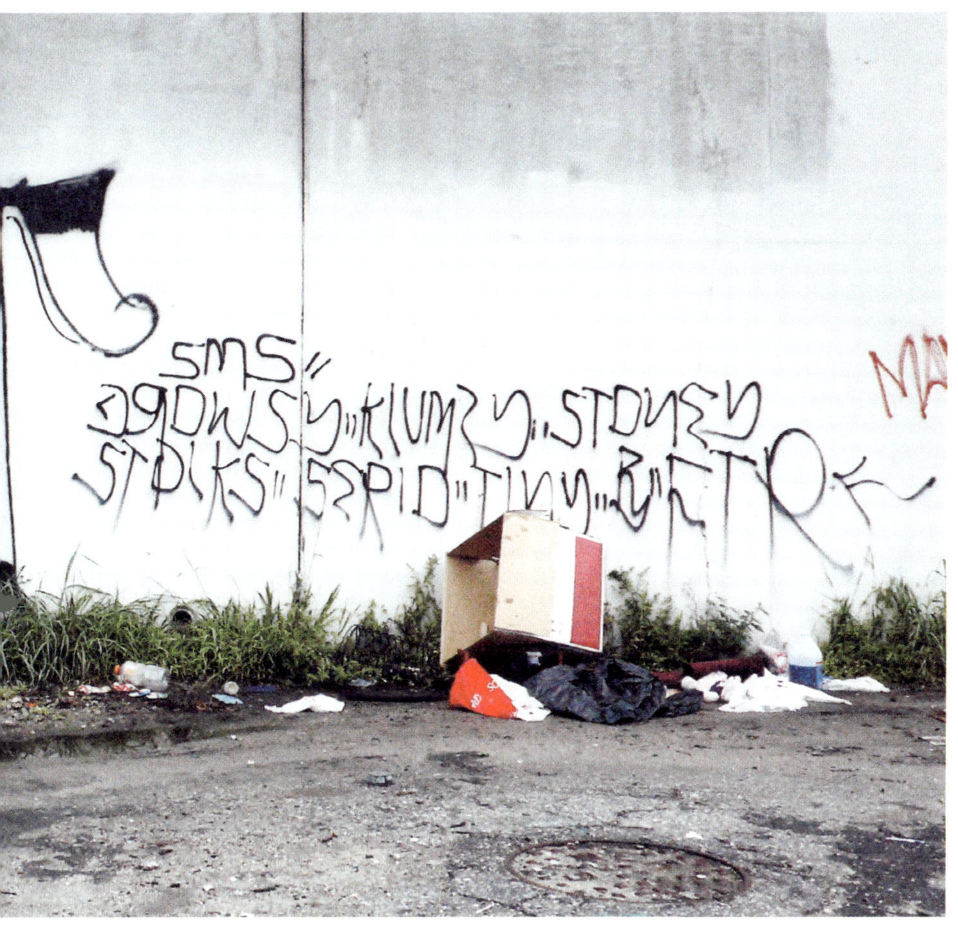

1
(RIFA)

SMS‖
DROWSY‖KLUMZY‖STONEY
STALKS‖SERIO‖TINY‖B‖FTR ←

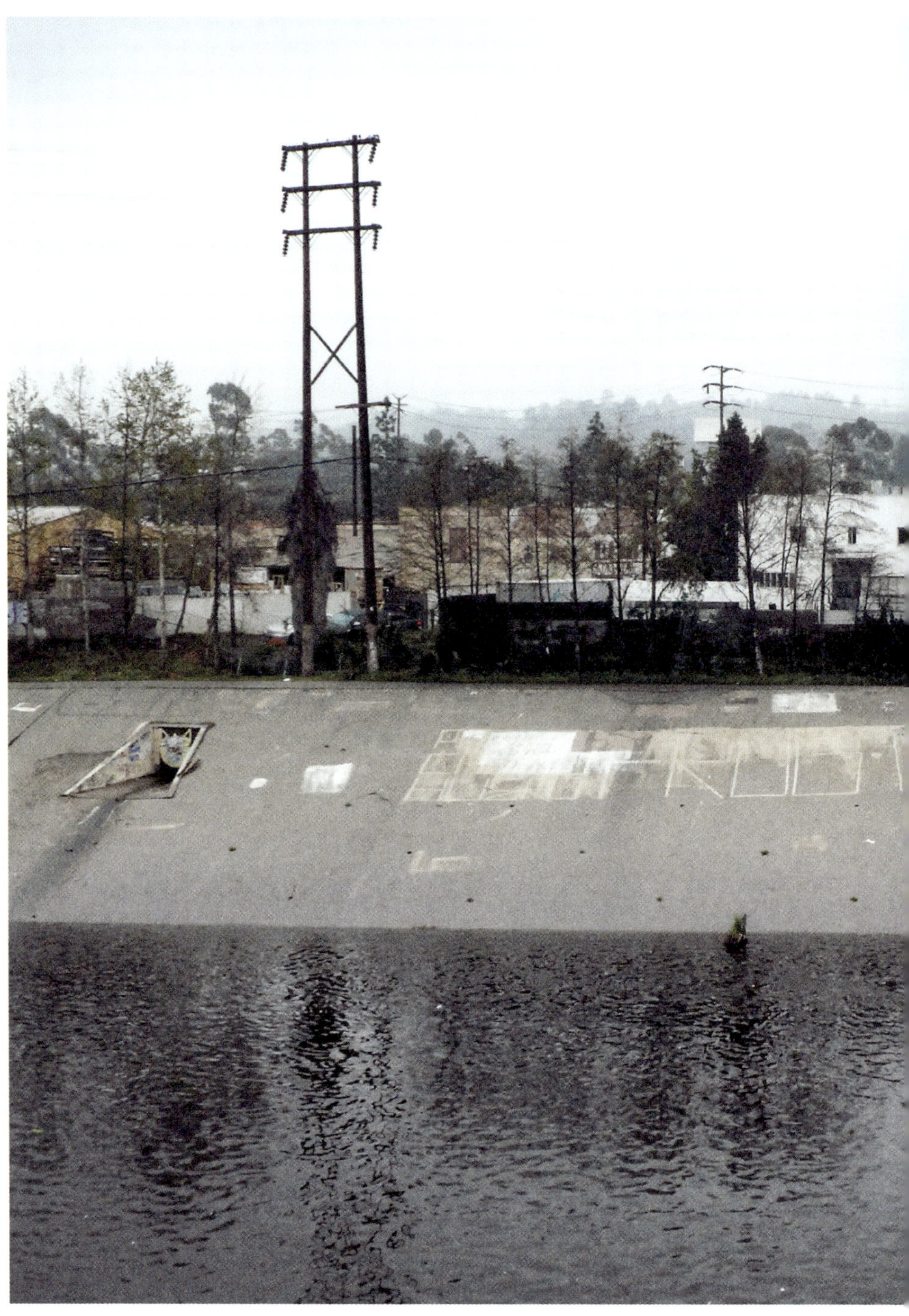

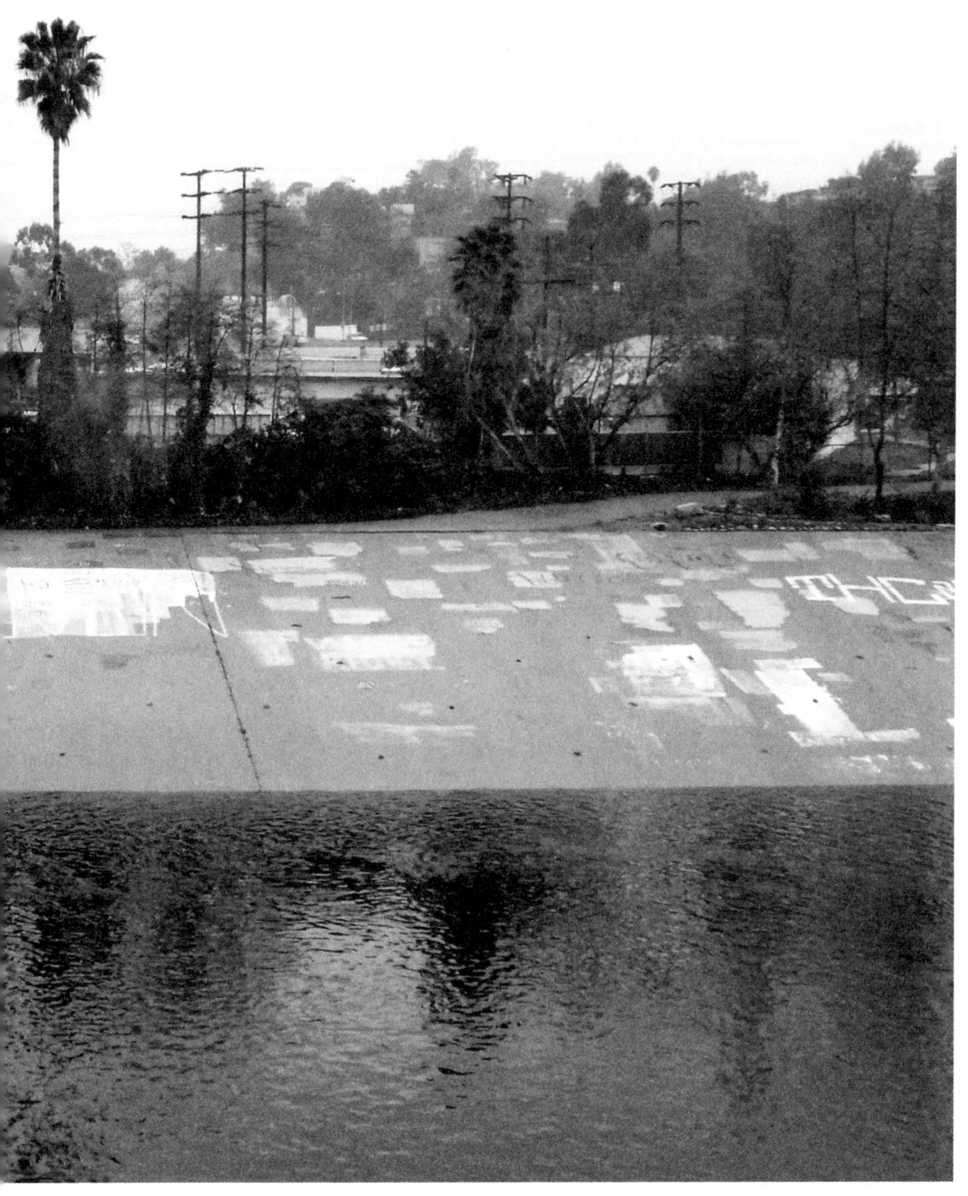

FROG·TOWN

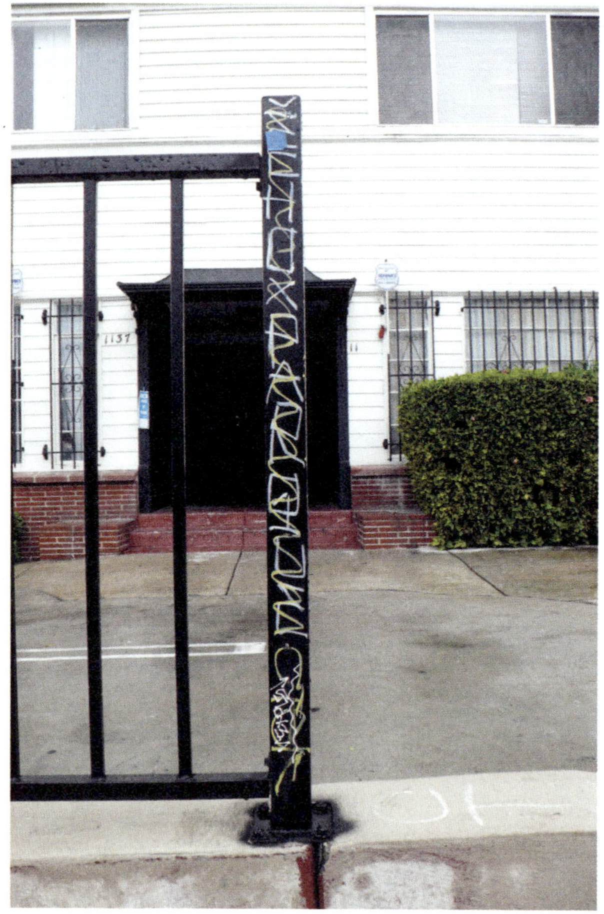

E
C
H
O
X
P
A
R
Q
U
E

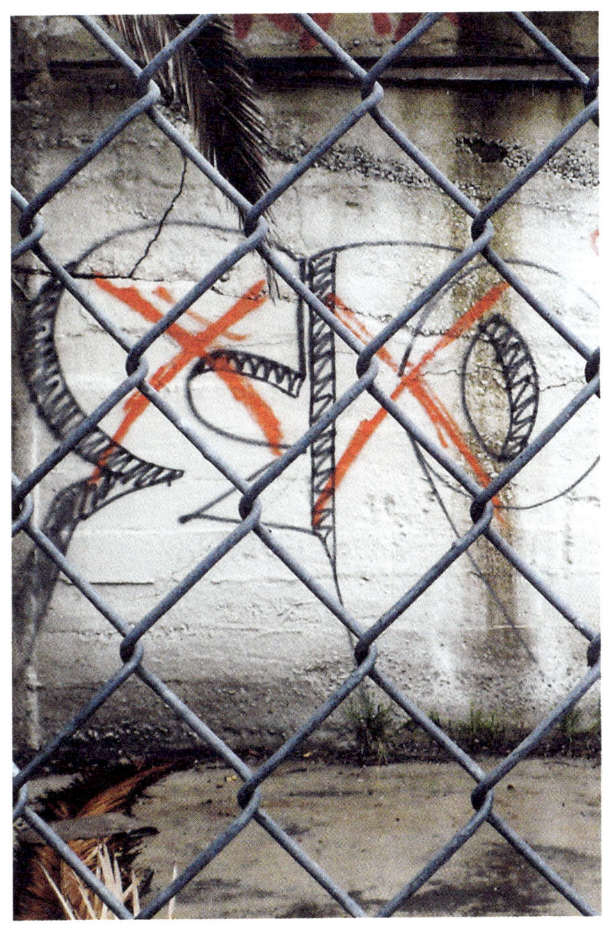

EP
(ECHO PARK GANG)

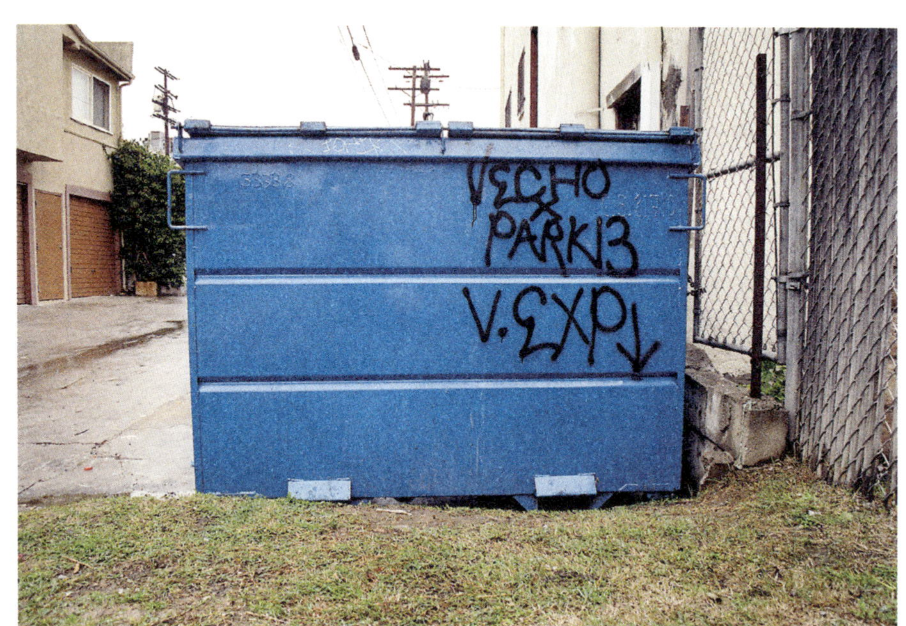

V (VARRIO) ECHO
×
PARK 13
V·EXP↓

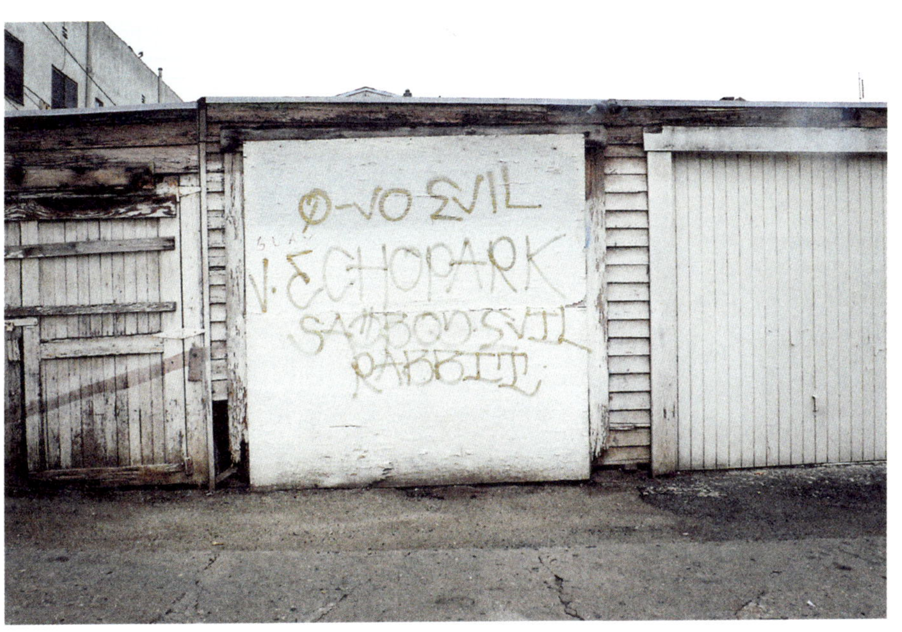

Q-VO EVIL
V · ECHOPARK
SADBOY · EVIL
RABBIT ·

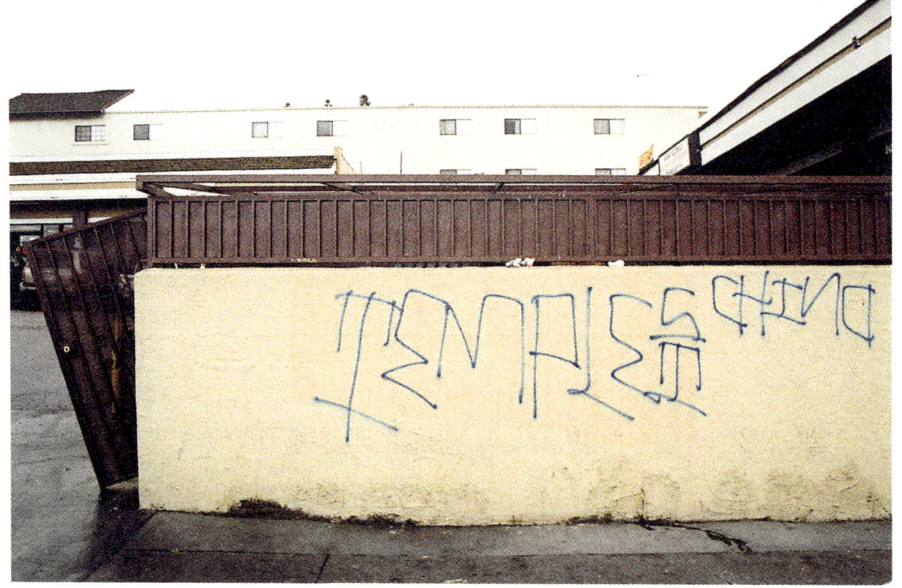

TEMPLE ST
(TEMPLE
STREET
GANG)

CHINO

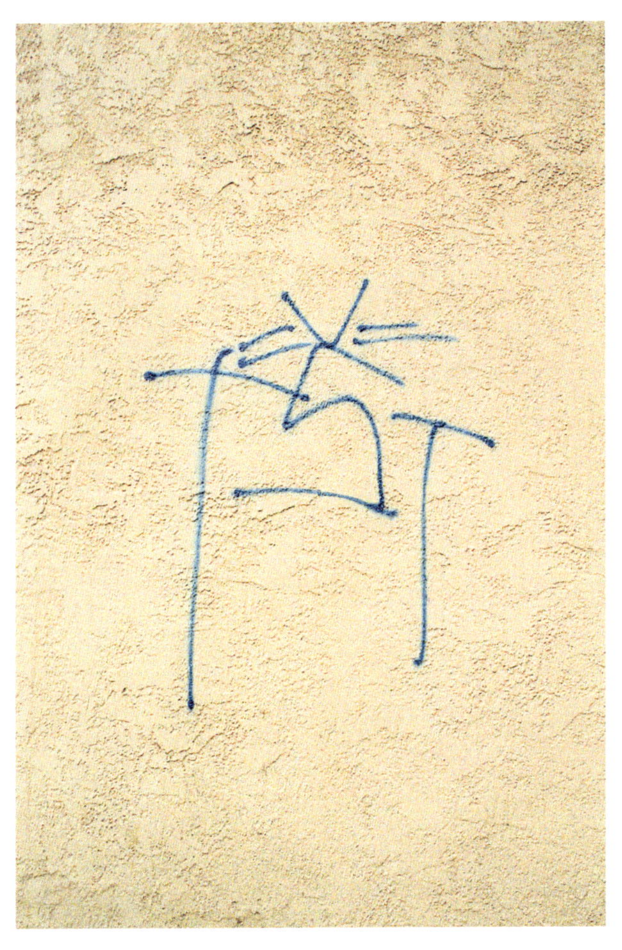

=V=
TST
(VARRIO
TEMPLE
STREET)

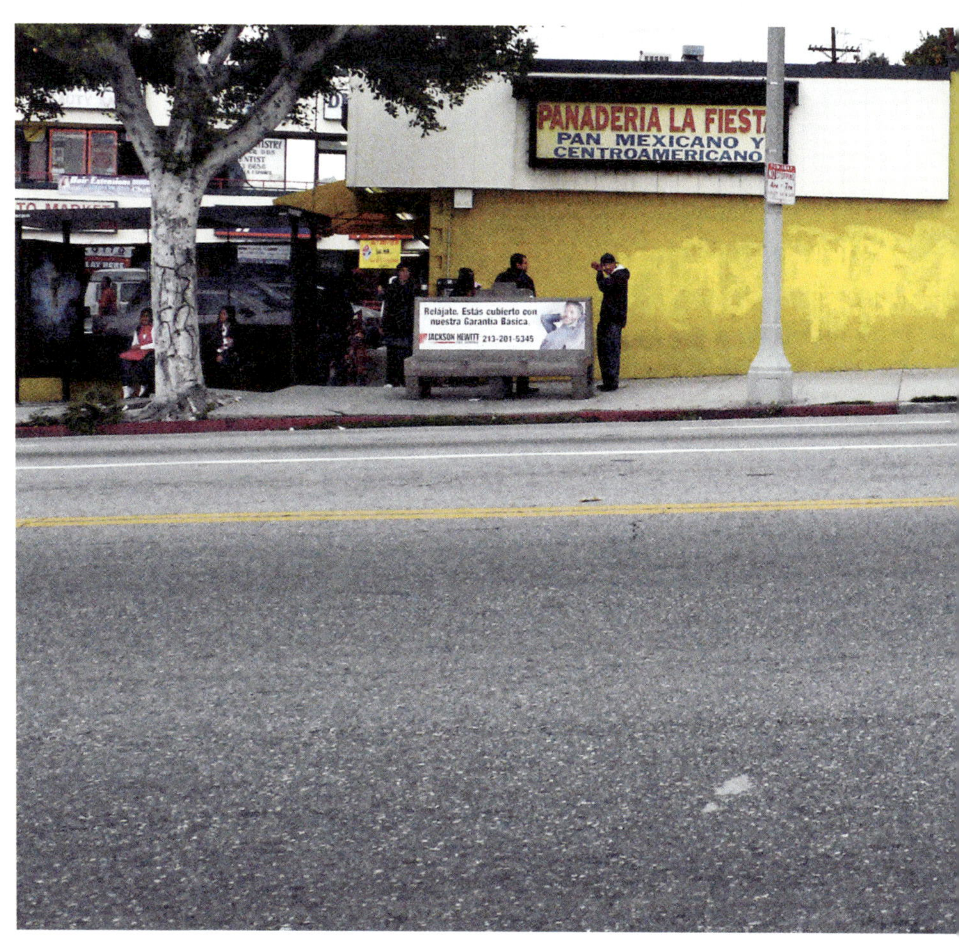
PANADERIA LA FIESTA
PAN MEXICANO Y
CENTROAMERICANO
Relájate. Estás cubierto con
nuestra Garantia Básica.
JACKSON HEWITT 213-201-5345

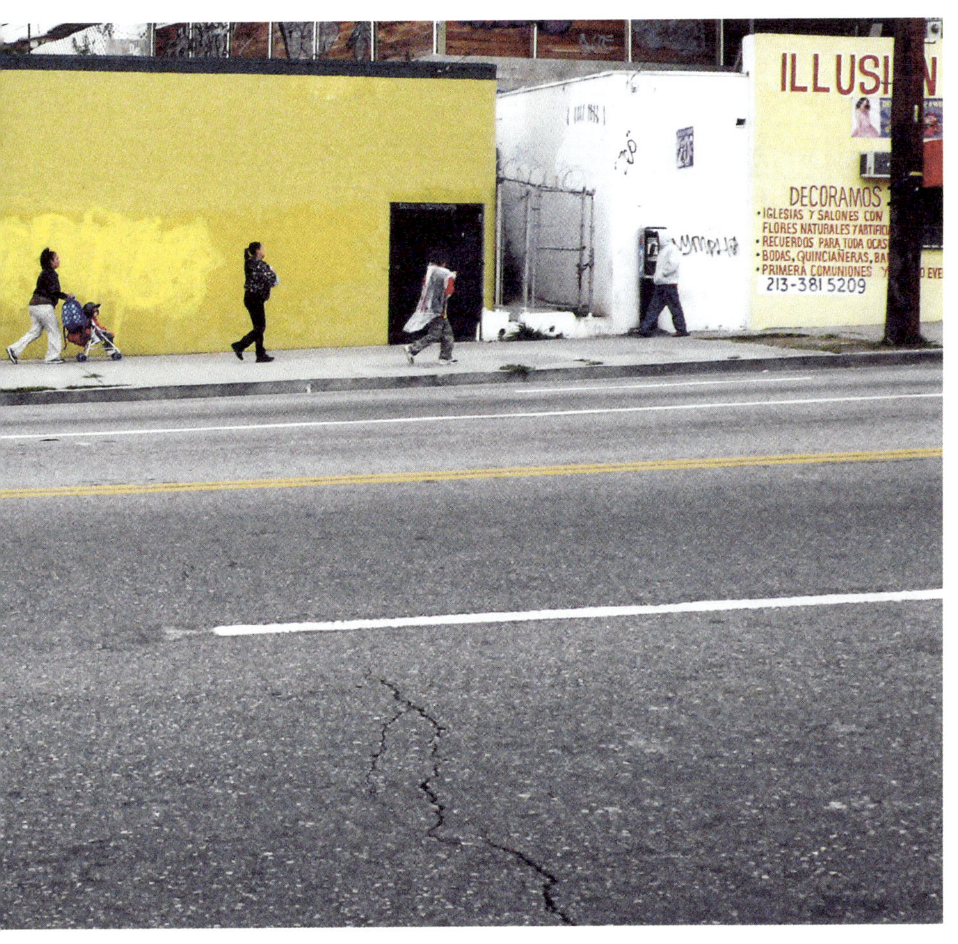

TEMPLE ST 13
(TEMPLE STREET GANG THIRTEEN)

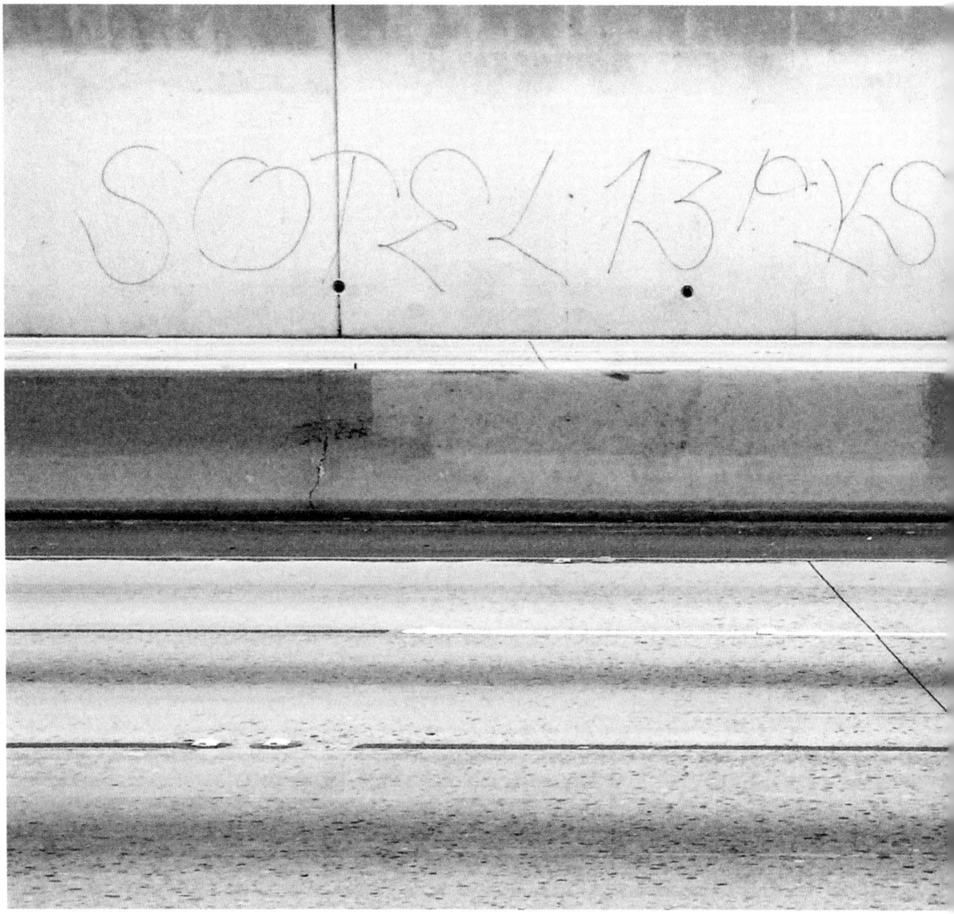

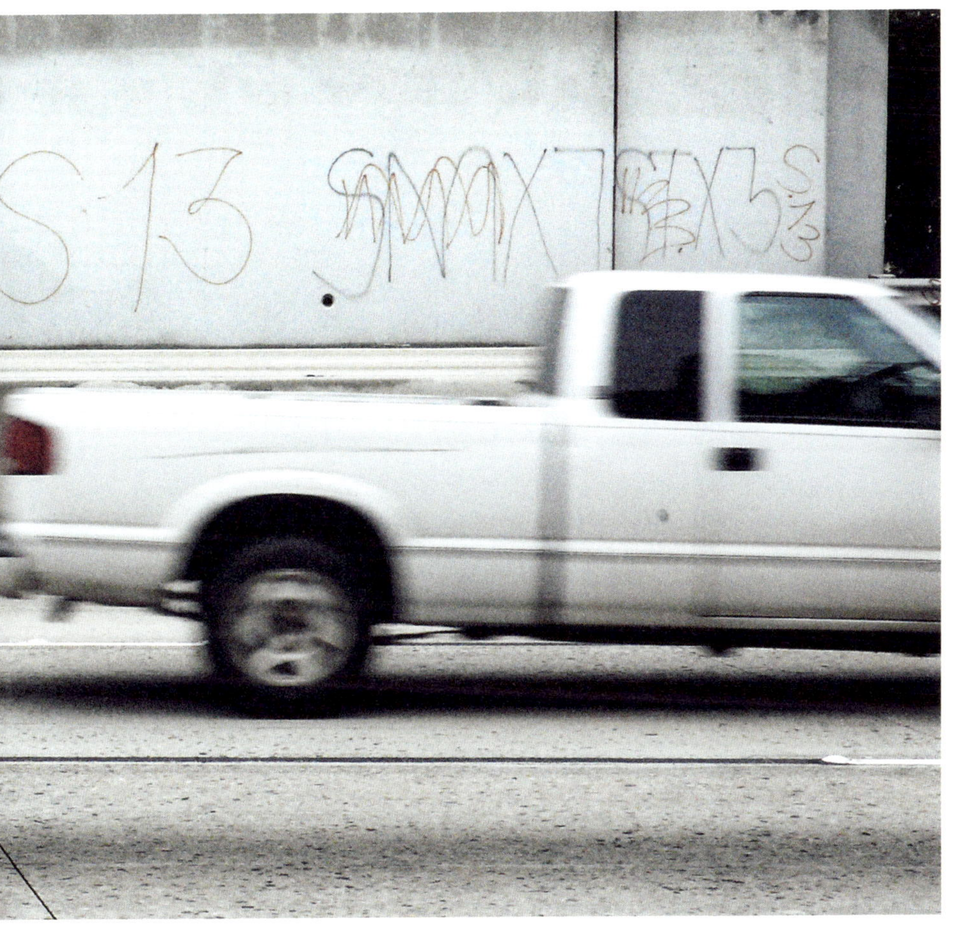

SOTEL·13 PYS V·S13 SMX7ST. X3 S·13
(SOTEL/SAWTELLE·TRECE, CLIQUE'S INITIALS) (VARRIO SOTEL·13)
(SANTA MONICA 17TH STREET TRECE)
(SOTEL·13)

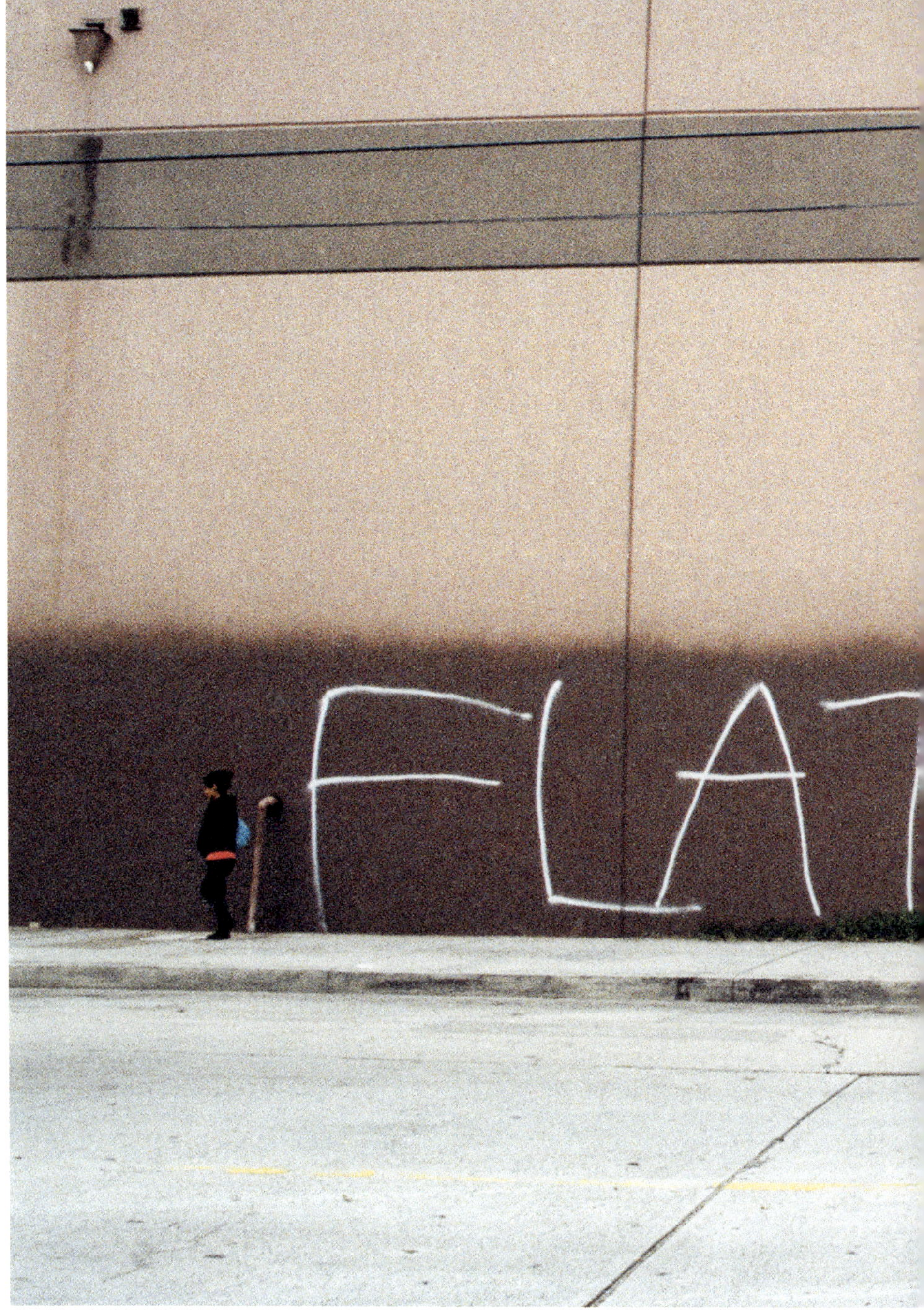

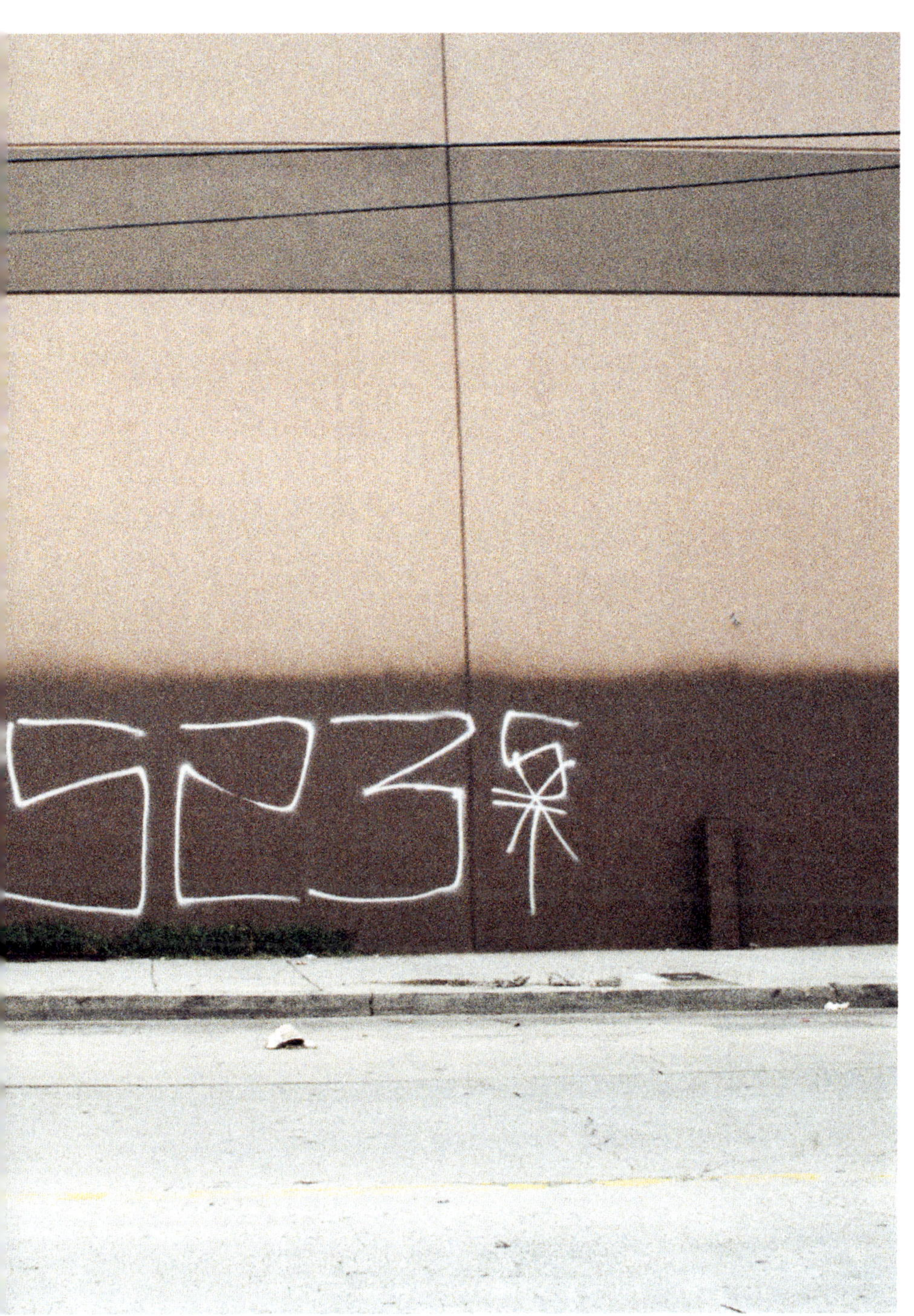

FLATS 23 ST
(PRIMERA FLATS
23 TH STREET GANG)

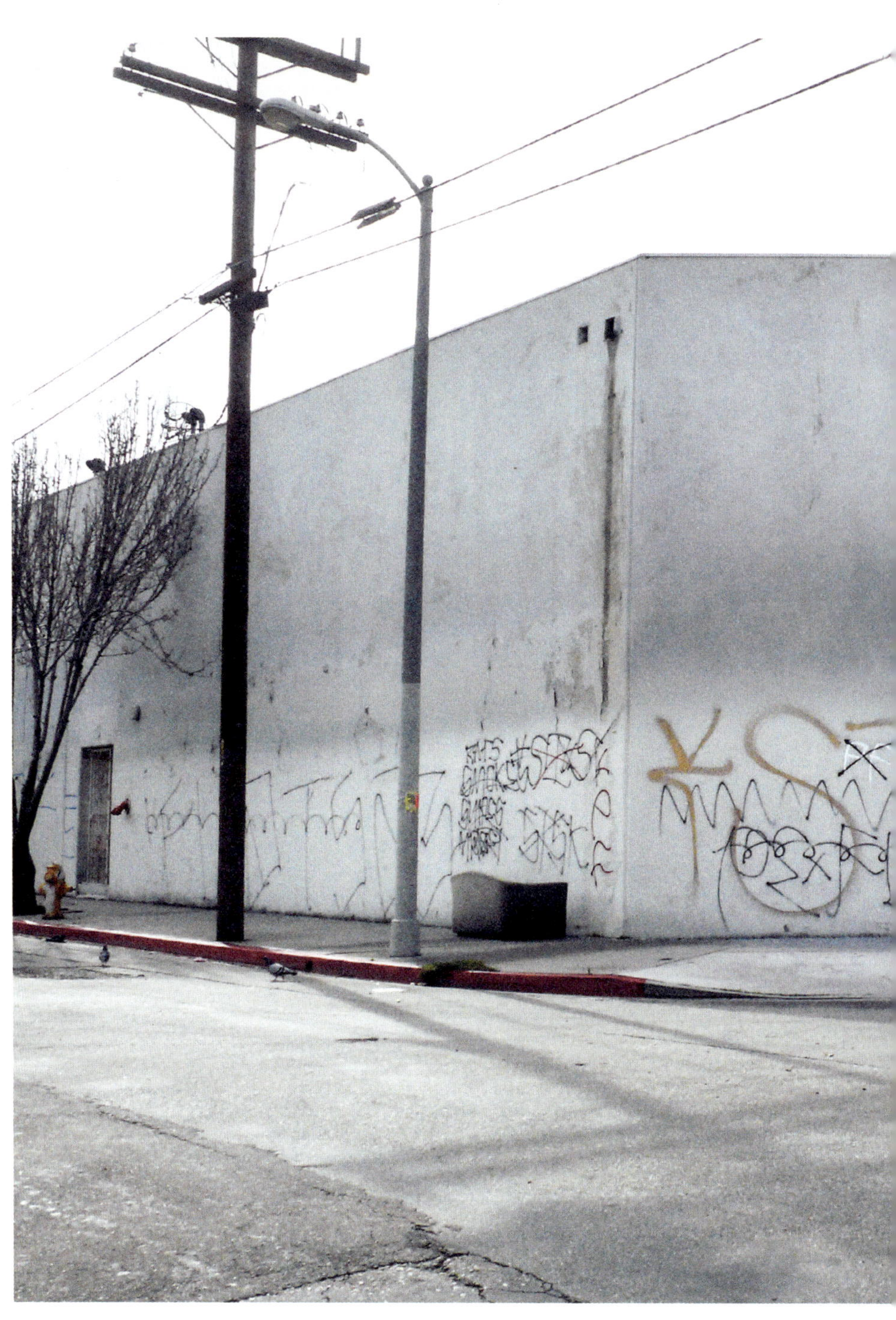

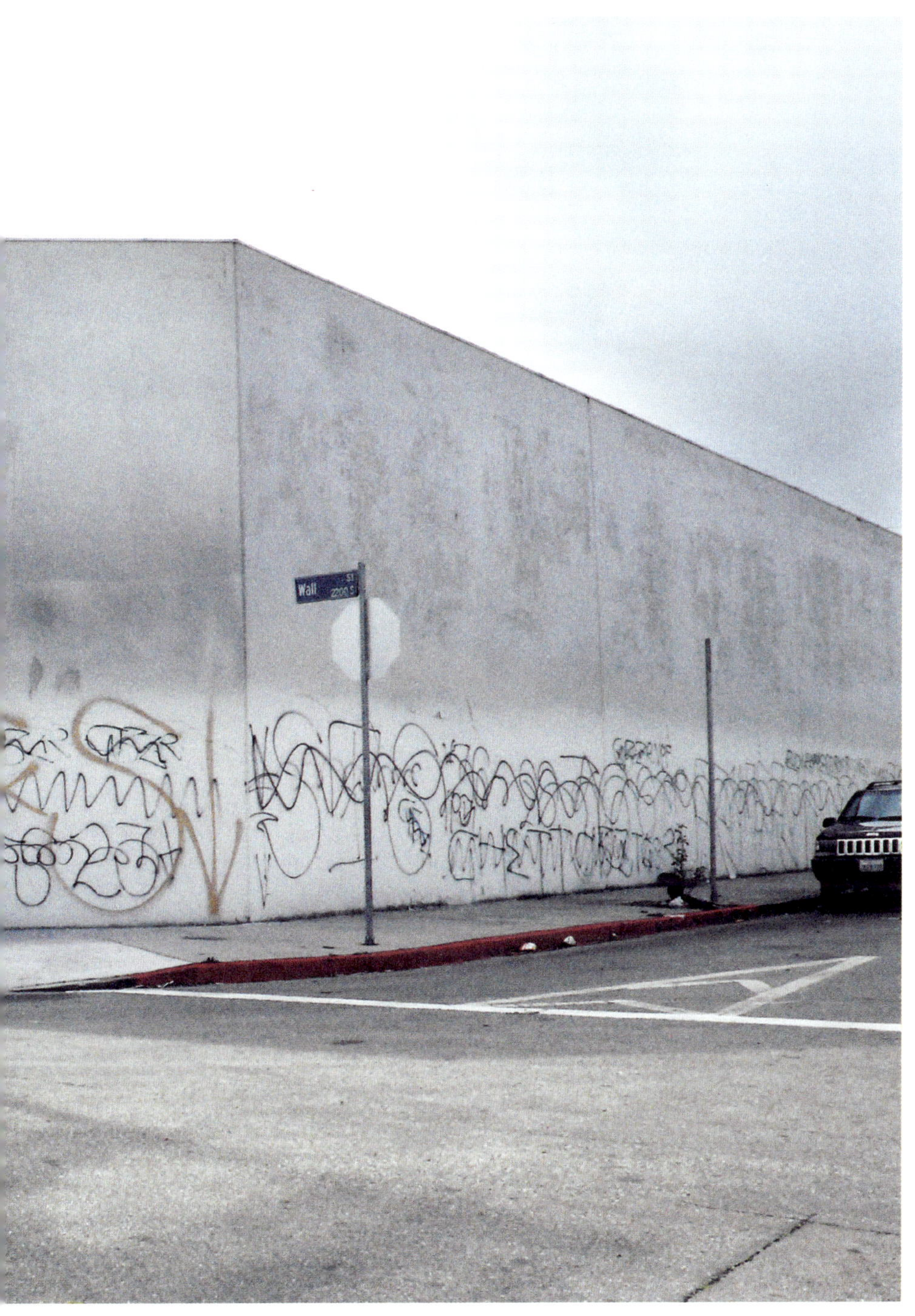

V ST × S↓
(VARRIO STREET SAINTS)
×××××××××××××××××××××××××
PE × FLATS 23↓
(PRIMERA FLATS 23 TH ST.)

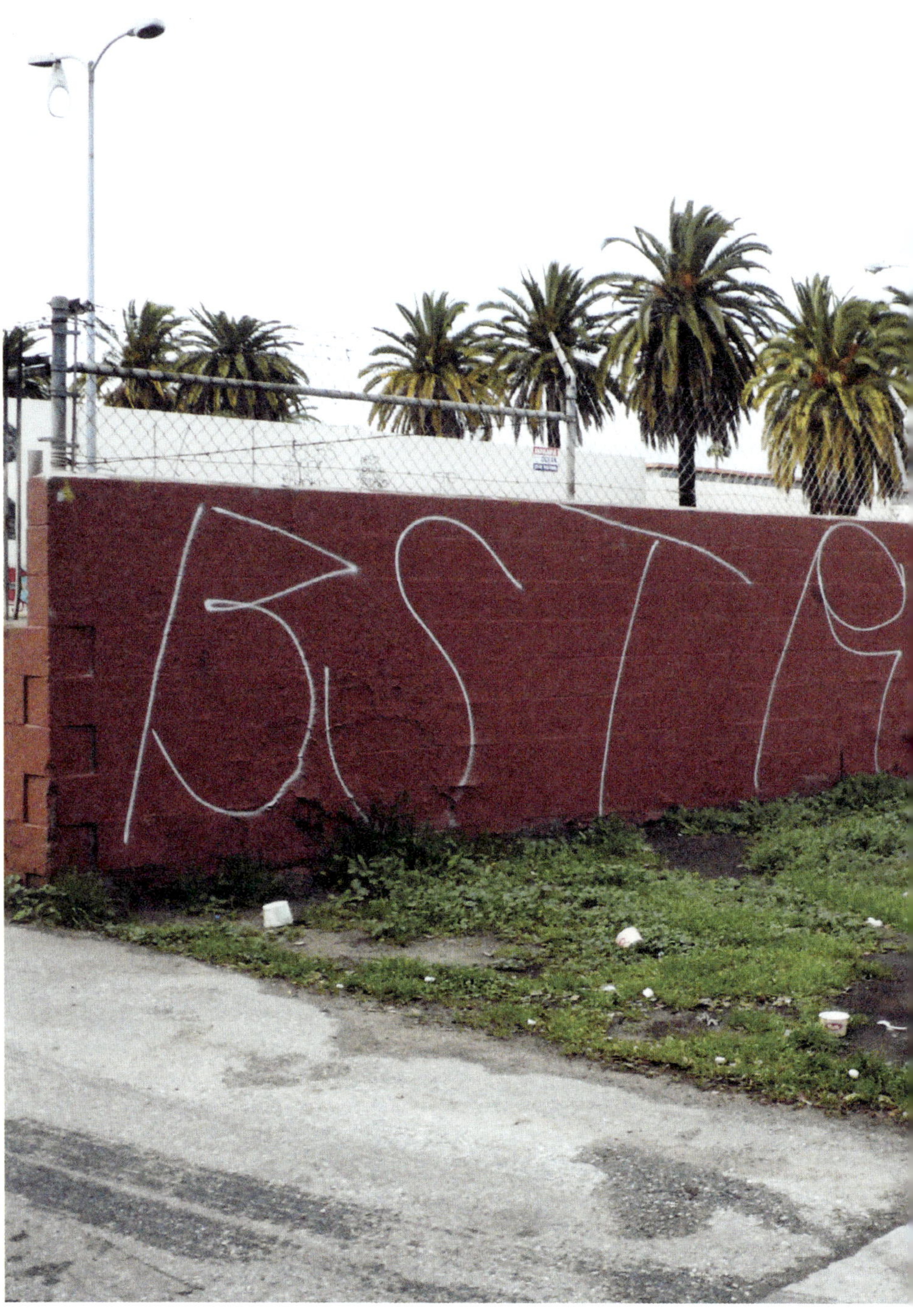

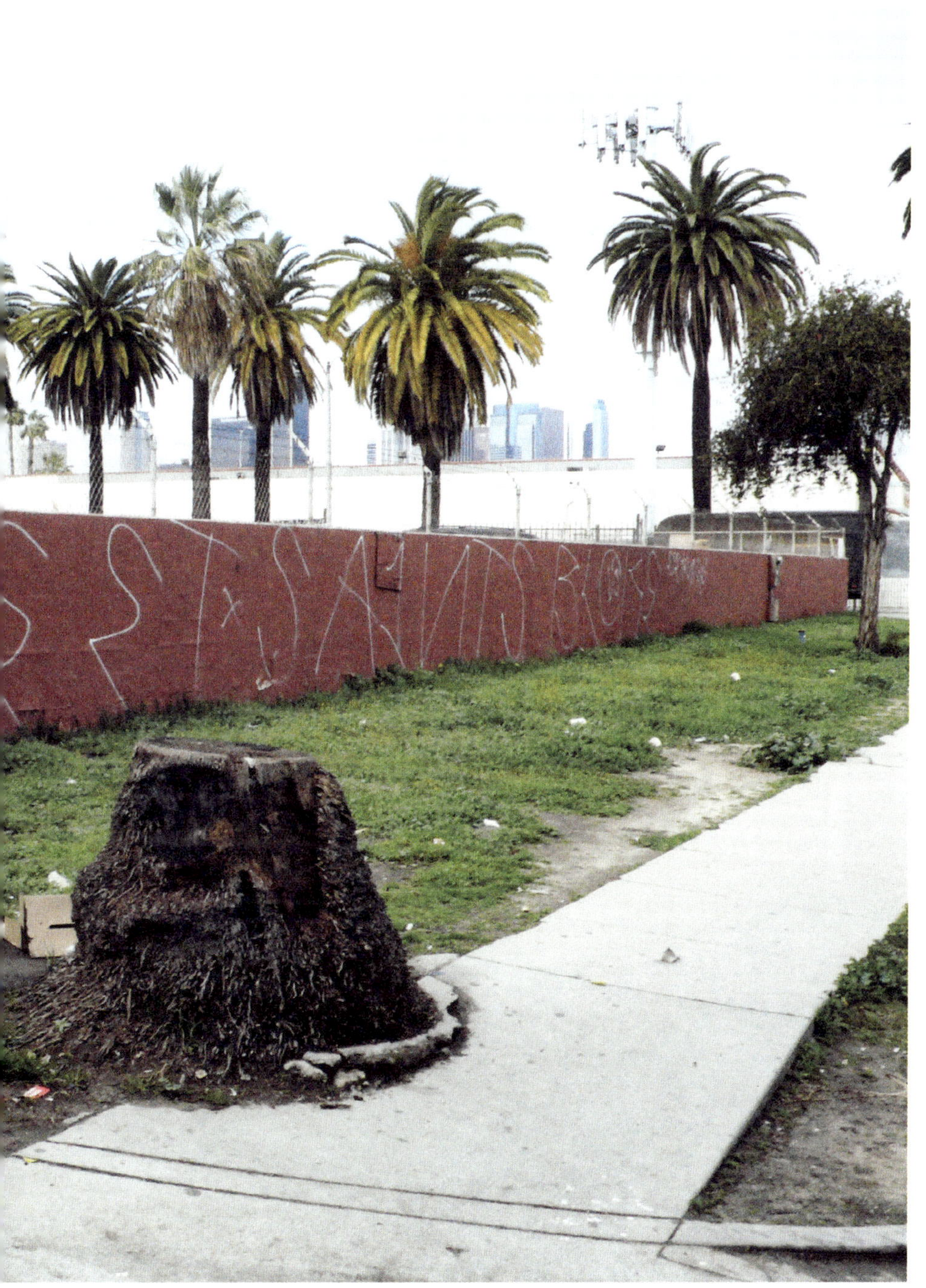

B (BARRIO) STREET×SAINTS BLOKE

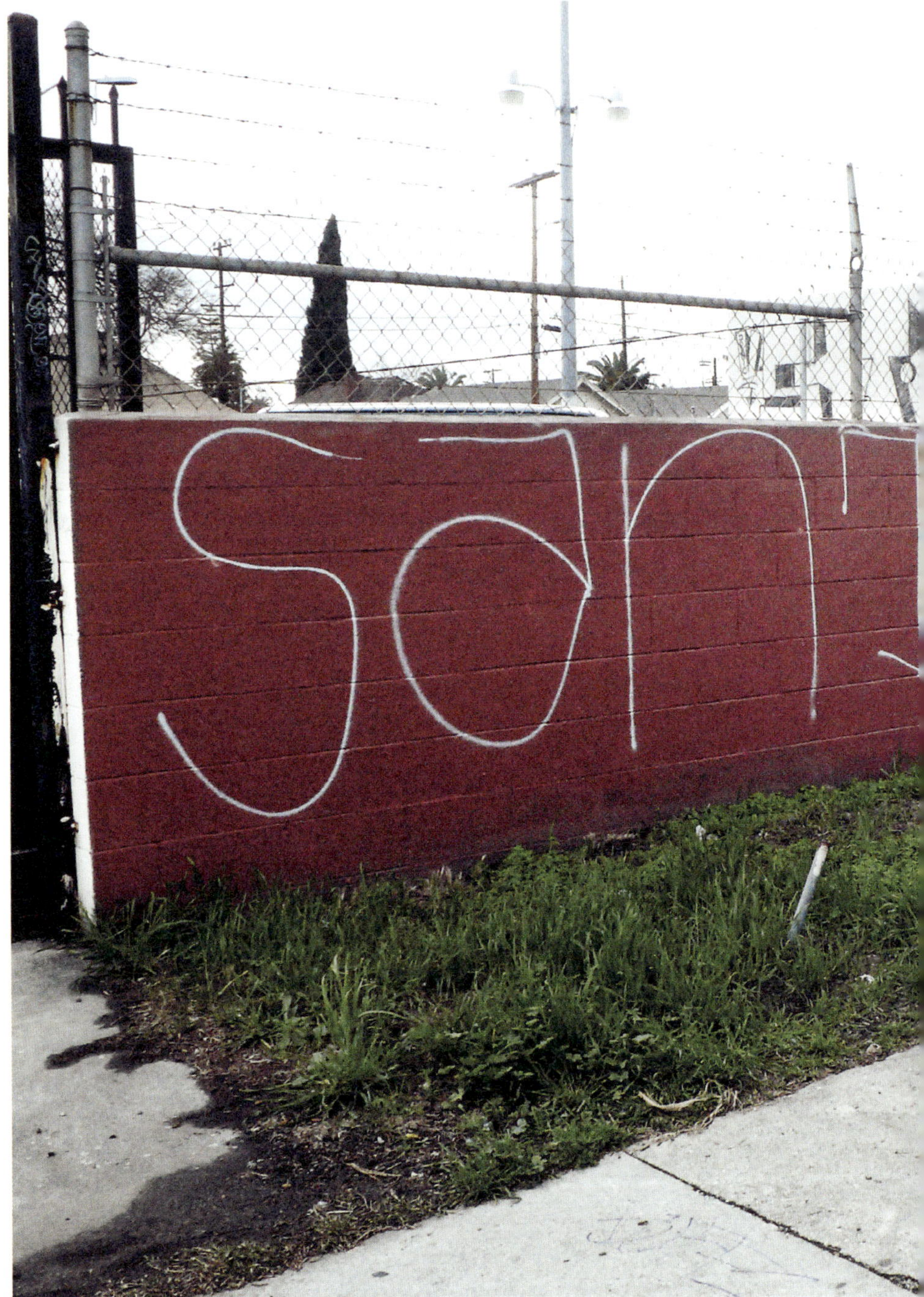

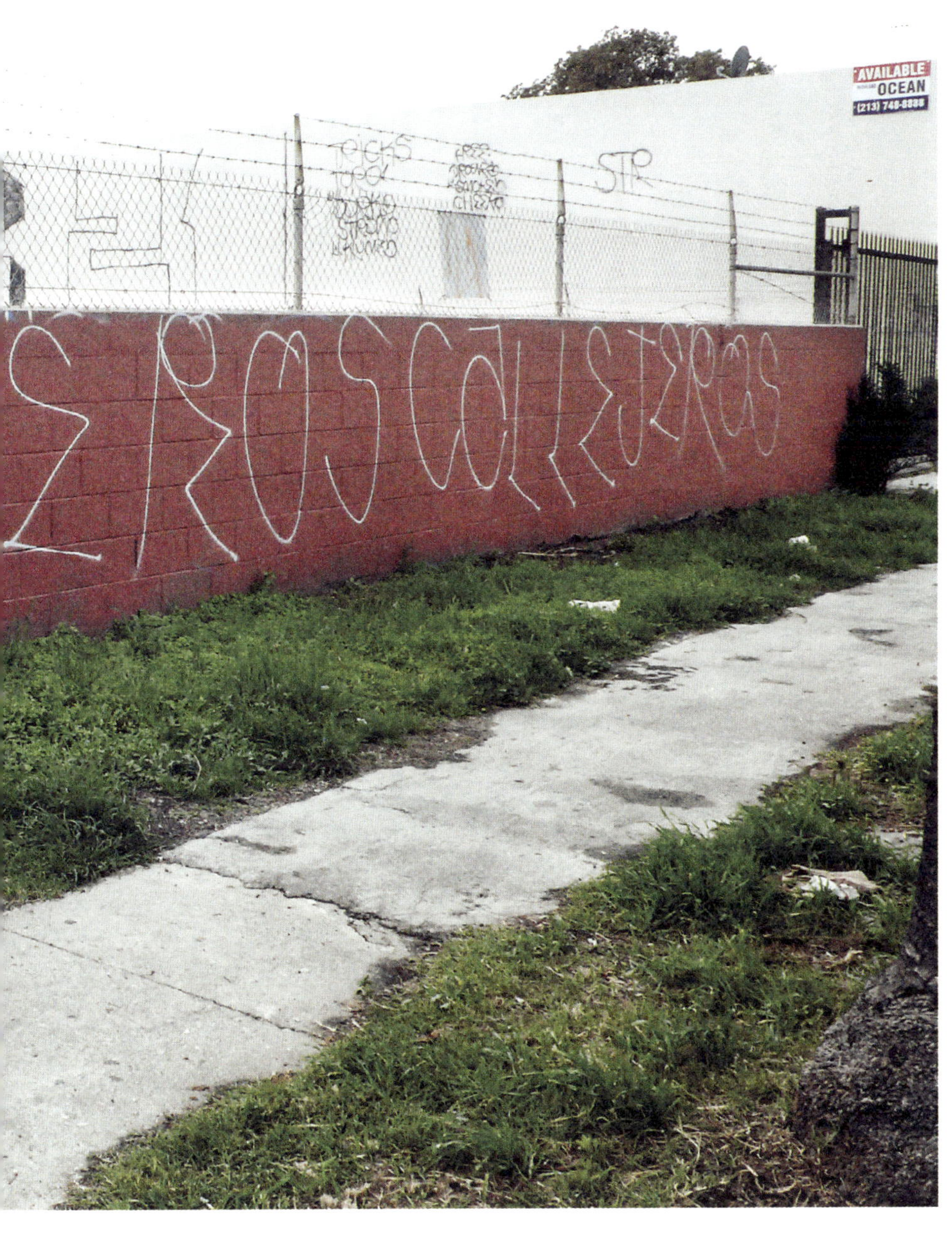

V ST·S 21
(VARRIO
STREET SAINTS
21TH STREET)

SANTEROS
CALLEJEROS

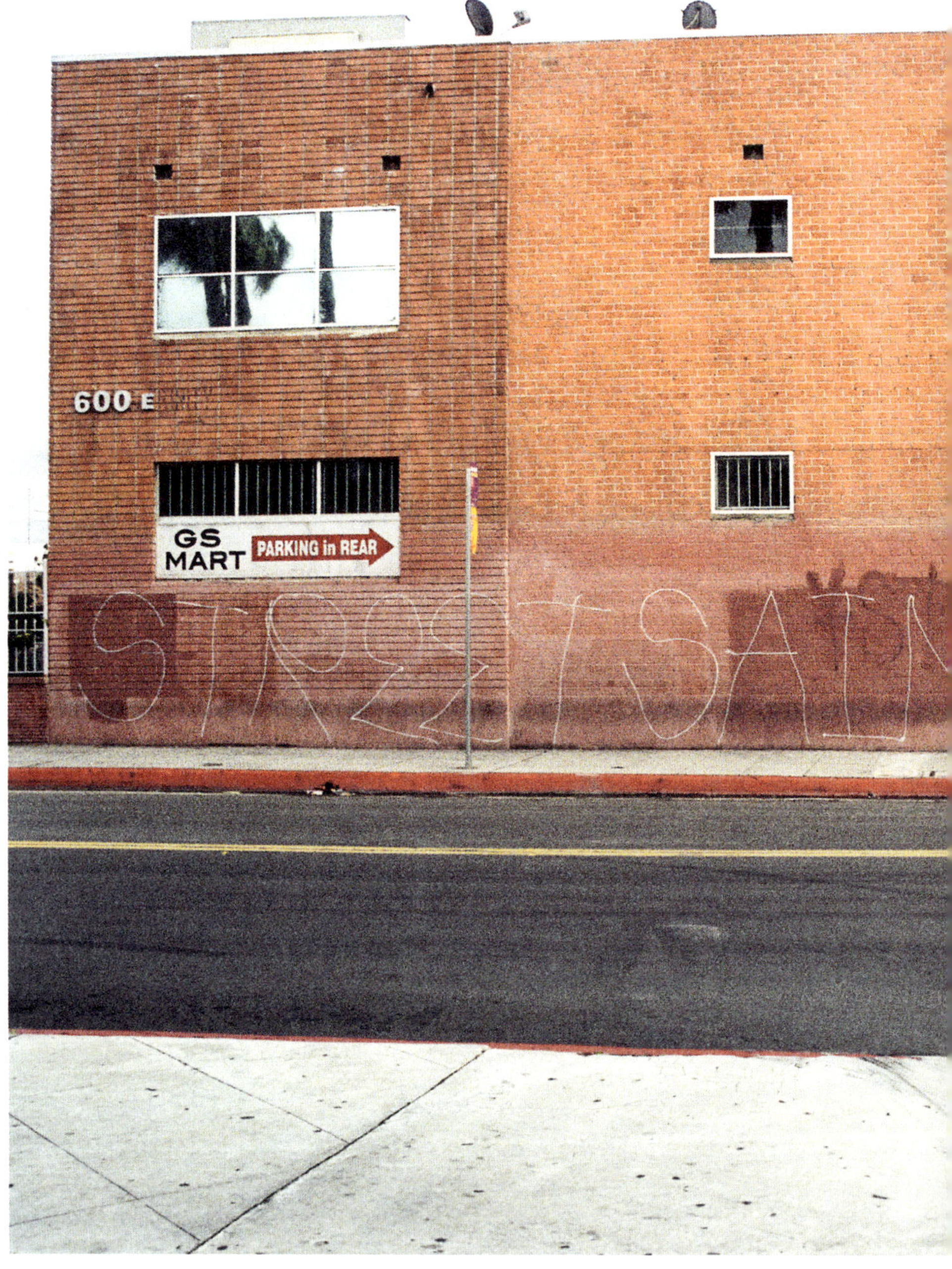

600 E
GS
MART
PARKING in REAR

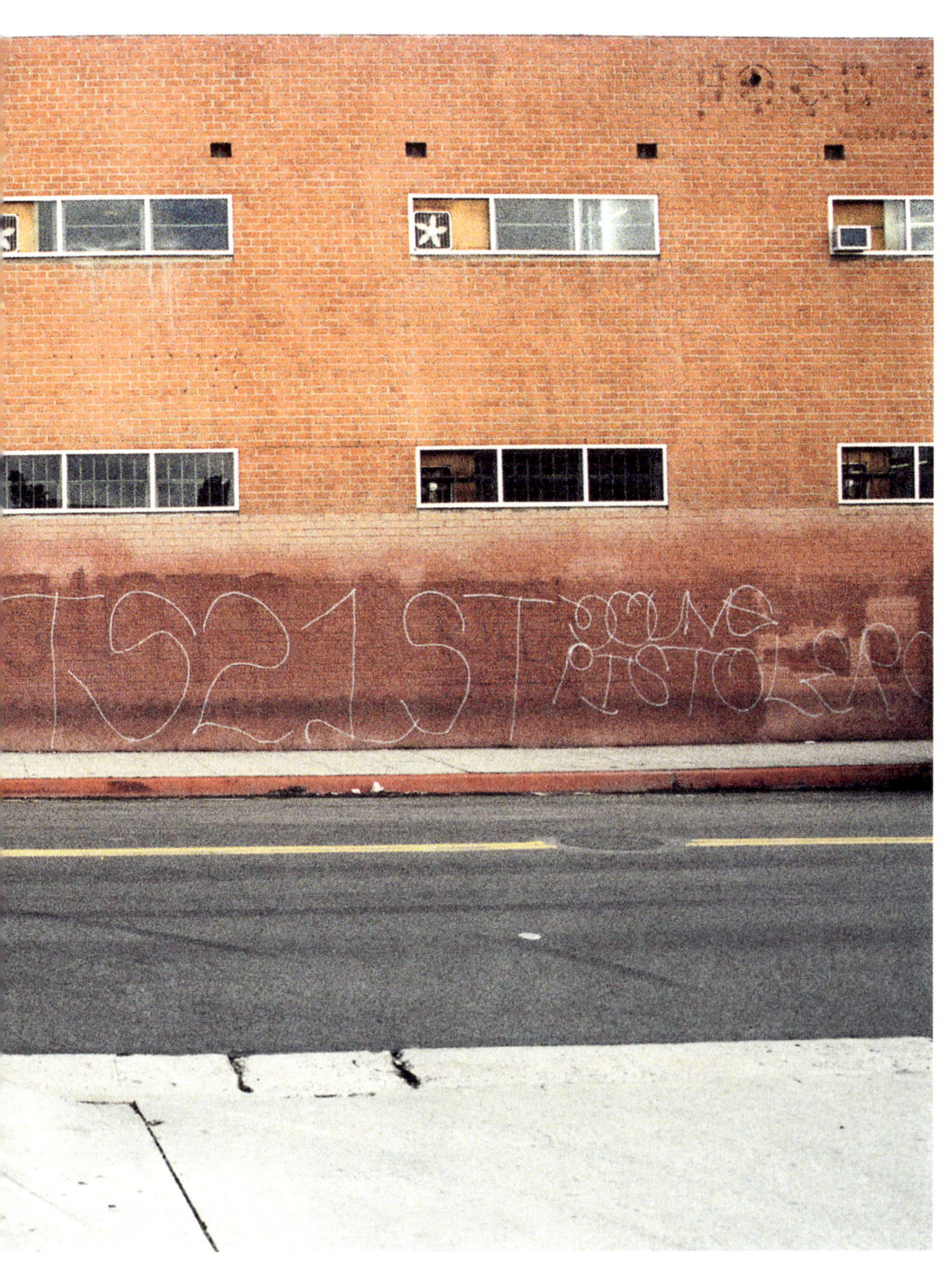

STREET SAINTS 21ST YOUNG PISTOLER[OS]

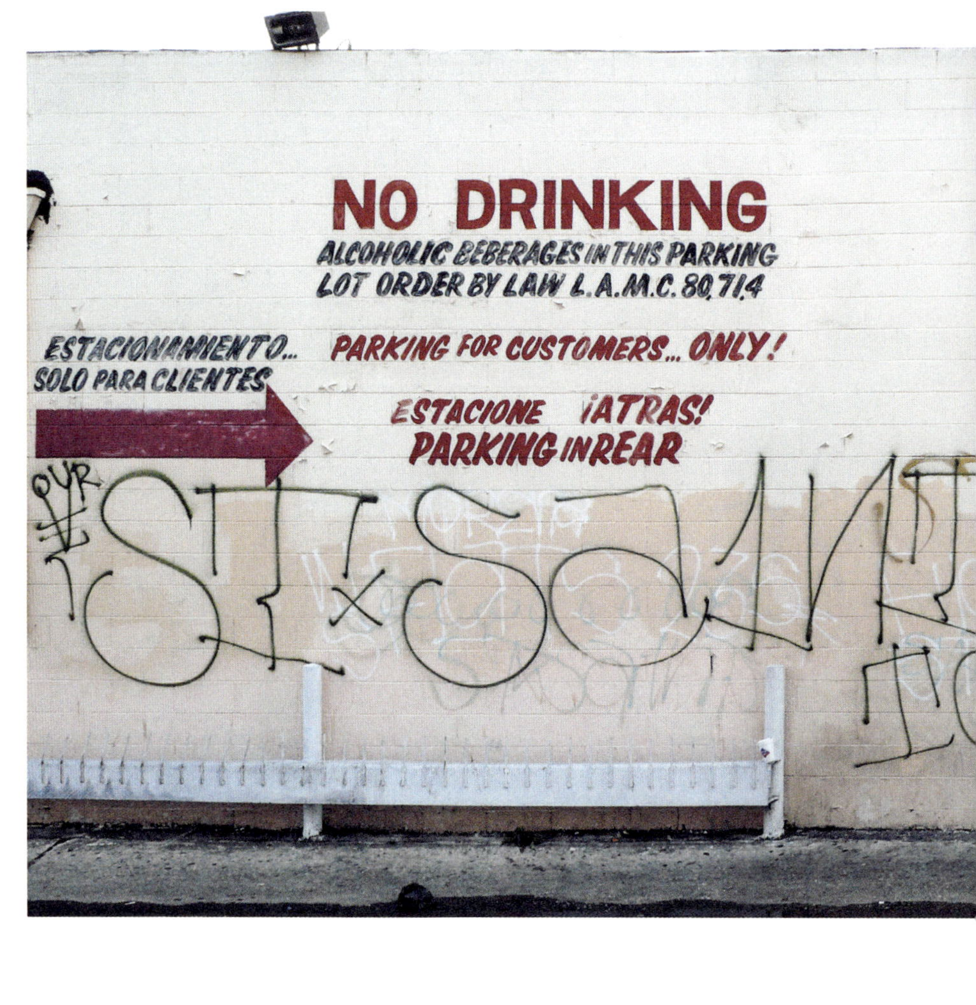
NO DRINKING
ALCOHOLIC BEBERAGES IN THIS PARKING
LOT ORDER BY LAW L.A.M.C. 80.71.4
ESTACIONAMIENTO...
SOLO PARA CLIENTES
PARKING FOR CUSTOMERS... ONLY!
ESTACIONE ¡ATRAS!
PARKING IN REAR

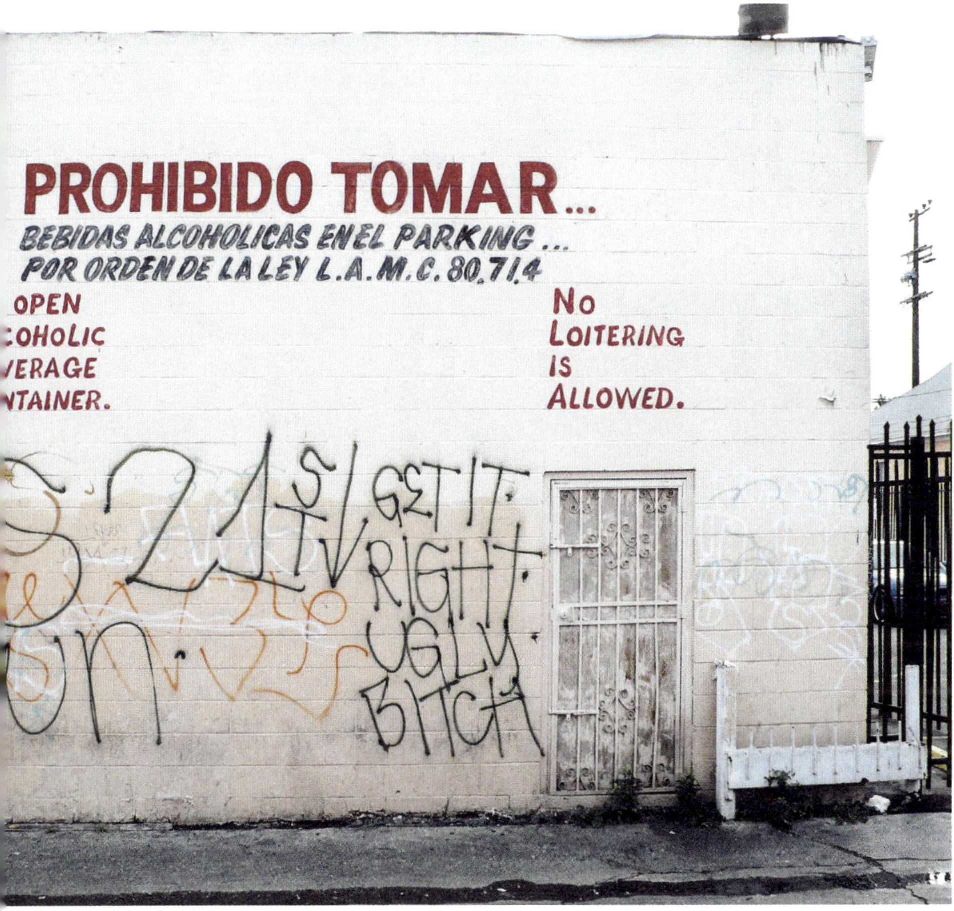

OUR V (VARRIO) STREET × SAINTS 21 ST ↓ TOWN
GET IT RIGHT UGLY BITCH (DARK GREEN)
MORENA WS (WEST SIDE) FLATS 23 ST / MORENA P(URO) F(LATS) 23 ST (WHITE)
WS (WEST SIDE) XV3 (18TH STREET GANG) LPS (ORANGE)

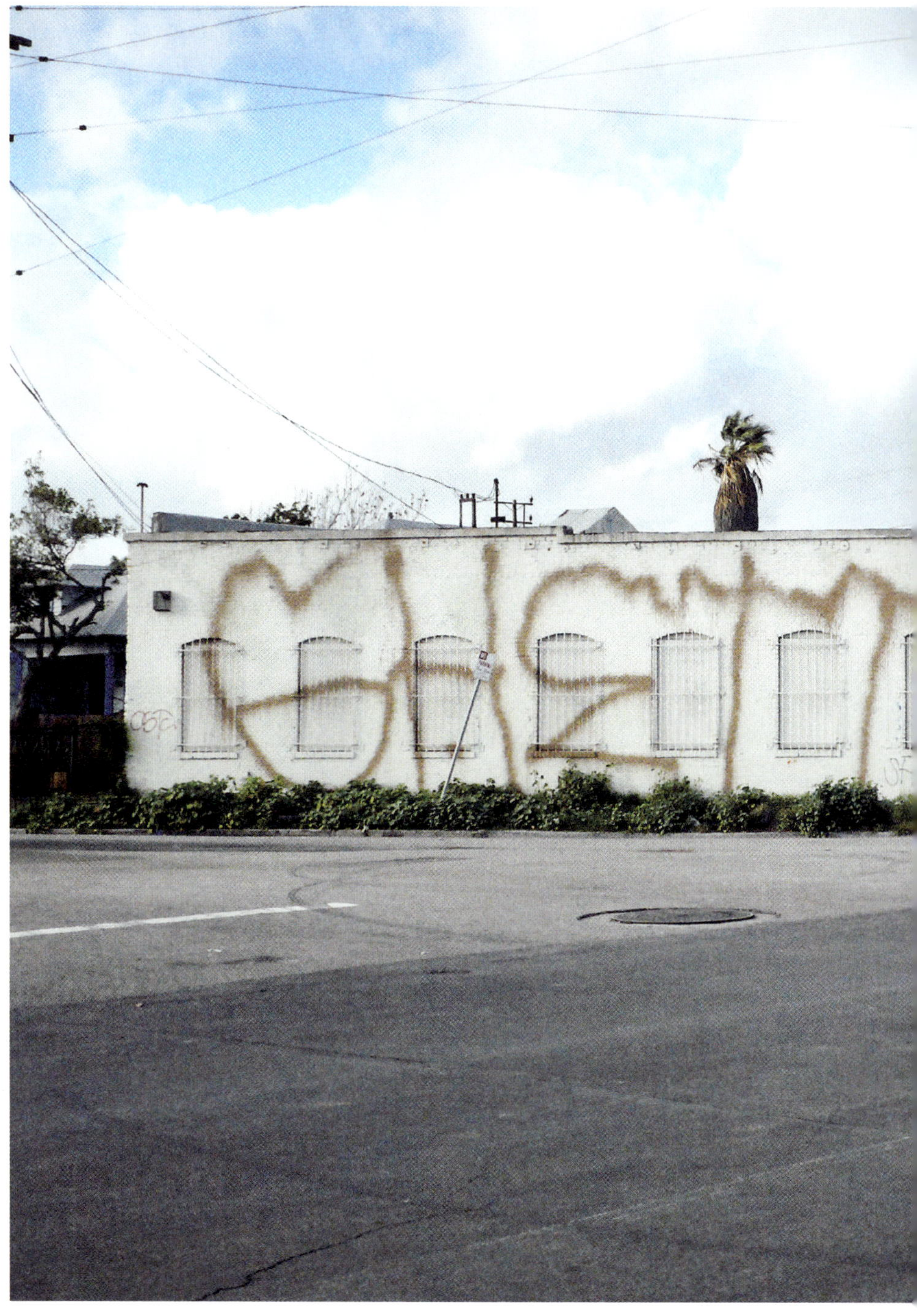

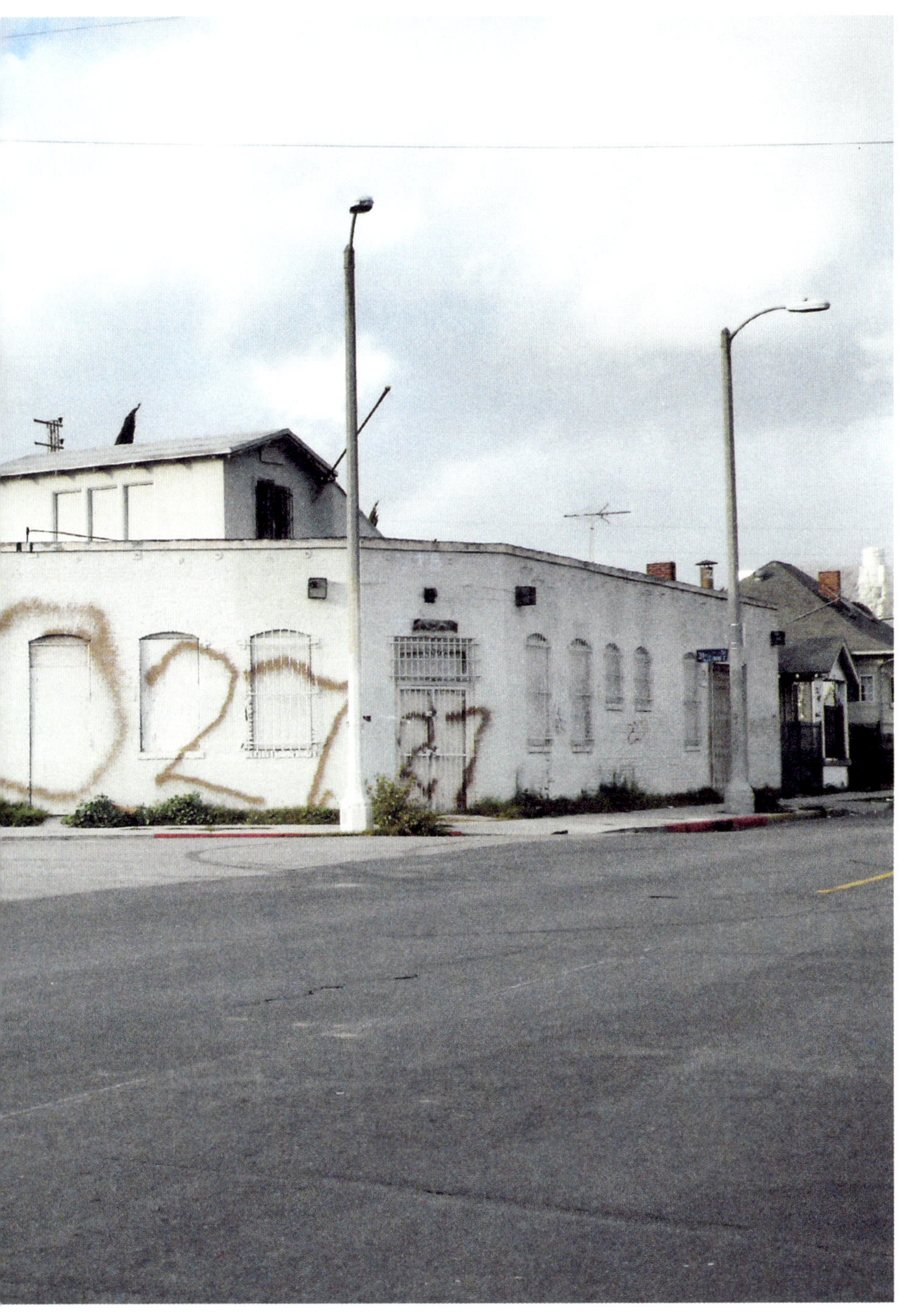

GHETTO 27
(GHETTO BOYS
27TH STREET GANG)

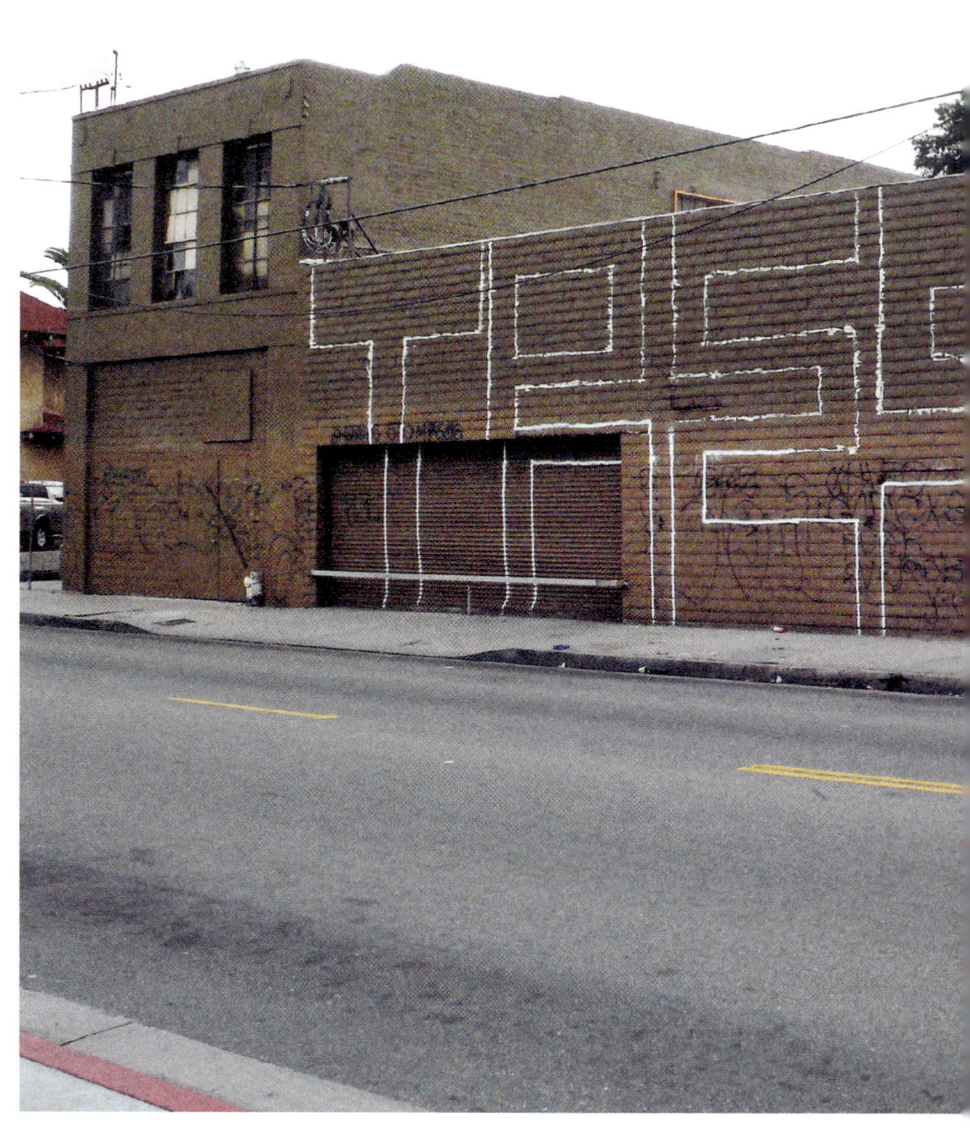

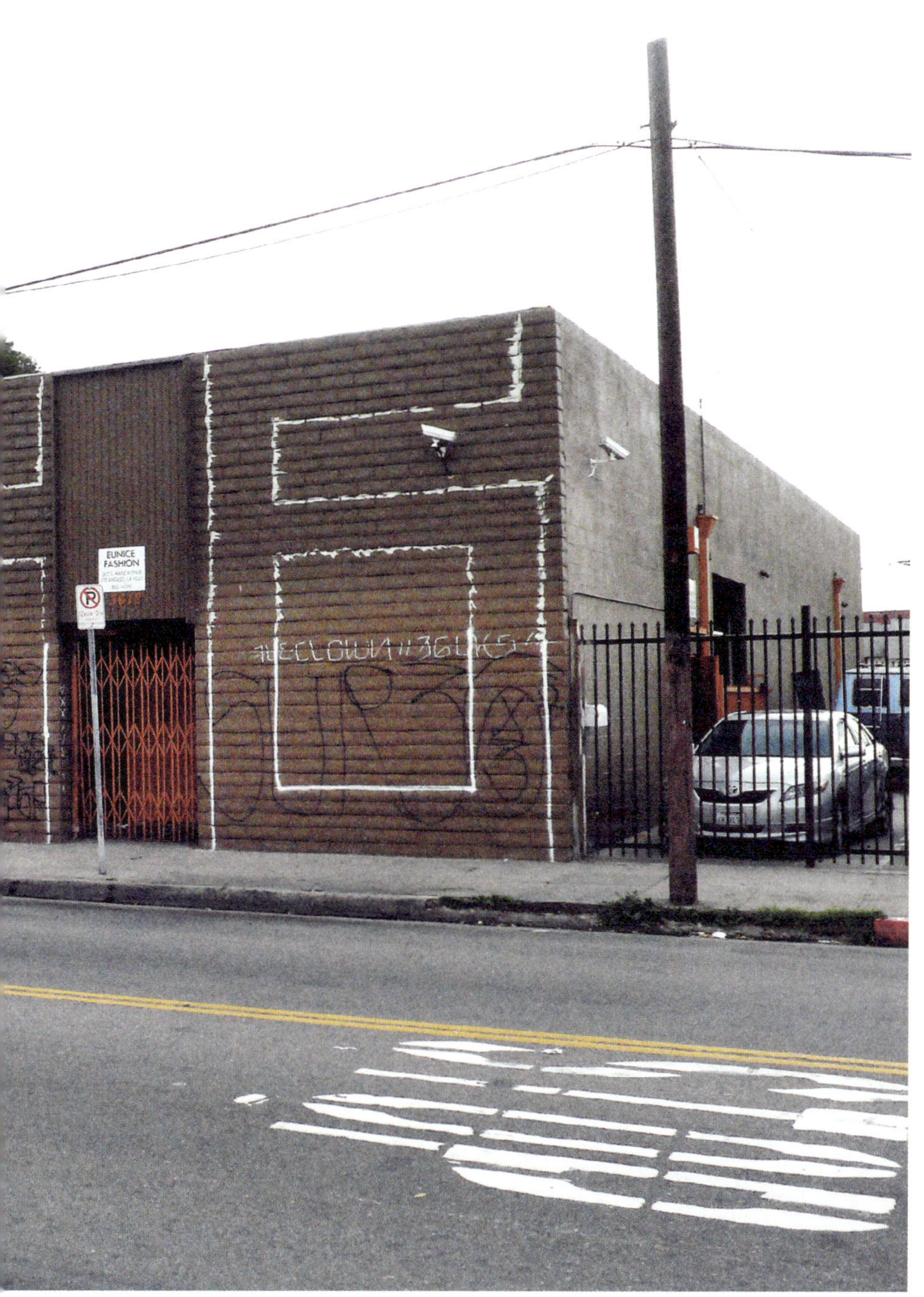

TRES 6
(SUR/SOUTH 36TH STREET GANG)

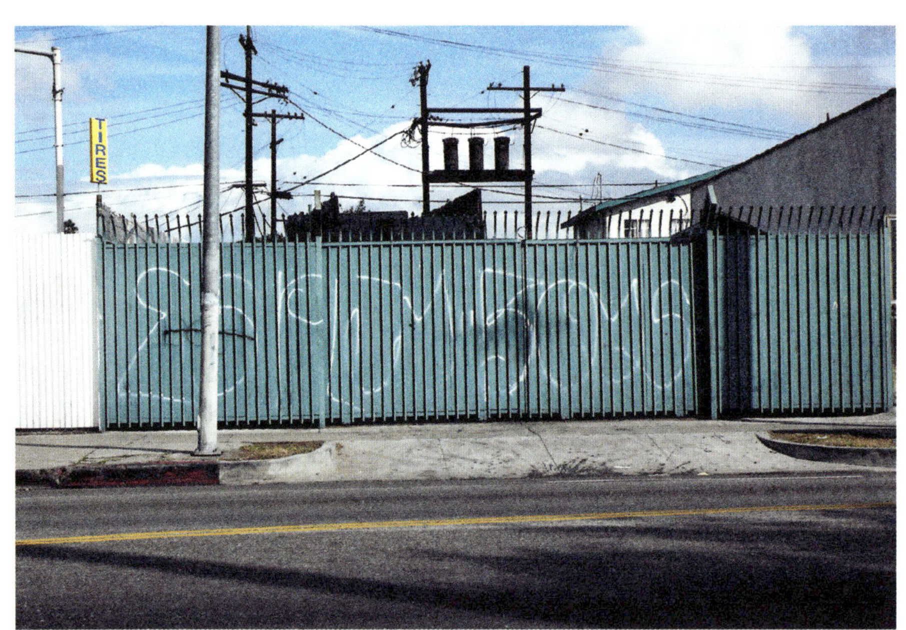

ES (EAST SIDE) PLAYBOYS

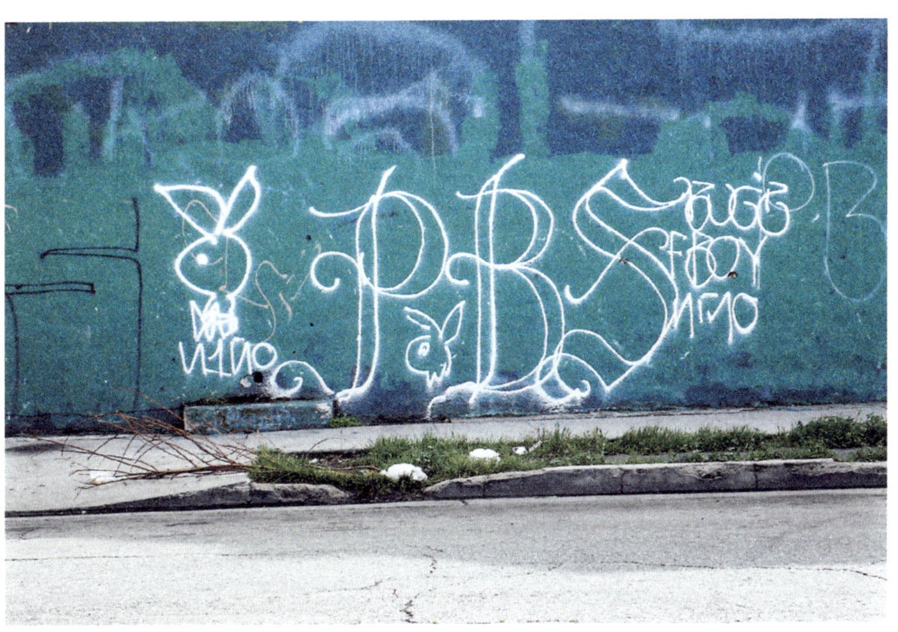

NIÑO PBS BUG'Z
  (PLAYBOYS) FBOY
    NIÑO

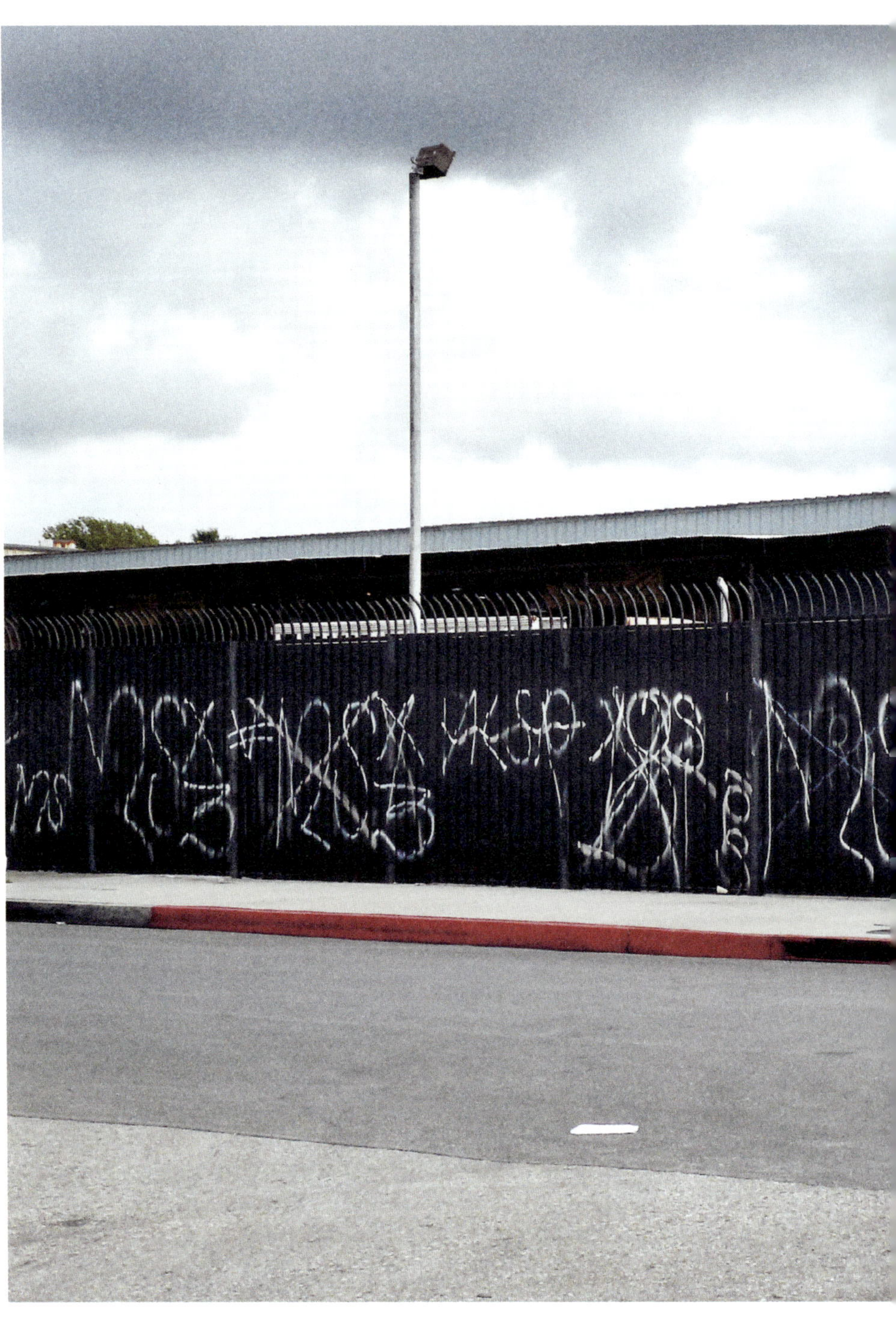

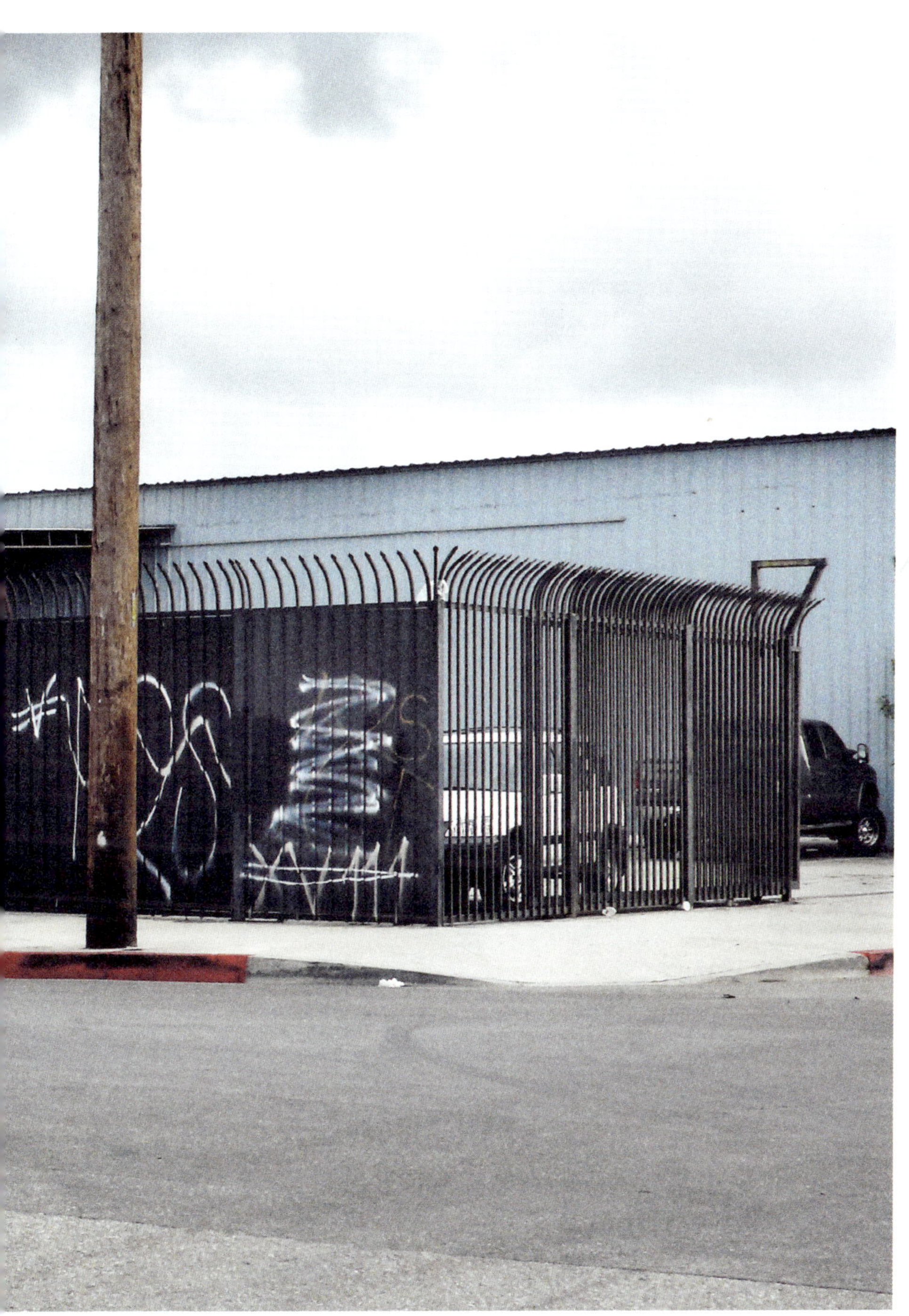

MSX3 VS. 18/XVIII ST
(MARA SALVATRUCHA TRECE)
(EIGHTEEN STREET GANG)

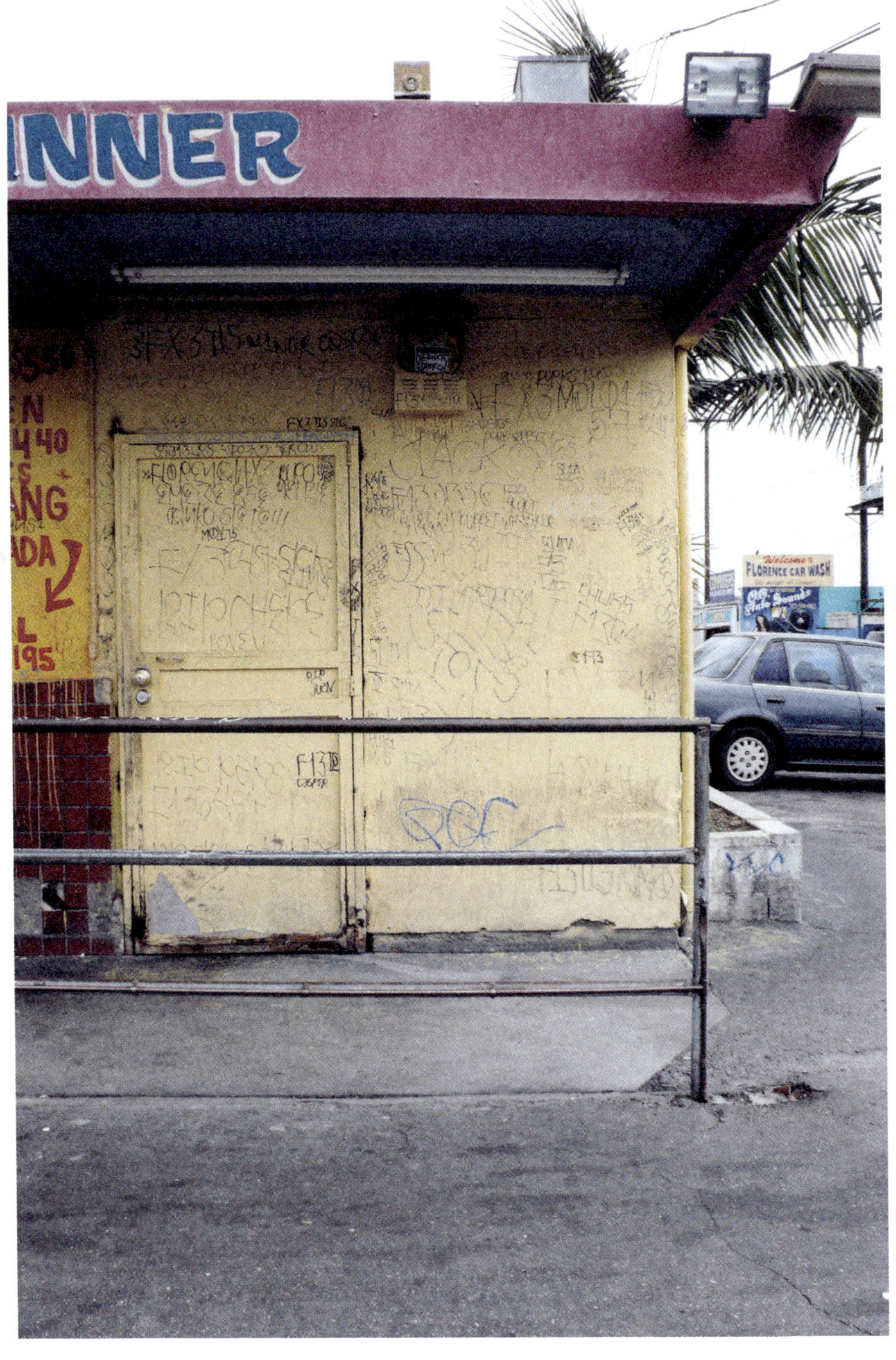

V FX3
(VARRIO FLORENCIA 13)
TLS (TINY LOCOS)
EME DE ESE / MDS (MALDITOS)
VARIOUS CLIQUES'
MEMBERS

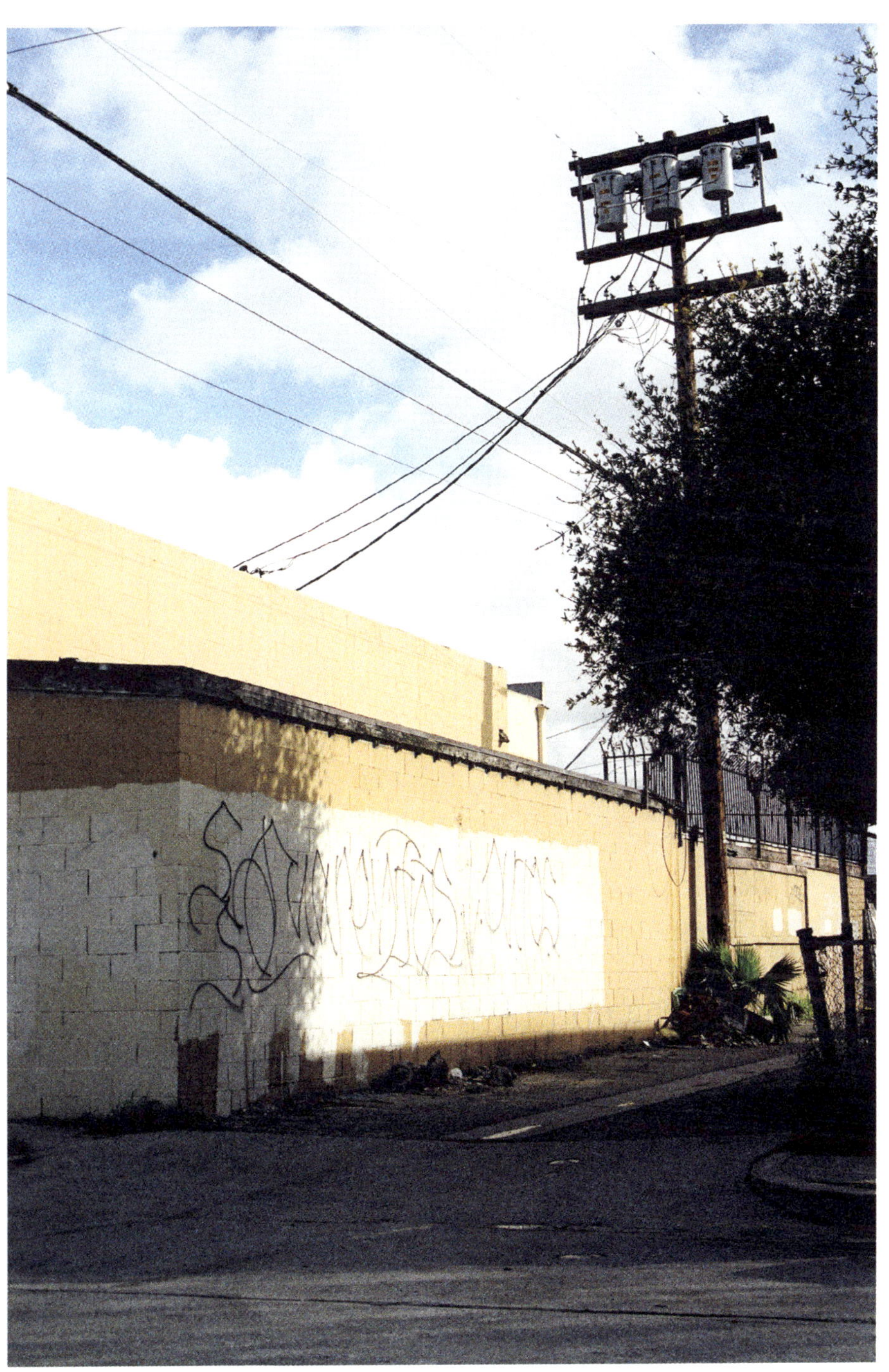

ss cuarentas↓putos
(SOUTH SIDE FORTIES' HERE MOTHERFUCKERS)

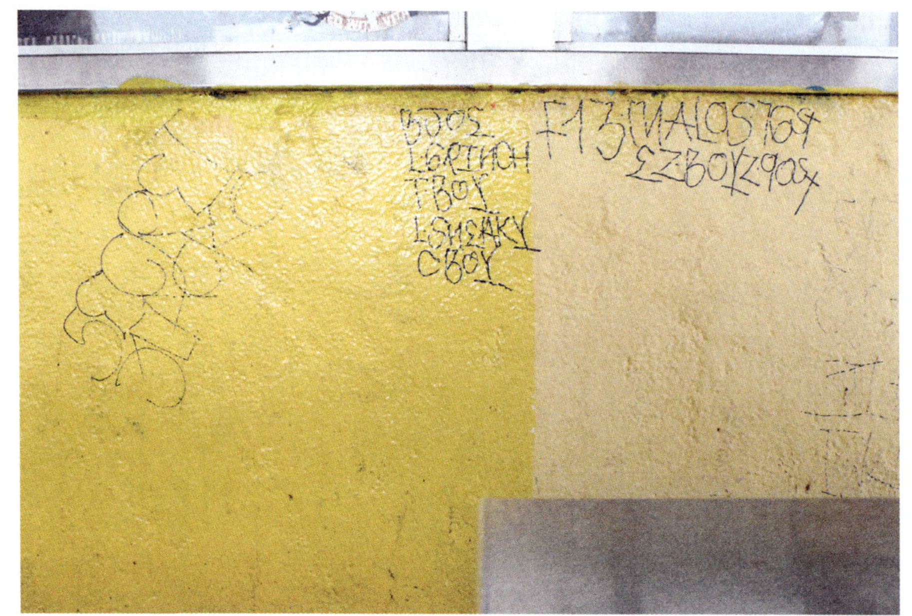

SECRET   BJOE   F13·MALOS·76ST
FLACKO   L·GRINCH   (FLORENCIA 13)
         T·BOY   EZ·BOYZ·90ST
         L·SNEAKY
         C·BOY

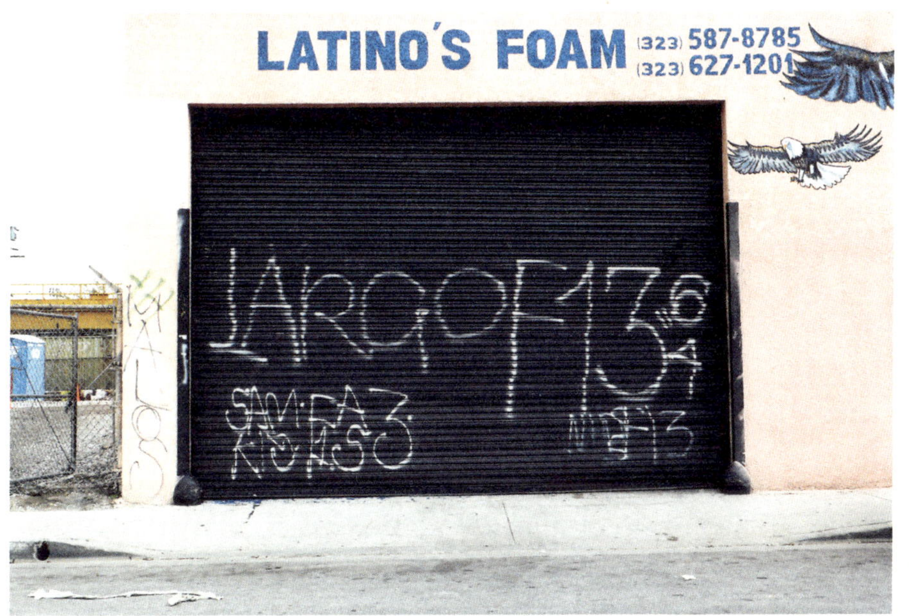

SAM KID ·F1AS3·   LARGO F13 64
(FLORENCIA TRECE,   (FLORENCIA
CLIQUE'S NAME)   TRECE 64 JT)

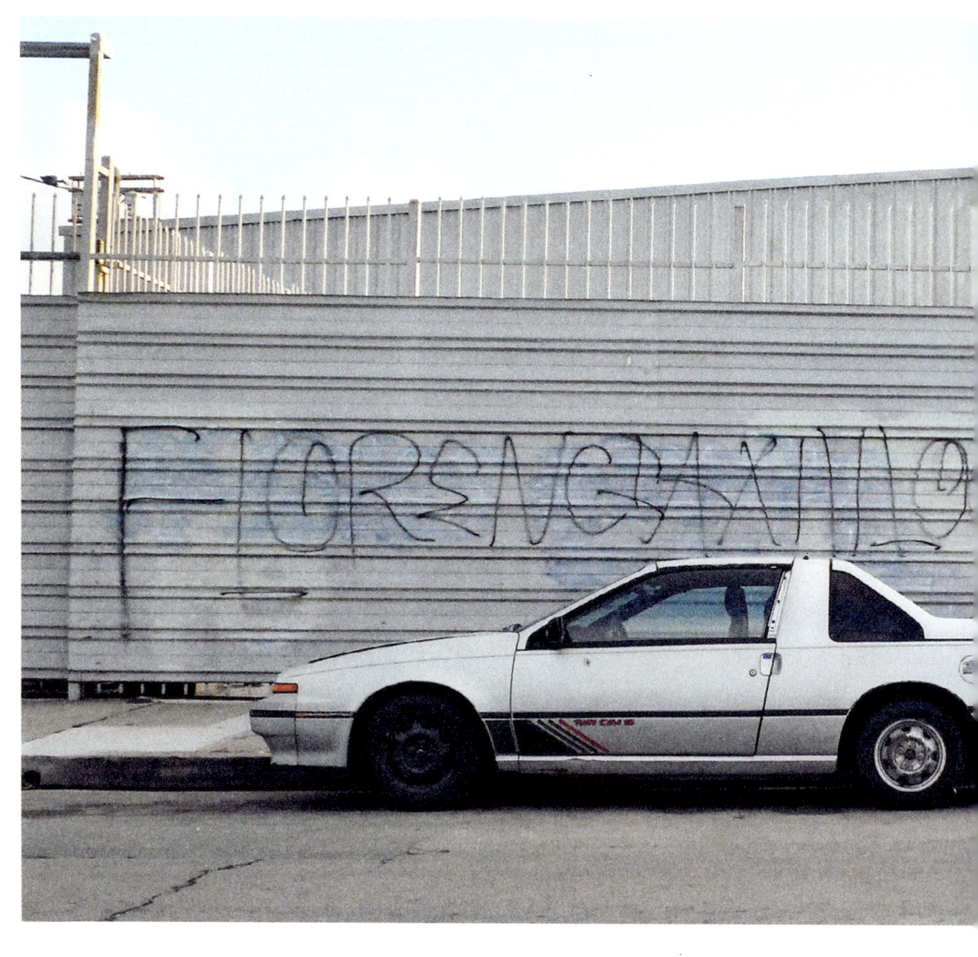

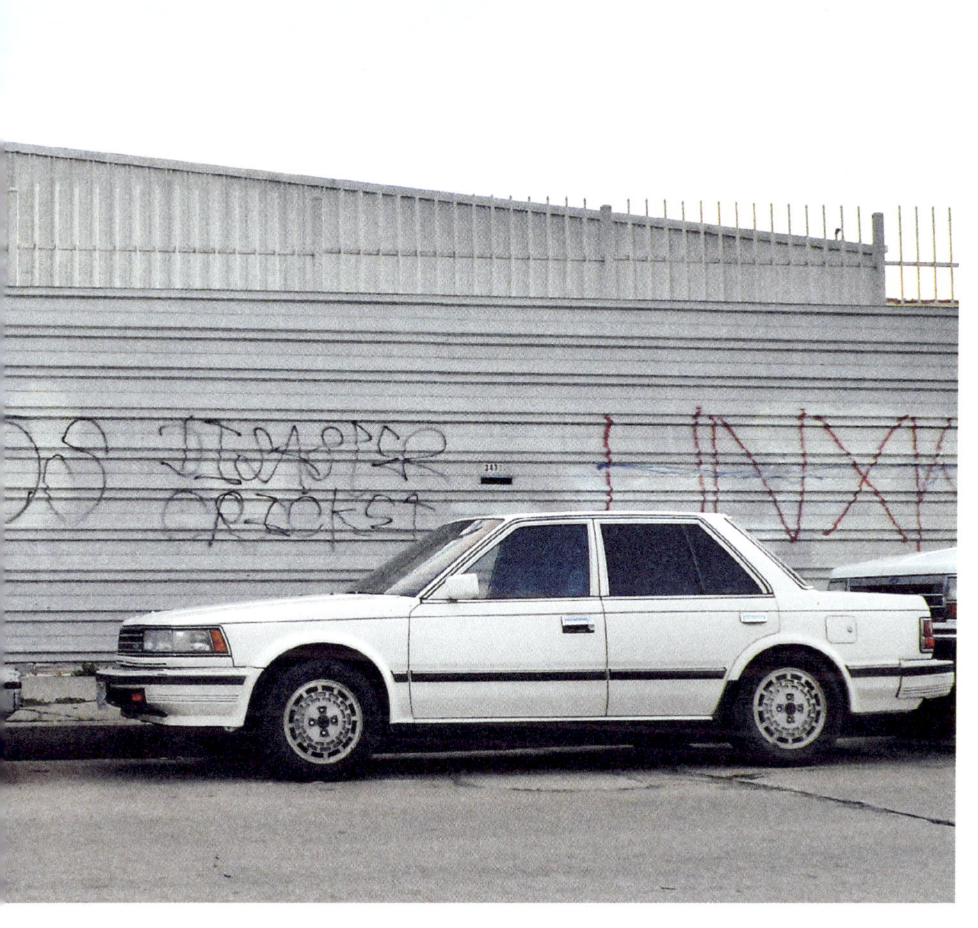

FLORENCIA XIII LOCOS   DISASTER   ~~UNXK~~
CRICKET

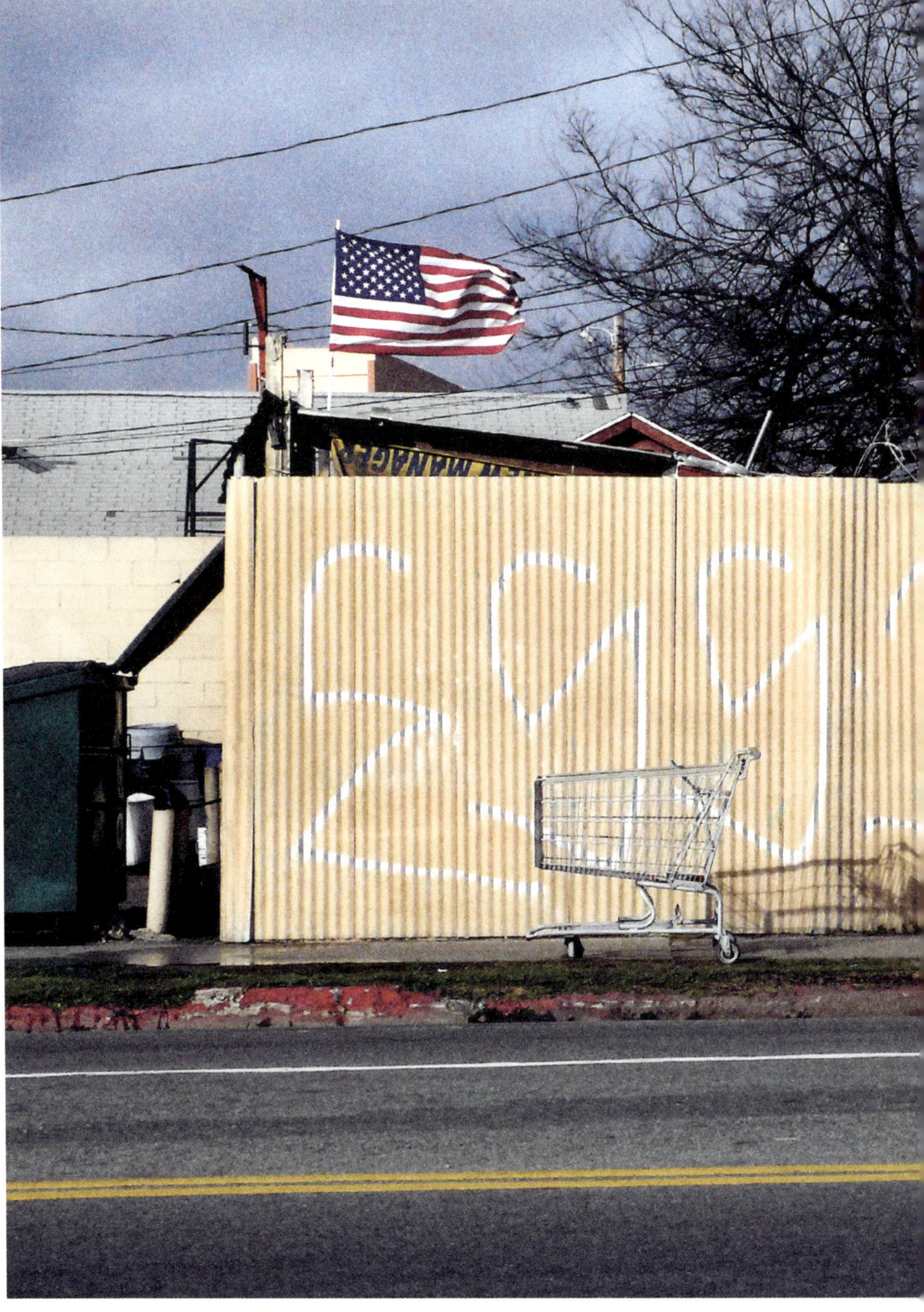

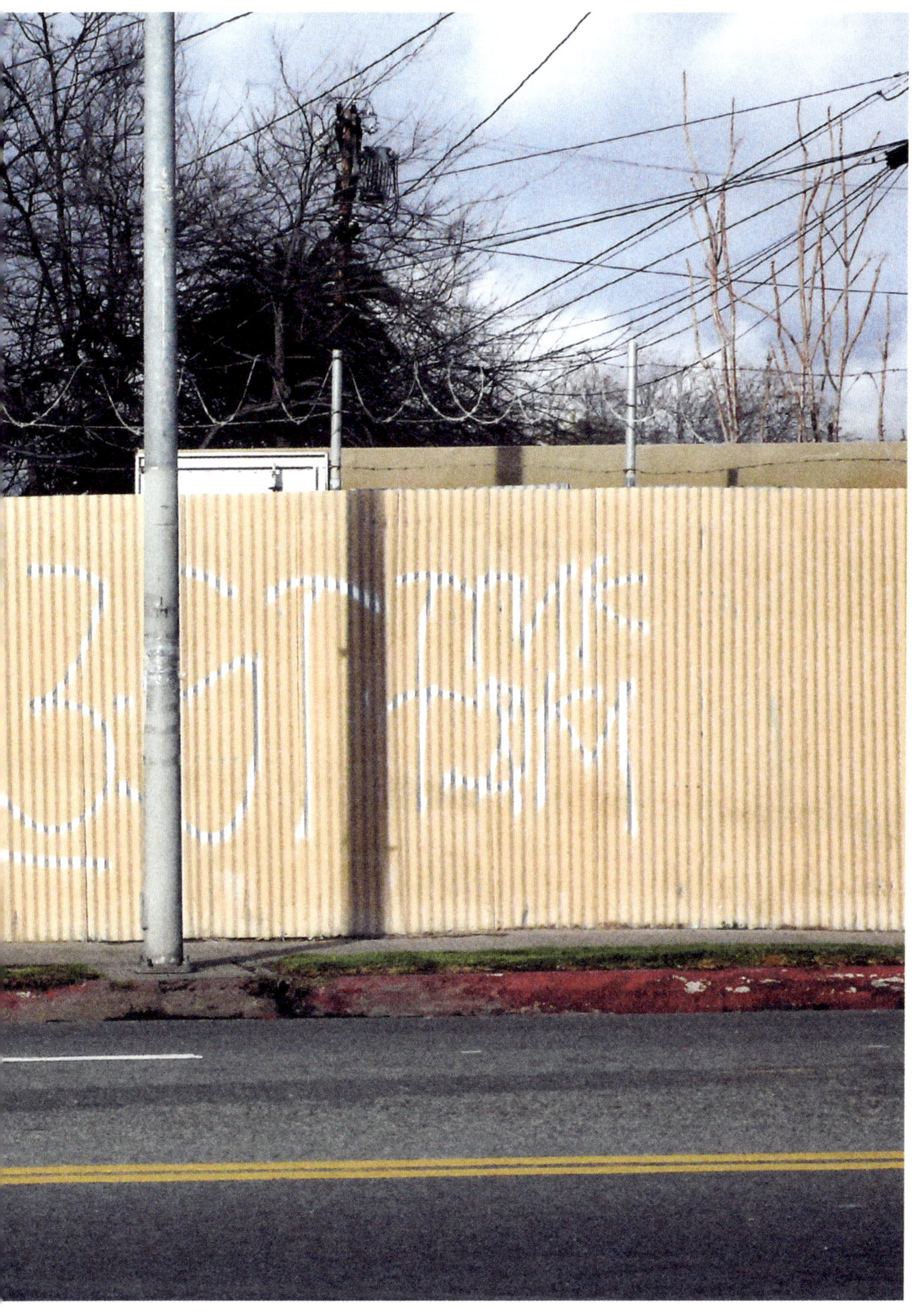

ESS·13·ST
(EAST & SOUTH SIDE
13TH STREET GANG)
TMK, TDK (TINY DUKES)

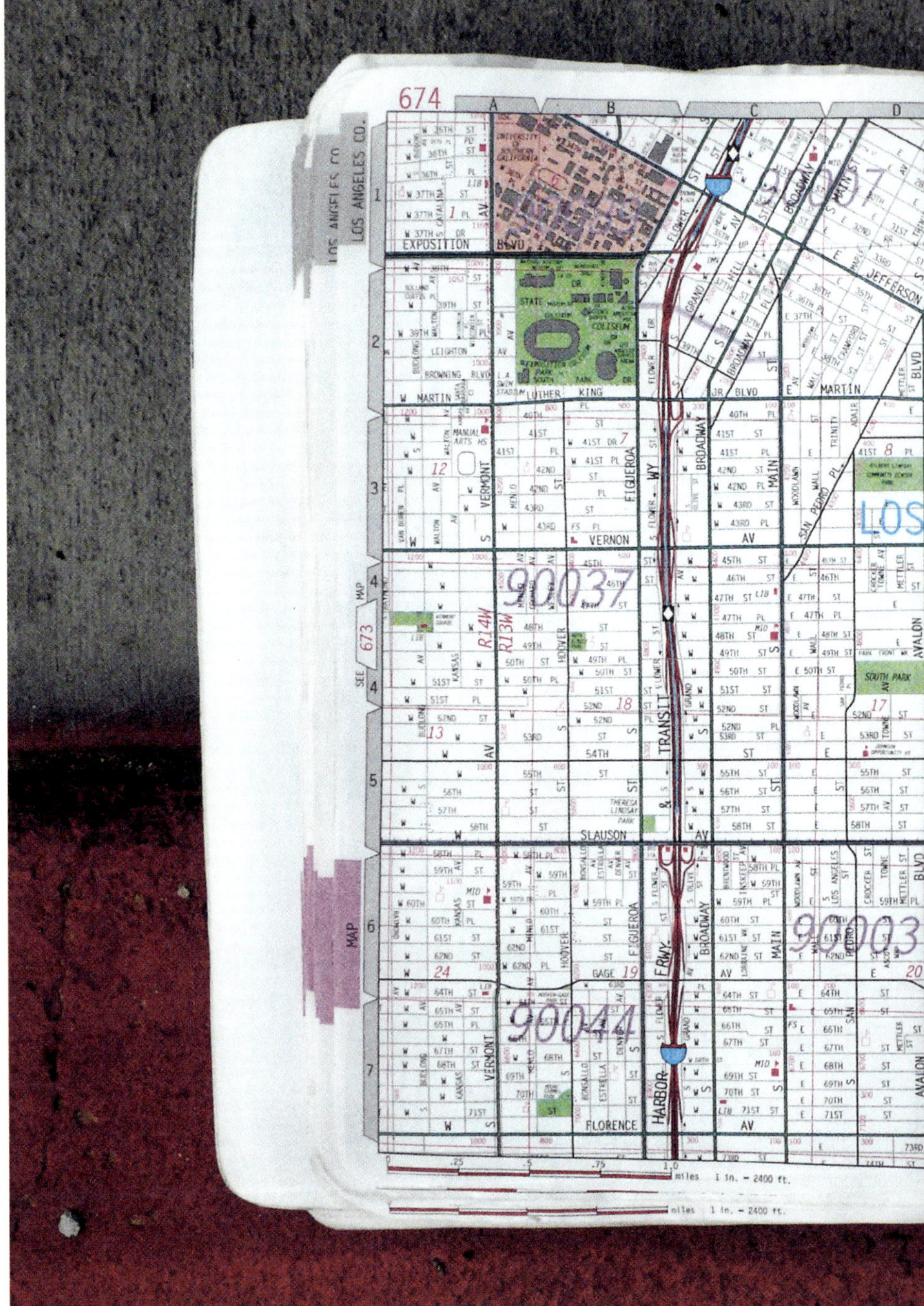

674
LOS ANGELES CO.
LOS ANGELES CO.
A   B   C   D
EXPOSITION   BLVD
STATE   DR
COLISEUM
MARTIN LUTHER KING   JR BLVD
MANUAL ARTS HS
VERMONT
FIGUEROA
BROADWAY
MAIN
SAN PEDRO
AVALON
VERNON   AV
90037
HOOVER
TRANSIT
GRAND
SOUTH PARK
JEFFERSON BLVD
E MARTIN
LOS
SEE 673   MAP
SLAUSON   AV
THERESA LINDSAY PARK
90003
90044
GAGE
FIGUEROA
HARBOR FRWY
BROADWAY
MAIN
SAN PEDRO
AVALON
VERMONT
FLORENCE   AV
MAP
miles   1 in. = 2400 ft.
.25   .5   .75   1.0
miles   1 in. = 2400 ft.

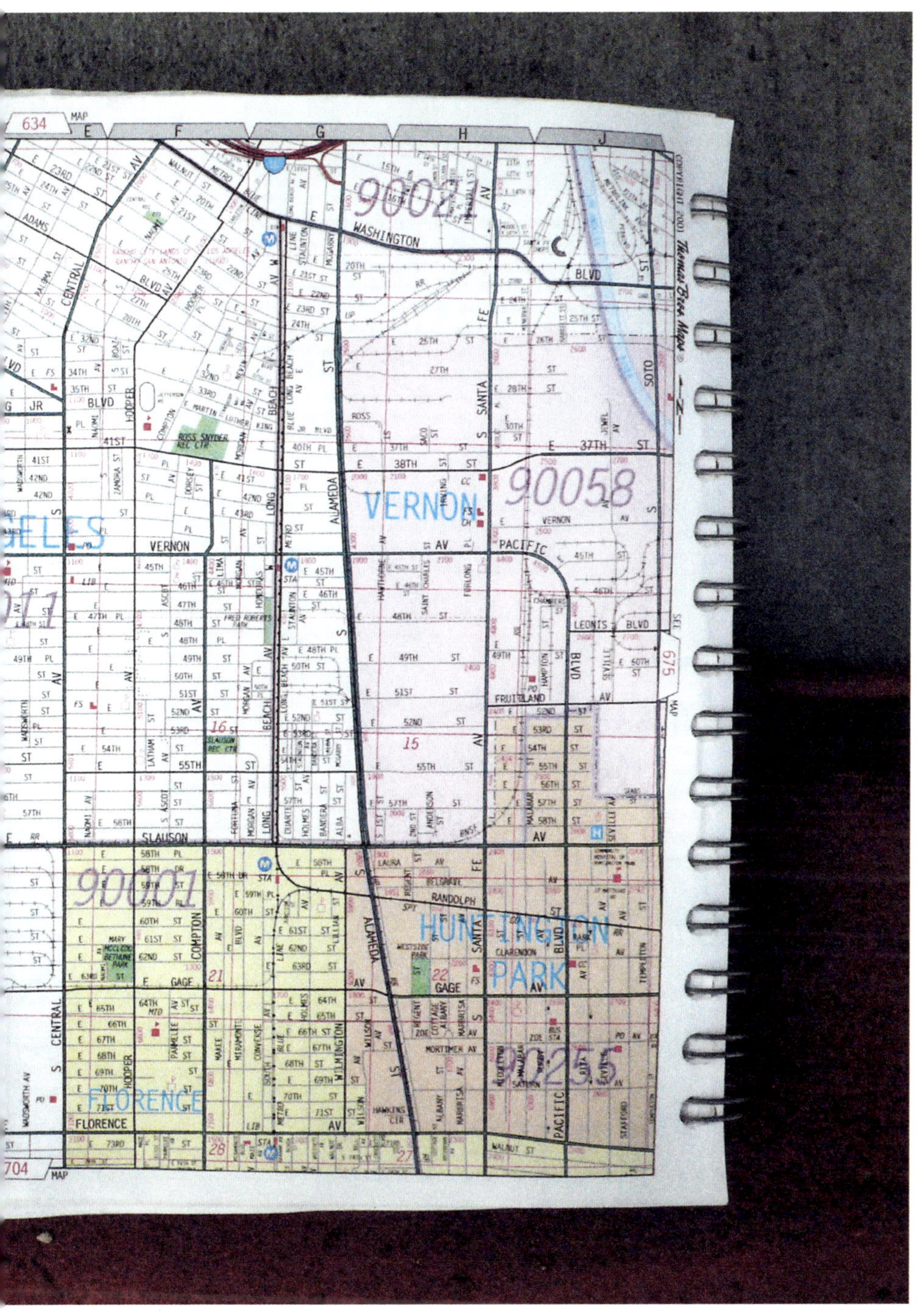
634
MAP
E F G H J
COPYRIGHT 2001
Thomas Bros Maps
N
90021
WASHINGTON
BLVD
SANTA FE
9010
VERNON
90058
PACIFIC
LEONIS BLVD
SEE
675
MAP
FRUITLAND
AV
15
16
SLAUSON
AV
90001
HUNTINGTON
PARK
GAGE
AV
21
22
90255
FLORENCE
AV
28
27
704
MAP
ANGELES
VERNON
FLORENCE
PACIFIC

Since the first publication in 2009, three of Howard Gribble's black and white photographs and six color photographs by François Chastanet were added with typographical transcriptions of the names and updated captions. Chastanet kept investigating Cholo handstyle origins and influences while regularly lecturing on this topic. His essay «The Gangster E» of this present edition has been updated with the latest available information: precisions are mainly concerning calligraphic and typographic models that probably shaped the emergence of the Cholo landmark letters and additional examples of the Cholo hand used on record sleeves from the 1970s. During this research, unresolved questions also came up about possible links with Chicago's gangster graffiti and blasons scene, that has existed since the 1950s, and using a similar Old English lettering aesthetics: Chicago was the second largest Hispanic community at that time after Los Angeles.

138

The iconographical context has also changed a lot since 2009, Instagram has notably permitted the publication of first hand new visual material detailing Cholo street handwriting with both valuable historical sources and current productions in the third decade of the 21st century. Many videos can now be found on YouTube on the history of Hispanic street gangs from different Los Angeles neighborhoods or veteranos interviews. Video tutorials explaining how to perform Cholo lettering are also available online.

On the back cover of this second edition, the typical *caló* slang expression *Con Safos* is used. Con safos or c/s was a phrase and symbol popular in the 1970s (as shown in many of Howard Gribble's photographs): usually placed centered at the end of the inscription, this mark symbolically protects the image of the name against erasure, it's a way of saying «the same to you» if someone defaces your wall signature or «don't mess with this». Its recurrent use disapeared over the years in the streets, but some veteranos and Chicano artists are nervertheless still using this acronym in the 2020s.

Born in 1944 in Wilmington, North Carolina, Gribble grew up in Southern California in the 1950s and 1960s, where he immersed himself in gang and lowrider culture associated particularly with youth from the barrios of the Mexican-American community. In the early 1970s he photographed examples of Latino gang graffiti, travelling throughout a wide geographic area in order to encompass a larger variety of styles and variations. In 2007, under the alias Kid Deuce, Gribble showed his archives for the first time on the photo sharing site Flickr. The collection entitled *The Golden Age of Gang Graffiti* proved to be unique, and the interest was enormous.

Dr. Chaz Bojórquez

Born 1949 in Los Angeles, Bojórquez is a resident of Highland Park East LA, California. Growing up, he was exposed to the uses, values, and craft of graffiti through neighbors and friends in the territory of «The Avenues», the area's dominant gang. Bojórquez began his art career by spray-painting alongside the concrete river banks of the Arroyo Seco. By the end of 1969, he had created a symbol that represented him and the streets – a stylized skull called «Señor Suerte» (Mr. Luck). It has become a gangster image of protection from death. Bojórquez is acknowledged as a pioneer and «Godfather of Los Angeles Cholo style graffiti» for more than 50 years. Considered one of the few artists who have successfully made the transition from the street to the gallery, Bojórquez is represented in numerous permanent museum collections, including The Smithsonian Institute: National Museum of American Art, National Museum of American History, National Museum of American Archives, Washington, D.C. In 2020, Bojórquez was awarded an Honorary Doctorate Degree of Humane Letters from Art Center School of Design, Pasadena, CA. He exhibits and lectures internationally, and performs «live painting» demonstrating his unique letter styles, as well as pursuing commercial and cultural projects.

François Chastanet

Born in 1975 in Bordeaux, France, Chastanet is an architect, graphic and type designer, documentary author, co-founder of TypoMorpho studio based in Bordeaux, France, and teacher of the Institut Supérieur des Arts et du Design de Toulouse / ISDAT. Through graphic design commissions, documentaries and teaching, he explores the relationship between architecture and written signs, from wayfinding typography to ephemeral handwritings. At the crossroads of epigraphy and paleography, he is currently conducting doctoral research at the École Pratique des Hautes Études / EPHE in Paris in joint supervision with the Atelier National de Recherche Typographique / ANRT on the evolution of Latin letterforms through six case studies of graffiti of names' handstyles in North and South America (Los Angeles «Cholo Writing», New York «Tags and Throw-ups» and Philadelphia «Tall Hands and Wickeds» in the United States, São Paulo «Pixação» in Brazil, Tijuana «Trepes» and Monterrey «Ganchos» in Mexico).

139

+ front +
endpapers
+

B (BARRIO)
FROGTOWN RIFA X3
CSL'S

BST
(BREED STRET)

WF
(WHITE FENCE)
SPS / CLS / MLS / TLS
THIS SINCE 1939

V (VARRIO) EAST SIDE
CERCO BLANCO
HOE TOWN

FLAT
(PRIMERA FLATS
GANG)

WS 18 ST
(WESTSIDE EIGHTEEN
STREET GANG)

MMV 187
(MARIANNA
MARAVILLA
187 / MURDER CASE)

PBS
(PLAYBOYS)

V BT LS X3
(VARRIO BIG TOP
LOCOS TRECE)

V STS↓
(VARRIO
STREET SAINTS)

V (VARRIO) HAZARD X3

SUREÑOS X3

V BNLS
WS BURLINGTON LS
(WEST SIDE
BURLINGTON LOCOS)
BEAVER · KIKO · CHILLS

PRIMERA FLATS 23
(PRIMERA FLATS
23 RD STREET GANG)

WS REBELS LS X3
(WEST SIDE REBELS
LOCOS TRECE)

VARRIO MMV
MARIANNA
MARA[VILLA]

ALL DAY!
LOS AVENIDA'S
43 RD

SMX7ST
(SANTA MONICA
17 TH STREET)
SNAPPER KRAZY

V · EXP
(VARRIO ECHO PARK)

es
V · W LOS · F
(EAST SIDE
VARRIO WHITE FENCE
LOS ANGELES)
· KANE (?) · SLEEPS ·

+ back +
endpapers
+

LA · COLONIA · WATTS X3

PURO FLATS 23 ST

AVE'S 43 DUST
(AVENUES 43 RD
STREET)

V ES BREED LA
(VARRIO EAST SIDE
BREED STREET
LOS ANGELES)

ES GERAGHTY LOMA
(EAST SIDE GERAGHTY
LOMA GANG)

V WF · MALOS↓
(VARRIO WHITE
FENCE MALOS)

VG×LOMA BSL1↓
(VARRIO GERAGHTY
LOMA, CLIQUE'S
NAME)

MARAVILLA RIFA
GAGE BOYS

EIGHTEEN STRE[ET]

V GEE MV
(VARRIO G / GAGE
MARAVILLA)

OUR V (VARRIO)
ST × SAINTS
TOWN 21 ST↓
GET · IT · RIGHT ·
UGLY · BITCH

V BHR TLS
(VARRIO BIG HAZARD
TINY LOCOS)
TOKER
CROW

BH
BIG HAZARD GANG
CAN'T FUCK BITCHES
××××
X3

V (VARRIO)
PRIMERA × FLATS
PPLAS

ES VLV R 13
(EAST SIDE
VARRIO LITTLE VALLEY
RIFA TRECE)

PF / V PF
(VARRIO
PRIMERA FLATS)

FX3
(FLORENCIA TRECE)

PELON
SUSPECT
VNE 13
(VARRIO NUEVO
ESTRADA TRECE)

ES · VE · ENE · EE
(EAST SIDE VNE
VARRIO NUEVO
ESTRADA)

· V · EXP ·
(VARRIO ECHO PARK)
SPORTY · SADBOY ·

ES V HAZARD 1
(EAST SIDE
VARRIO HAZARD
NUMBER ONE)

EIGHTEEN ST
(EIGHTEEN
STREET GANG)

V CE × ELE R
(VARRIO C×L
CARNALES RIFA)

14·COLONIA·WATTS 3